SYRIA's
DEMOCRATIC
YEARS

PUBLIC CULTURES OF THE MIDDLE EAST AND NORTH AFRICA

Paul A. Silverstein, Susan Slyomovics, and Ted Swedenburg, *editors*

SYRIA's
DEMOCRATIC
YEARS

Citizens, Experts, and
Media in the 1950s

KEVIN W. MARTIN

INDIANA UNIVERSITY PRESS

Bloomington & Indianapolis

This book is a publication of

INDIANA UNIVERSITY PRESS
Office of Scholarly Publishing
Herman B Wells Library 350
1320 East 10th Street
Bloomington, Indiana 47405 USA

iupress.indiana.edu

Cataloging information is available from the Library of Congress

ISBN 978-0-253-01879-3 (cloth)
ISBN 978-0-253-01887-8 (paperback)
ISBN 978-0-253-01893-9 (ebook)

1 2 3 4 5   20 19 18 17 16 15

for my parents

Contents

Acknowledgments

WORK ON THIS book began more years ago than I like to recall. Thus I have many to thank. I must begin by expressing my gratitude to the members of my research committee, Walter Armbrust, James Gelvin, John Ruedy, and especially my mentor, Judith Tucker, for their support, guidance, patience, and good cheer. I would also like to thank the many current and former faculty members at Georgetown University who contributed to this project and/or my professional training. These include Jon Anderson, Belkacem Baccouche, Roger Chickering, Michael Hudson, John McNeill, David Mehall, James Millward, Aviel Roshwald, Suhail Shadoud, John Voll, and the late Hanna Batatu and Hisham Sharabi. In the same vein, my Arabic instructors at Middlebury College's School of Languages, Sinan Antoon and Ahmad Karout, were instrumental in preparing me for my research and residence in Syria.

Initial research was made possible by a Fulbright Research Grant from the Institute of International Education, a Fulbright-Hays Doctoral Dissertation Research Fellowship from the U.S. Department of Education, and various travel, research, and writing grants from Georgetown University's Graduate School of Arts and Sciences and Department of History. Subsequent travel and research for this book were supported by a New Frontiers in the Arts and Humanities Exploration Traveling Fellowship from the Office of the Vice Provost for Research at Indiana University, and an Overseas Research Grant from the Office of the Vice President for International Affairs at the same institution. I offer my sincere thanks to all.

I conducted the bulk of the research for this book at the Hafez al-Asad National Library, the Center for Historical Documents, and the Institut Français du Proche-Orient (IFPO), formerly known as the IFEAD, in Damascus. Additional research was conducted at the American University of Beirut's Jafet Library, and the U.S. National Archives in College Park, Maryland. Many thanks to the staff and officials of these institutions for their assistance. I must express additional appreciation to the faculty and staff at IFPO, which served as my base throughout two years in residence. Two of the institute's former directors, Dominique Mallet and Floréal Sanagustin, provided me with research affiliation and permitted me to pursue specialized studies with members of their excellent faculty. Most notable of the latter were Hasan 'Abbas, Maher Charif, and (once again!) Ahmad Karout, who were true teachers, mentors,

ix

colleagues, and friends. In addition, Steve Seche, Sahar Hassibi, Jessica Davies, and the staff of the American Cultural Center in Damascus provided valuable institutional support.

My enduring gratitude is due to Abdul-Karim Rafeq, former chair of the Department of History at Damascus University and professor emeritus at the College of William and Mary. Professor Rafeq, who has generously and ably mentored two generations of American researchers in Syria, has repeatedly and unselfishly bestowed upon me the benefits of his vast knowledge and experience, and otherwise provided advice and support since my first spell of Arabic language study in Damascus more than sixteen years ago.

While pursuing language study and conducting research in Damascus, I was privileged to enjoy the company of a host of friends and colleagues, both old and new. Special thanks to Robert Bain, Samar Farah, T. J. Fitzgerald, Garner Gollatz, Hugh Jeffrey, Tricia Khleif, Kinda Lamʿa, Joshua Landis, Justin Lenderking, Laith Moseley, Goetz Nordbruch, Kristin Shamas, Anders Strindberg, Steve Tamari, Malissa Taylor, and Clay Witt for their conversation, camaraderie, and kindness.

During these and subsequent residences in Damascus, I incurred many debts that can never be repaid in full. It is no exaggeration to say that I was frequently overwhelmed by the kindness, generosity, and hospitality offered to me by an extraordinary number of Syrians. Ghiyath Shadoud facilitated my initial introduction to Damascus with unfailing generosity and good humor, all the while voluntarily acting as the most patient of Arabic teachers. Amer Dahi, who I met by happy accident on a dangerously dilapidated Karnak Company bus to Beirut, has contributed enormously to my research and my knowledge of modern Syrian history, and will ever be one of my dearest friends. Through Amer, I made the acquaintance of Professor Hanan Qassab Hasan, who kindly welcomed me into her home, shared her memories, and patiently submitted to a lengthy interview.

For years Sami Moubayed has graciously shared his encyclopedic knowledge of Syrian history and continued to assist my research in many other ways. I will always have fond memories of sitting with Sami outside restaurants and cafes, engaging in hours of conversation and banter, our laughter frequently erupting from within clouds of exhaled argileh smoke. I also tender my very special thanks to Mazen al-Masri and Mohammad "Moe" Sukiyya, who remain the truest friends possible. Finally, I offer my abiding affection, respect, and gratitude to Abu ʿUbada, a man of towering integrity and dignity, without whose knowledge, energy, and ability to find rare books and periodicals, this work would have been all but impossible.

I must also note the contributions of my graduate students at Indiana University, whose presentations and discussions in my colloquia have often prompted me to rethink my approach to primary sources in ways fruitful for my research and writing. In particular, I want to thank Danie Becknell, who helped me prepare the bibliography for this book, and the graduate students who served as my research assistants for this and other projects, Hicham Bou Nassif, Walter Lorenz, Bilal Maanaki, Ghassan Nasr, and Ahmad al-Qassas, who saved me countless hours poring through sources and found some true jewels in the process.

Current and former colleagues at Indiana University read and provided comments on drafts of this book, suggested useful secondary sources, or provided support and friendship. Chief among them are Salman al-'Ani, Çigdem Balim, Heather Blair, Erdem Çipa, Guadalupe González Diéguez, Christiane Gruber, John Hanson, Ambassador Feisal Istrabadi, Zaineb Istrabadi, Stephen Katz, Paul Losensky, Manling Luo, David McDonald, Abdulrazzaq Moaz, Michelle Moyd, Kaya Şahin, Nazif Shahrani, Kevin Tsai, and John Walbridge.

Several old friends assisted in critical ways. Tsolin Nalbantian informed me of the contents of the al-Malki files in the special collections of the Jafet Library, and has encouraged and supported me through every stage of this project. Doaa' H. El Nakhala did a superb job of preparing the manuscript in record time. Laurie King proofread and provided valuable editorial suggestions for an earlier draft of this manuscript. My dear friends Sara Scalenghe and Chris Toensing did the same for numerous drafts of this work and others. Ilana Feldman did all of the above and much more for the final draft of this book, which is far better as a result of her efforts. Needless to say, I am solely responsible for any shortcomings that remain.

Fulsome thanks are also due to the staff at Indiana University Press, my sponsoring editor Rebecca Tolen, her assistant, Mollie Ables, and my project editor, Nancy Lightfoot, who swiftly and professionally shepherded this book through the publication process. I am grateful to Maggie Hogan and Alex Trotter, who did such rapid, excellent work on editing the copy and compiling the index, respectively. I also offer my thanks to the members of the editorial committee for the Public Cultures of the Middle East and North Africa series, and to the press's anonymous readers, who offered welcome encouragement and criticism of the submission draft.

Elements of chapters 4 and 5 first appeared in a paper presented in January 2014 at the Annual Meeting of the American Historical Association. I am grateful for the helpful comments I received. Elements of the introduction and chapter 1 appeared in modified form in "Peasants into Syrians?," *International*

Journal of Middle East Studies 41, no. 1 (2009), 4-6; and "Presenting the 'True Face of Syria' to the World: Urban Disorder and Civilizational Anxieties at the First Damascus International Exposition," *International Journal of Middle East Studies,* 42, no. 3 (2010), pp. 391-411. I am grateful to Cambridge University Press for permission to reprint.

Finally, I must thank most of all my late parents, both of whom pushed me to pursue every educational opportunity. Their love, hard work, and sacrifice have made my life so much richer than they could have imagined.

Notes on Transliteration

Most of the sources used in this book were written in Modern Standard Arabic. When transliterating Arabic words from such sources, I have used a simplified version of the *International Journal of Middle East Studies* system, eliminating all of the diacritical marks except for the ayn (') and the hamza ('). I have transliterated some titles, place names, and personal names in dialectal form, e.g., Tabibuka becomes Tabibak, al-Maliki becomes al-Malki, and so forth.

SYRIA's
DEMOCRATIC
YEARS

Introduction

The Virtuous Citizen and the Postcolonial State

On May 5, 1955, the Syrian Defense Ministry journal *al-Jundi* (The Soldier) published attorney and radio show host Najat Qassab Hasan's encomium for the Syrian Army's deputy chief of staff, Colonel 'Adnan al-Malki, who had been assassinated on April 22. Entitled "Sahib al-Raya" (The Standard Bearer), the article begins by describing a solemn ceremony held on Syria's first Independence Day, April 17, 1946. "At that historic moment," the Syrian president, Shukri al-Quwwatli, presented a newly designed army standard to a group of officers that included then–First Lieutenant al-Malki. According to Qassab Hasan, President al-Quwwatli, the officers, and "tens of thousands of men" witnessing the event "wept like children," while the schoolchildren in attendance "displayed the humility and reverence of men."[1]

The ceremony that Qassab Hasan described instantiated a foundational premise of the young Syrian state's constitutionally prescribed distribution of power, the subordination of military to civilian authority. By receiving the army's flag from President al-Quwwatli, al-Malki and his colleagues publicly acknowledged the legitimacy of the civilian executive's authority over the armed forces. But the display of emotion, whether real or apocryphal, can only be explained by the perceived import of a momentous reality: with the end of the French Mandate, for the first time in history, all of the armed forces on Syrian soil were under the command of that country's citizens. In other words, the consecration of this flag signified the Syrian armed forces' transformation from a colonial police force into a true national army, the signal characteristic of sovereignty and a necessary precondition for the pursuit of "national" developmental goals.

Furthermore, the putative solemnity of the ceremony was evidence of a widespread perception: the most pressing and challenging task facing the vulnerable new Syrian state was pedagogical—the tutelage of citizens. And the placement of this eulogy in *al-Jundi* was doubly significant. Its appearance in a Defense Ministry publication endowed Qassab Hasan's tribute with

1

the state's imprimatur, officially declaring it part of an exercise in national pedagogy, an impression enhanced by the journal's status as one of Syria's most widely circulated periodicals. Furthermore, the fact that a Defense Ministry weekly ostensibly published by and for enlisted men had such extensive circulation is evidence of the military's desire to reach the "hearts and minds" of the general populace as well as its ability to demand state resources for this purpose.

Qassab Hasan's account was published during a period (1954–1958)—retrospectively designated "the Democratic Years"—that witnessed a flourishing of diverse media production, including newspapers, magazines, and radio broadcasts, unequaled before or since. At this moment of intense hope and anxiety about the future of the Syrian state, mass media was a central site for the elaboration of the postcolonial developmental project. This book surveys this rich media landscape to explore the articulation of normative citizenship, through a discourse instructing Syrians and other Arabs about the qualities they should aspire to embody: self-discipline, rationality, and service to family, state, and nation.

This study also focuses on a particular form of media production, the media of expertise. I use this term and "expert media" to refer to a specific genre of pedagogical literature, a "mirror for citizens" that was the modern, developmentally informed analogue of its Ottoman-era predecessor, the *nasihatname,* or guidebooks composed for the edification of monarchs.[2] Expert media encompassed state radio programming and state- or privately published outlets in the form of weekly or monthly illustrated journals—as opposed to daily newspapers—nominally targeting a particular professional audience. Yet thanks to varied content (e.g., sports, entertainment, science, the arts) and state subsidies or corporate advertising revenue, these publications sought, and reached, a mass audience.

The oft-repeated goal of these journals' pedagogical project was the "moral and material" uplifting of Syria's population through the inculcation of citizenly virtues.[3] In pursuit of this objective, the authority of various forms of modern developmental expertise—science, medicine, the law, and the military arts and sciences—was deployed to produce an idealized depiction of the citizen, the agent of progress and irreducible subject of politics in a democratic system. As the act of defining—"elucidating the features of"—the citizen is, of necessity, both inclusionary and exclusionary, these texts also enumerated and classified deviations from the qualities of this normative figure.[4]

The Democratic Years were the turning point of a period in which Syria's regional significance can scarcely be overstated. Syria was the cradle of pan-

Arab nationalism and the first state to experience both military dictatorship and the free and fair election of a civilian government, to allow communists full political participation, to attempt an effacement of the spatial-political order produced by the post–World War I settlement, and to execute a comprehensive transformation of its political economy. Syria was also the perennial leader of opposition to American influence in the region and to the political normalization of Israel. It was both the site of the longest experience with populist authoritarian government and the locus of the century's fiercest and most prolonged contest for regional hegemony, the fabled "struggle for Syria," in which domestic, regional, and global actors battled to determine the country's foreign policy orientation. In short, Syria was the late twentieth century's crucible of ideological conflict and change in the Arab world, its experience foreshadowing and/or exemplifying a number of macro-historical trends in the region.

One of these regional trends, the trajectory toward authoritarian government, is central to this study. The institutional conflict through which this system was imposed and consolidated in Syria—the armed forces' repeated intrusion into and eventual capture of the political sphere—is a leitmotif of the scholarly literature, which has been dominated by political economy, international relations, and social history approaches. To date, no monograph has focused on the cultural phenomena informing this process. Hence this book employs a cultural history approach to augment and nuance the historiography of the post–World War II Arab world. It examines print and broadcast media during a turning point in Syrian and regional history, the hopeful period prior to the erection of an authoritarian system that has only recently been challenged. In the process, the book illuminates the ways in which media was used as a vehicle to popularize the urgency of developmental imperatives and normalize authoritarian solutions to the problems confronting Syria and its neighbors.

In addition to a vast array of state- and privately owned mass media, this analysis draws on personal interviews; the memoirs of journalists, politicians, and military officers; biographical dictionaries; archival collections; clandestine publications; legal depositions and other court records; and relevant American diplomatic correspondence. A cultural history approach is qualitative, emphasizing subjective experiences of historical events and processes rather than attempting to uncover an objective reality underlying these phenomena. It also assumes that "linguistic practice, rather than simply reflecting social reality," can serve as an "instrument of (or constitute) power."[5] Thus these sources are read as much for their deployment of language to represent reality as for their factual content. A cultural history approach is also more inclined to analyze systems of signification on their own terms rather than as mere reflections of said reality. In sum, as Lynn Hunt observed, "The central task of cultural history" is the "deciphering of meaning."[6] In this vein, this book constitutes a departure from the "high politics" of "leaders" featured in previous studies, devoting attention instead to the discourse lying outside or at the margins of this field. In the process, it seeks to uncover the operation of "technologies of governmentality" on "political society," the realm in which most Syrians experienced the modern and the postcolonial.[7]

Among the modern state's most significant technologies of power are the legal and military arts and sciences. Expertise in these fields is particularly crucial for vulnerable, developing states, which perceive the orderly mobilization of human and material resources as existential imperatives. Thus print and broadcast media are employed to stimulate, inform, and guide popular aspirations and anxieties in ways beneficial to the state. In post-independence Syria, expert media constituted the primary venue for such efforts.

THE POSTCOLONIAL STATE/CONDITION

Syria's modernizing reformers of the post-independence period shared a characteristic with their counterparts throughout the developing world, a profound anxiety that many (if not most) of their countrymen were not "up to the task" of practicing citizenship. This contention—the ill-preparedness or incapacity of the population for rational action and civic responsibility—was a fundamental premise of colonial thought, yet one that nationalist elites persistently attempted to refute. Thus the postcolonial narrative of the nation was highly ambivalent, as male, urban, educated, and ideologically oriented experts "masqueraded as the universal" while devoting extraordinary energy and resources to a project that belied that universality. This contradiction constitutes the "fundamental plot," the predominant narrative trope, of the postcolonial period in Syria.[8]

Other elements of these experts' discourse reveal striking epistemic continuity with the ideas of Syria's colonial-period predecessors. As the newly independent states of the Arab East were all the products of imperial/colonial enterprises that produced vast bodies of knowledge—"a way of ordering the world . . . inseparable from social organization"—the similarities should not be surprising.[9] The French Mandate officials who governed Syria in its first decades promulgated a narrative of "civilizing" and "uplifting" Syria's masses. This French narrative was perfectly in keeping with their own imperial pretensions, as well as the language of the League of Nations Covenant, which adjudged the populations of the former Ottoman Empire "not yet able to stand by themselves under the strenuous conditions of the modern world."[10]

The sincerity of their anti-imperialist and Arab nationalist pronouncements notwithstanding, Syria's post-independence political and intellectual elites internalized these European narratives and adopted—in revised form—the "mission" at their core. Thus in the public discourse of 1950s Syria, the perceived link between the country's immature state of development and the persistence of its various internal divisions is palpable. Nationalist ideologues saw these divisions as the shameful remnants of the colonial experience, when French authorities' Machiavellian strategy of divide and rule encouraged and exacerbated ethnic and sectarian differences in an effort to prevent the emergence of a broad-based resistance movement. Accordingly, the effacement of difference, that is, the populations' various deviations from the norms of urban, literate, gendered, republican citizenship, was the most urgent and pervasive "social problem" under discussion.

Another conspicuous feature of the pedagogical project in Syria is the variety in forms of expertise that it mobilized.[11] The significance that the postcolonial state attributed to the law, modern science, medicine, and a professional civil service of managerial bureaucrats has been widely noted.[12] In Syria, these more common forms of expertise were deployed alongside those of the military and security establishments to inform the construction of modern citizenship, a practice visible during the Democratic Years and the authoritarian periods that preceded and followed them.

These multiple forms of expertise found ideal vehicles for their affirmation and dissemination during Syria's Democratic Years. State publications and a national broadcasting service established under the authoritarian regime of Colonel Adib al-Shishakli (1949–1954), which immediately preceded the Democratic Years, in conjunction with the repeal of that dictator's draconian press regulations, created unprecedented opportunities for those wielding professional expertise and harboring developmental aspirations. This new media environment provided multiple instruments for the presentation of an otherwise elite discourse to mass audiences, facilitating the transformation of this conversation into a pedagogical project, a discourse about the people propagated to the people with the aim of educating and uplifting them.

For example, the journals of the security establishment—*al-Jundi* (The Soldier), *Majallat al-Shurta wa al-Amm al-'Amm* (The Journal of the Police and Public Security), and *al-Majalla al-'Askariyya* (The Military Gazette)— circulated far beyond the agencies' personnel and featured contributions from members of the intelligentsia practicing a variety of professions in the public and private sectors. Precise circulation figures are unavailable for these specialized journals, and mass audience reception to their content is now largely unrecoverable. Nevertheless, we do have extensive information about these press vehicles and ample evidence of the messages they persistently and collectively sought to convey.

One lesson frequently imparted in the pages of these periodicals is the modern citizen's proper perception of and relationship with the "security man." In one such article, Public Security Police Inspector Mustafa al-Hajj Ibrahim frankly acknowledged the image problem confronting the public servant. Some Syrians saw in him an eternal adversary, one from whom the citizen must hide. Others viewed the security officer as a "corrupted" person who sought to please his superiors by any means, even at the expense of the citizen. Still others thought of him as a creature apart, operating in a space separate from the society of citizens. Although such views were common, they were, al-Hajj Ibrahim averred, not only mistaken, but the product of defective "consciousness."[13]

Fortunately, al-Hajj Ibrahim continued, there were other citizens with sound consciousness who correctly perceived the security man as the one who guarded and protected their security, and thus preserved their freedom. Citizens who possessed the appropriate consciousness realized that, unlike the security man of the colonial past, who was the hired lackey of foreign occupiers, professional officers at this time served the interests of the people. Thus, he believed, citizens should confide in and trust the security man, knowing that such reliance upon the state was their only source of protection. The intended message of this and similar articles is clear: respect for and cooperation with members of the security forces was an index of the modern citizen.[14]

Security expertise was deployed to teach the citizen to trust state officials and to inculcate a spirit of sacrifice on behalf of both state and nation. Expert discourses in other fields, such as medicine, science, and law, contributed to this project by presenting images of "the virtuous citizen" from their specific perspectives. This citizen (almost always gendered male) respected the rights of women while simultaneously acknowledging and exercising his patriarchal responsibilities. He also saw no contradiction in celebrating the advances of scientific progress while valuing many aspects of Islamic "tradition."

The virtuous citizen was, above all, self-consciously part of a collectivity. Yet his was a "multilevel" citizenry, variously delimited as Syrian, Levantine, or Arab.[15] It was not always clear, however, if the entirety of Syria's population could be incorporated into these larger wholes. One such, usually unspoken, concern was sectarian difference, which was referenced obliquely (through the mention of a family name or a place of origin) if at all, but was not the object of a specific pedagogical project. The differences that did figure explicitly and prominently in these texts were those associated with the urban-rural divide, with special concern expressed about the backwardness and ignorance of those residing in the countryside.

This perspective is evident in Director-General of Syrian Broadcasting Ratib al-Husami's editorial "The Citizen and the Radio." Decrying Syria's divisive class and regional distinctions, al-Husami asserted that radio is one of the state's most powerful tools for effacing such differences and "uplifting" the peasant and tribesman, who constituted the "overwhelming majority of the homeland's sons." Al-Husami then lamented the poverty, lack of education, and "primitive life" of those inhabiting Syria's "desert" and "desolate steppes," declaring that these "Bedouin" and "nomads" remained ignorant of the modern world and of the "affairs of their country," making them "unlike any [citizens] in the advanced world," which he associated with Germany, England, France, and the United States.[16]

EXPERT MEDIA AND THE PEDAGOGY OF DEVELOPMENT

Al-Husami's assertion of radio's developmental agency addresses one of the key issues of this study, the significance of mass media in the processes of producing citizens *and* legitimizing the experts who acted as the arbiters of citizenship. During the Democratic Years, the popular press, both state and private, was the critical space for the articulation of modern citizenship, the expression of professional expertise, and the interaction of these experts with their interlocutors, the members of the public presumably in need of education. This interaction took place not only in countless daily acts of readership, but also in advice columns through which Syrians sought the counsel of experts. The perceived urgency of citizen building is indicated by media experts' frequent invention of readers' queries when their actual correspondence did not serve this objective.

But this work was not confined to editorials or "serious" advice columns. It was also performed via the apparently frivolous genre of the cartoon. Two cartoon strips that appeared in the Defense Ministry's illustrated weekly journal *al-Jundi* exemplify this practice. Entitled "Those Who the People Scorn" (figs. I.1, I.2), these cartoon panels depict an oafish character engaging in a variety of behaviors that arouse horror in "the people," that is, his

FIGURE I.1 "Those Who the People Scorn." *Al-Jundi*, September 1, 1955, 6.

more refined fellow urbanites. He dresses and grooms himself in unseemly or absurd fashion and chooses particularly inappropriate settings in which to spread gossip. He also scolds his wife and uses foul language in public, and in numerous other ways displays a complete lack of "manners" as understood by those around him. *Al-Jundi* was a logical venue for the publication of these instructional cartoons, as the army's post-1949 expansion made it one of the most visible agents of Syria's rapid urbanization during the period. The overwhelming majority of military personnel in the streets of Syria's cities were new enlistees from rural areas, a fact that did not go unnoticed by long-term residents of Damascus, Aleppo, and Homs. Damascenes, in particular, were often alarmed by this influx of "country people," as these generally less well-educated and less sophisticated recruits were euphemistically known.[17]

But the comic strips' featured character is not depicted as a soldier or a peasant. He sports a Western-style business suit and tarboosh, the latter a passé symbol of social status. He is, however, clearly a parvenu incapable of enacting the identity to which he aspires, and so ignorant of appropriate deportment and speech that he is gleefully unaware of the displeasure evident on the faces of those around him. This depiction raises another potential category of exclusion from "proper" citizenship—class—that can operate independently or in association with gender, sect, or place of origin.

FIGURE I.2 "Those Who the People Scorn." *Al-Jundi,* September 22, 1955, 42.

MODERN DEVELOPMENTAL EXPERTISE

Developmental expertise has had enduring significance in the modern history of the Arab world.[18] In the postcolonial period, indigenous experts used mass media to both disseminate their views and enact their expert personas. The chapters that follow focus on three distinct and yet related figures who wielded professional expertise in fields crucial to the establishment, maintenance, and development of the modern state: medical science, the law, and the "arts of war." These experts' agency was not fixed, unbounded, or unchallenged. It required the deployment of various forms of knowledge and the application of specific skills. It had to be repeatedly asserted and performed, often in novel and surprising ways that call into question the relationship among individual agency, the performance of "work," and the—now deemed naive—high-modern conception of the expert as objective, disinterested, and apolitical.

The first of these experts, the attorney Najat Qassab Hasan, employed a variety of modern media to promote his vision of progressive reform. His most famous effort, the weekly radio program entitled "The Citizen and the Law," earned him lifelong prominence and the sobriquet "the radio attorney." At the very center of Syrian politics was Colonel 'Adnan al-Malki, the deputy chief of staff of the Syrian Army, whose April 1955 assassination provoked a torrent of rhetoric about the professional soldier as citizen and agent of national development par excellence. Al-Malki was virtually unknown to the Syrian public during his lifetime, acquiring a public persona only after his death. As an "expert" and an educator of the Syrian public, al-Malki was a product of the media. Finally, Sabri al-Qabbani was a politically engaged physician who used broadcast and print media to spread the twin gospels of science and progress to listeners and readers throughout the region, an audience he defined as "the citizens of the Arab East."

Moving in intersecting professional, political, and social circles, all three of these figures were well known to one another. In 1949, al-Qabbani served as an adviser to Syria's first military dictator, General Husni al-Za'im, whose patronage facilitated al-Malki's rapid rise through the ranks of the Syrian Army.[19] Al-Qabbani had also known Qassab Hasan since at least 1947, when both contributed to a variety of nationalist and satirical journals. Finally, Qassab Hasan was a neighbor and friend of al-Malki's brother Riyad, and Qassab Hasan's younger brother Burhan had long been a close army comrade of 'Adnan. More importantly, the three shared a space that constituted the center of gravity in post-independence Syrian politics. Although none had any formal association with a political party at the time of his prominence, all three displayed progressive, reformist tendencies and impatience with the speed of Syria's development that led them, despite espousing "democratic" ideals, to cooperate with Syria's postwar military dictators.

In addition, all of these men enjoyed privileged relationships with and access to mass media outlets. Qassab Hasan's personal connection to the first director-general of Syrian Broadcasting, Ahmad 'Isseh, facilitated the arrangements for his radio program, which made his name and voice familiar to most Syrians and paved the way for his subsequent television and book-publishing career.[20] Sabri al-Qabbani's relative Sabah (brother of the famous poet Nizar al-Qabbani) was 'Isseh's successor as broadcasting tsar, and Sabri's successful radio program and columns in a variety of state and privately owned publications enabled him to attract sufficient capital from advertisers to establish his own journal, *Tabibak* (Your Doctor), which reached subscribers from Morocco to Iraq.[21] Finally, al-Malki's name and visage dominated the majority of Syria's popular media for almost two years, and became well known to Egyptians, Lebanese, Jordanians, Iraqis, and Saudi Arabians as well. This posthumous prominence can be understood, in part, as a product of his previous role in mass media. One of al-Malki's duties as deputy chief of staff for operations was the supervision of the Military Cultural Committee, which served as the editorial board of *al-Jundi,* Syria's largest-circulation periodical during the period and the journal that initiated his posthumous lionization.[22]

In contrast to specialized, professional journals like *al-Nashra al-Iqtisadiyya li Ghurfat al-Tijara* (The Economic Bulletin of the Damascus Chamber of Commerce), *Majallat Kulliyat al-Tarbiyya* (The Journal of the College of Education), and *Majallat Niqabat al-Muhandisin* (The Journal of the Engineer's Union), the expert media featured in this study were mass media whose content and wide circulation bespoke their publishers' desire to speak to much broader audiences.

In sum, Syria's literate, radio-listening public could not have remained unaware of these three experts, or of their main message—the absolute necessity of reforming and strengthening Syria and the Arab world. Furthermore, in all three cases, the precondition for achieving this goal was the construction of a new Arab subject, an "autonomous male citizen" who was embedded in the "wider social and national order."[23] In the process, segments of the population who deviated from the norms of Arab, male, urban, literate, and heterosexual became objects of developmental attention.

STRUCTURE OF THE BOOK

This study consists of seven chapters. Chapter 1 presents a historical overview of the Democratic Years (1954–1958) in Syria. It argues that the period was distinctive for its freedom of public expression, and thus its proliferation of broadcast and print media, sources that reveal extraordinary hope and anxiety about Syria's future.

The remaining six chapters are organized into three parts, each pair of chapters focusing on the discourse produced by or about a single public figure. Within each pairing, the initial chapter analyzes the construction and articulation of a particular type of developmental expertise and authority, while the second explores the forms of citizenship that these "authoritative discourses" produced. Chapters 2 and 3 explore the relationships among the citizen, the state, and the law by analyzing the published writings of Najat Qassab Hasan, the "radio attorney." Chapter 2 focuses on Qassab Hasan's demonstration of his authority as an expert interpreter and reformer of Syria's complex, syncretic legal system. Chapter 3 analyzes the characteristics of his pedagogical project's idealized subject, the "virtuous citizen" in the form of the rational, self-disciplined, and civic-minded patriarch.

Chapters 4 and 5 analyze the discourse produced about Colonel 'Adnan al-Malki, the recently assassinated deputy chief of staff of the Syrian Army.

The media-disseminated narratives of al-Malki's life and death transformed him into a "the martyr of Arabism," while providing powerful institutional support for long-present authoritarian and antidemocratic impulses in Syrian politics.[24] Chapter 4 analyzes the propagandistic use of mass media and various forms of state power to valorize Syria's politically ambitious officer class and reify their preeminent role in Syrian politics through the destruction and intimidation of their opponents. Chapter 5 explores these media campaigns' celebration of the redemptive power of sacrifice, which gave meaning to politically motivated violence and produced a new, heroic representation of citizenship, the "martial citizen."[25]

Chapters 6 and 7 analyze the medical and scientific writings of the physician, medical journalist, and broadcaster Sabri al-Qabbani, who employed paradigmatic elements of nationalist ideology to present an idealized historicization of medical science, and appropriated the rhetorical modes, structures, elements, and devices of Islamic discourse to dispense his scientific, yet highly normative, rulings. Chapter 6 explores al-Qabbani's use of advertising revenue from multinational pharmaceutical manufacturers to both validate his medical and scientific authority and facilitate the mass distribution of his developmental vision throughout the Arab world. Chapter 7 analyzes al-Qabbani's efforts to demarcate the "libidinal economy" of the region, defining and delimiting the proper sexual and reproductive practices of his developmental vision's agent, the married, heteronormative "conjugal citizen."

This book's focus on the developmental discourse of these media celebrities locates their concerns within a set of interrelated developments in the region: the emergence of the sovereign, postcolonial nation-state; the appearance of truly mass media; and both institutions' focus on the raw material of developmental mobilization, the citizenry. In exploring the above, this study's narrative follows several interrelated trajectories—from the abstract to the concrete; from nature to society, and then to nation-state; from law to science, and then to the violent application of both; and from persuasion to coercion. In this way, it traces the course of a postcolonial state's failed experiment with democratic governance, and its initial abandonment and subsequent readoption of authoritarian solutions for its manifold and seemingly intractable problems. The work concludes by attempting to locate the Democratic Years and the pedagogical project of its modern experts within the historical processes that produced the country's authoritarian outcome, arguing that in this, as in so many other ways, Syria's post-independence experience exemplifies that of the region.

1 Syria during the Democratic Years

On February 24, 1954, military dictator Colonel Adib al-Shishakli resigned as president of Syria and fled the country, thereby ending a five-year period ("The Era of Military Coups") during which all political activity in Syria had been circumscribed by the will and objectives of senior military officers. Four years later, on February 21, 1958, the United Arab Republic (UAR), a pan-Arabist union of Syria and Egypt, was proclaimed, producing a three-year subsumption of all political activity beneath several layers of corporatist mass-mobilization organizations that operated under the authority of Gamal Abdel Nasser and his local surrogates. The interim period of 1954–1958, remembered locally as the "Democratic Years," provides the temporal framework of this book.[1] The retrospective designation of this period expresses a widely held revulsion for the periods of war, oppression, and occupation that preceded 1954, as well as equally intense disappointment with the increasingly brutal and repressive regimes that followed.

From 1516 to 1918, the area comprised by the Syrian Arab Republic, like most of the countries in the region we now call the Middle East, was part of the Ottoman Empire. At its height, the empire, one of the great "world empires" of the early modern period, stretched from the Balkans to Yemen and from the Mediterranean coast of North Africa to the Persian Gulf. Syria owes its existence to the post–World War I settlement that destroyed the empire. In the Levant, the First World War was truly calamitous. An Allied naval blockade, combined with Ottoman requisitions of foodstuffs and ethnic cleansing campaigns, yielded malnutrition, disease, and civilian casualties on a scale unimaginable in Europe. In Damascus, Ottoman wartime governor Jamal Pasha's imprisonment and execution of Arab nationalists earned him the appellation *al-Saffah* ("the shedder of blood"), and resulted in renaming the city center Martyrs' Square. The chief legacies of the wartime experience were profound bitterness, the spread of Arab nationalist sentiment, and longings for independence from "foreign" governance.

These sentiments were heightened by British wartime promises of an Arab Kingdom that encompassed much of the Arabian Peninsula, including most of Syria. But the British also made other wartime allies conflicting promises that were, unlike their pledges to the Arabs, upheld by the new League of Nations. Thus arbitrary borders were drawn separating British and French mandate territories, the French receiving present-day Syria and Lebanon and the British taking Iraq and Palestine, the latter comprising present-day Israel, Jordan, and the Palestinian Occupied Territories.

French armed forces invaded Syria in July 1920, defeated the armed forces of the short-lived Kingdom of Syria at the Battle of Maysaloun, where they created Syria's first military martyr, Defense Minister Yusuf al-'Azma. The French then put King Feisal and his government to flight, carved the Republic of Lebanon from Syrian territory for the benefit of their Christian clients, divided the remaining territory into several mini-states, and ruthlessly crushed any overtly expressed opposition to their political and economic domination. After twenty-six years of economic stagnation and social unrest under French occupation, Syria finally achieved its sovereignty in 1946.

The ensuing flourishing of post-independence optimism—an attitude captured in Najat Qassab Hasan's eulogy for 'Adnan al-Malki—soon gave way to disgust with the corruption and incompetence Syria's civilian politicians displayed during the First Arab-Israeli War (1948–1949). As a result, many Syrians rejoiced when General Husni al-Za'im staged the country's first military coup in April 1949. Al-Za'im and his eventual successor, al-Shishakli, brushed Syria's traditional political elites aside and initiated sweeping legal, constitutional, bureaucratic, economic, social, and political reforms designed to accelerate Syria's development. As a result, both strongmen were initially supported by a majority of Syria's reform-minded journalists, entrepreneurs, professionals, and intellectuals.

Syria's abortive experiment with democracy was terminated by another short-lived experiment, the United Arab Republic that merged Syria and Egypt (1958–1961). A subsequent attempt to reestablish the old political order ended with yet another military coup in March 1961, initiating a chaotic period of successive coups, counter-coups, mass arrests, bloody street battles, and increasingly more repressive forms of governance culminating in the populist-authoritarian dictatorship of Hafez al-Asad (1970–2000).

Thus for many who lived through the postwar period, the Democratic Years became the focus of nostalgic reflection, a hopeful interregnum between periods of occupation and disillusion.[2] Such attitudes are understandable, as these years featured the restoration of civilian government and the constitution of 1950, a document that afforded, in Syria's historical experience, unprecedented freedoms of speech, press, and association.[3] These events were soon followed by the "first free election in the Arab world," featuring universal adult suffrage, candidates from across the ideological spectrum, secret ballots, private voting booths, and extraordinary measures to prevent fraud and corruption.[4] In this way, the Democratic Years later seemed the antithesis of the subsequent "Arab malaise" or the "widespread and deeply seated feeling that Arabs have no future, no way of improving their condition."[5]

While this period is now seen as one of general optimism, it actually featured increasing tension and political instability, as the old system of resource allocation, under which personality and patronage networks administered by the traditional elites controlled the lion's share of economic activity, broke down. The political arrangements devised to serve and perpetuate this segment's interests also disintegrated in the 1950s. This breakdown was manifested in increasingly complex social stratification and the incessant realignment of classes, personalities, and interest groups, resulting in the intensification of social conflict and the presentation of alternative models of political, social, and economic relations. One manifestation of this new environment was labor unrest. Private and public sector employees struck or threatened to strike over salaries, benefits, and working conditions throughout the summer and fall of 1954.[6] As a result, the lot of many civil servants was improved, and new links were forged between wageworkers and leftist political parties.

THE LEGAL CONTEXT OF CITIZENSHIP

In Syria, urban elites had been laboring to "fashion" the "identity of that historically unique subject"—the citizen—since the late-Ottoman Tanzimat (1839–1876), a period of modernizing reforms that included numerous liberalizing edicts; a new land code; extensive revisions of the empire's commercial, civil, criminal, and penal codes; a constitution; and the establishment of a parliament.[7] The Tanzimat initiated a process of defensive developmentalist reforms that persisted in the empire's successor states long after its dissolution.

The French Mandate period (1920–1946) produced a system of "colonial citizenship" that was rigorously gendered and hierarchical, imposing on "citizens" all the obligations inherent to a civic-republican order while bestowing few of its rights. Syria's first post-independence governments were content to maintain this system, neglecting to address its structural anachronisms and gender inequalities.[8] Ironically, it took the authoritarian regimes of al-Zaʿim and al-Shishakli to spur the drafting of a new constitution and the reform and streamlining of Syria's welter of Ottoman and French legal codes. Al-Shishakli repealed and replaced the French Mandate legislation on nationality in stages (1951, 1953), oversaw the drafting of a more liberal constitution in 1950, and promulgated a new Personal Status Code in September 1953 (Legislative Decree 59).[9] While the key elements of al-Shishakli's subsequent Peronist-style authoritarian presidency were dismantled, his previous reforms were retained, providing the structural basis for a relatively more democratic social and political order after his overthrow.

The Personal Status Code, part of al-Shishakli's broad program of top-down legal and social reform, was particularly significant, and was supported by most reformist intellectuals. At the time of its enactment, the 1953 code represented the most fully realized example of a continuing, region-wide project—the reconciliation of the *shari'a* with the perceived imperatives of modern state and economic development by reference to various European civic and criminal codes.[10]

The constitution of 1950 is another case in point: It defined Syria as a "sovereign Arab Republic with a democratic parliamentary regime"; eliminated legal designations based on gender, class, and other distinctions; and simultaneously invoked "the will of God and the free wish of the people." It also guaranteed "freedom of belief" while stipulating Islam as the religion of the country's president, designating the *shari'a* as the "main source of legislation," and restricting the government's "respect" and "protection" to the practices of "theistic religions . . . consistent with public order."[11] In other words, this syncretic document gestured to the norms of both parliamentary democracy and modernist Islam, while retaining one of the authoritarian state's most critical presumptions, the right to intervene into the "private" sphere in the name of public order.

The 1950 constitution also provided the framework for the discussion of citizenship during the Democratic Years. Although the citizen is clearly the subject of this document—the term *muwatin* (citizen) appears more than twenty times—the concept is never explicitly defined in relation to nationality or criteria like birth, naturalization, or parentage. What is clearly articulated, however, is the drafters' conception of citizenship. While several articles bestow equality of rights and opportunities, the overwhelming emphasis is on duties and responsibilities. For example, "every citizen" is expected to "contribute his life, effort, wealth, and knowledge" to "the republic," to display a "spirit of sacrifice," and to fulfill his "sacred duty" through "compulsory" military service."[12]

Thus the operative definition of citizenship at the outset of the Democratic Years was "civic-republican" (emphasizing duties) rather than "liberal" (emphasizing rights), striking a tenuous balance between individual freedoms and the authoritarian requirements of the developing state, while ultimately favoring the latter. This perspective is evident in the expert media discourse featured in this study.[13] These experts usually elaborated the citizen's duties through concrete, minutely detailed examples while celebrating rights as vague abstractions or subsuming them within the concept of "virtues." Prominent among the latter were various forms of "judgment," "strength," and "self-discipline," individual qualities deemed critical to the development and advancement of a vulnerable, young state.[14] Those asserting or lauding modern expertise incessantly celebrated civic virtue in the form of service to God, family, state, and nation.

The noblest expression of this civic virtue was the fulfillment of patriotic duty through military service. The ideal of the "citizen-soldier" entailed the "ultimate sacrifice"—life itself—on behalf of the state. Since military service had, until quite recently, been an exclusively male endeavor, citizenship was "a status invented by men for men."[15] Syrian discourses about civic virtue consistently displayed this gendered conception of citizenship, either ignoring women altogether, or celebrating their "gentle," "civilizing," and subordinate role in the making of virtuous citizens.

THE POLITICS OF POSTCOLONIAL DEVELOPMENT

A leitmotif of the literature on modern Syria is the prolonged conflict that ended in the establishment of a populist-authoritarian dictatorship and its inventory of political, economic, social, and cultural consequences. The "struggle for Syria" actually comprised the dynamic interaction of several interrelated global, regional, and domestic contests that unfolded in the fields of high politics, political economy, and culture.[16] Scholars who privilege an internal struggle disagree over the identity of the key players, variously favoring social classes or political actors who commanded the loyalties of ethnic, confessional, or regional groupings. Viewed from the outside, the struggle appeared to be a contest between regional and/or global powers, for instance, Egypt versus Iraq or the United States versus the Soviet Union.[17]

During the Democratic Years, Syrian domestic politics shifted decidedly leftward, and the country pursued a foreign policy of alignment with Egypt and nonalignment in the international sphere. 'Adnan al-Malki's life and death were critical in the foreign policy sphere, as he was an advocate of the

ESS (Egypt, Syria, Saudi Arabia) alignment and Syria's joint-military defense pact with Egypt.[18] The response to al-Malki's murder eliminated the sway of officers receptive to American influence, and accelerated the progressive, anti-Western trends in parliament and the army. During late 1955 and early 1956, a "progressive, anti-Western, and deeply pro-unionist" coalition emerged in Syria's parliament based on an alliance of the Ba'th Party, "red millionaire" Khalid al-'Azm, and Communist Party General Secretary Khalid Bakdash.[19]

In early 1956, these forces formed a "Progressive National Front" in parliament. Later in the year, the Suez Crisis and a failed U.S./British/Iraqi coup attempt further discredited pro-Western politicians and intensified leftist tendencies in parliament, the army, the state bureaucracy, and the populace.[20] A second U.S. coup attempt failed in 1957, producing a diplomatic crisis, the movement of Turkish NATO troops to Syria's northern border, and invasion hysteria among the Syrian public.[21] In the same year, new electoral successes for the Progressive Front led to the signing of a trade and cooperation agreement with the Soviet Union.[22] Finally, a conflict within the Progressive Front in late 1957 produced a political crisis, which was finally resolved when a coalition of leftist military officers and progressive politicians accomplished the "dissolution of Syria's existence as an independent state" by compelling the country's absorption into a pan-Arabist union with Egypt, the United Arab Republic.[23]

The Syrian armed forces played a significant role in these processes throughout the Democratic Years. Upon independence in 1946, the government of urban notables viewed Syria's army, an institution trained, equipped, and commanded by French officers, and which included sizeable numbers of Circassian, 'Alawi, Druze, Isma'ili, and Christian commissioned and non-commissioned officers, with suspicion and unease.[24] These tense civil-military relations deteriorated markedly after independence, as the civilian government slashed the size and budget of the army, then awarded military supply contracts to corrupt or incompetent cronies. Both measures yielded disastrous results on the battlefields of the First Arab-Israeli War of 1948–1949, producing widespread, bitter resentment, a major contributing factor to the army's decision to seize power in 1949.[25]

Despite pledging a permanent "return to the barracks" immediately after deposing Adib al-Shishakli in February 1954, the army soon began to interfere in the composition of cabinets, attempted to influence legislation, drew a series of red lines in foreign policy, and otherwise made its collective opinion known to civilian politicians, foreign governments, and the public. A newly predominant clique of army officers—largely a single generational cohort—

[handwritten margin note: relationship between civilian government and military]

attempted to remake the institution in its own image, to forge a collective, professional identity that would "preclude subnational and primordial allegiances," thereby completing the army's transformation from a despised instrument of French imperialism populated by groups of suspect loyalty into a corps of citizen soldiers.[26]

Yet in 1955, the Syrian armed forces were ill equipped to realize this citizen-building agenda. The inherently political institution was riven by open ideological conflict and, beneath the surface, by tensions based on personality, class, sect, and regional origin.[27] Initially, al-Malki's murder only heightened these intra-army and civil-military tensions. This background explains why left-leaning Sunni Arab officers adopted al-Malki as "their" martyr, as his transfiguration would add a sacred component to the "progressive" developmental legitimacy and provide an admirable weapon with which to attack and intimidate their rivals, both within and without the armed forces. Although developmentalism seeks the combined operation of robust security institutions and the rule of law, the former often trumps the latter, as it did in the Syrian case.

In the midst of this ideological conflict, the majority of those participating in the struggle for Syria agreed on one critical issue. Just as no Syrian public figure of the period could earn political capital by displaying anything but reverence for Arab nationalism, confidence in the necessity and inevitably of progress through development was equally mandatory. National development, in all its moral and material forms, was understood to be the mission of every government, be it civilian or military, and of every political party, whether revolutionary or reactionary, and of every individual who had a significant public voice.[28]

In sum, a developmental episteme couched in the metanarratives of progress and modernity underpinned and delimited the discourse of both experts and high politics with which these ideological conflicts were waged. As a result, the period 1946–1958 witnessed "the rapid expansion of state intervention in the economy." Again, the authoritarian regime of Adib al-Shishalki led the way, pursuing corporatist and autarkic policies on an unprecedented scale. Yet the restoration of civilian government did not result in a return to the laissez-faire policies of the old notables who governed Syria in the period immediately after independence. Instead, a broad consensus emerged that the "the postcolonial politics of state and economy building" demanded that the former intervene more directly in the latter.[29]

Such an effort, however, would require strengthening the state's institutions and expanding their powers. Progressive/leftist politicians embraced this agenda most ardently, as it enhanced opportunities to intensify social and economic transformation, mobilize popular forces, and ameliorate the plight of workers and peasants. Advocates of these objectives routinely justified them as essential preconditions for economic growth and development.[30] Most advocates of development, both inside and outside the realm of high politics, thus betrayed concerns that nascent state institutions were inadequate for the task. These anxieties would ultimately privilege order and stability over individual freedoms, in Syria and throughout the region.

THE CITY AND THE COUNTRYSIDE

Like most cities in the developing world, Damascus was a very different place in the 1950s than it had been a generation earlier. The city's population grew from 359,000 in 1950 to 530,000 in 1960, a 4 percent annual increase. During this period, Syrian private investment also expanded rapidly, causing a marked rise in national income that was concentrated in urban areas.[31] Syria experienced a concomitant rise in aggregate literacy to approximately 44 percent, with 53–60 percent literacy in Damascus.[32] As the middle class grew in numbers, the lifestyles of the bourgeoisie became visible features of urban life.[33] Hanan Qassab Hasan, daughter of "radio attorney" Najat Qassab Hasan, described the Syrian bourgeoisie's origins, outlook, and ambition: "This stratum, an emerging new class, the professional, educated bourgeoisie . . . as a rule, emerged from or below the median. . . . By that time [the 1950s] they were sufficiently well educated and becoming large enough in numbers to have some impact. And the meaning of modernity was to them, and to us, the power to advance the world."[34] This transformational ambition was a signal characteristic of the postcolonial expert media of Najat Qassab Hasan, Sabri al-Qabbani, and 'Adnan al-Malki's panegyrists.

The distinguishing characteristic of the bourgeoisie in any society is the perception that they are identifiably different from those who are located above and below them in social class hierarchies. There is also the sense that they are something new, distinguishable from all who came before and indicative of those who will follow. In other words, they signify the future. The bourgeoisie of 1950s Damascus possessed the requisite education and fluency in the "idioms of modernity" to envision a future very different from Syria's past.[35] The media discourse featured in this study spoke both to and on behalf of this stratum, telling them who they were and who they should aspire to be.

The urban landscape of Damascus changed in other ways as well. As the city continued to expand to the north and west, the Old City and its environs, and the patterns of commercial and social life associated with these areas, were progressively marginalized and/or idealized as historical artifacts. Public transportation systems, new types of commercial and residential architecture, wider and straighter streets, and new patterns of work, entertainment, and leisure that had been introduced in the late Ottoman and Mandate periods now became the norm rather than the exception. Furthermore, this new environment facilitated, for good or ill, a greater degree of anonymity in social relations than previously possible. The city became a place "where strangers are likely to meet."[36]

The 1950s also witnessed the expansion and consolidation of new, modern spaces, both physical and conceptual, in Damascus. Physically, this new space was centered on—but not limited to—the new "downtown" of Damascus, an assortment of contiguous neighborhoods known collectively as al-Salhiyya. Conceptually, it entailed a variety of activities and experiences that American contemporaries would have called nightlife: the cinema, theater, restaurants, nightclubs, hotels featuring entertainment complexes, dances, concerts, and special-occasion parties in public places.

Damascenes who possessed sufficient means could enjoy many such bourgeois experiences in the city center, as merchants provided a host of urban, mostly nocturnal pleasures and an equal number of associated services. The state played a considerable role in this process. During the period under question, the most significant manifestation of this support was the Damascus International Exposition. Inaugurated in September 1954, the exposition necessitated substantial investment in infrastructure and stimulus for tourism, increasing demand in every sector of the hospitality industry. It also spawned film, book, and other festivals, attracted foreign interest and participation, and provided a model for the presentation of modernity. Located to the southwest of al-Salhiyya in and around a former city park/racecourse on the southern edge of the "Beirut road," the exposition's construction symbolized the consolidation of the western expansion of "Damascus proper" that had been underway for a generation.

According to all the evidence, the bourgeoisie of 1950s Damascus believed they had the "right to the city."[37] But the sector of Damascus's population that increased most dramatically during this period was wageworkers, a category that included a growing commercial and industrial proletariat, who contributed to the labor unrest.[38] Most of these low-wage workers were recent immigrants from the countryside, where conditions were starkly different. In those areas, poverty, poor or nonexistent infrastructure, and the relative absence of schools, hospitals, and government services remained the norm for the "majority of the homeland's sons."[39]

A summary of healthcare statistics provides a glimpse of this reality. A 1954 World Bank survey conducted with the cooperation of the Syrian government documented a total of only 3,000 beds in Syrian government hospitals, and a total of just 1.23 beds per 1,000 inhabitants in all public and private facilities. Furthermore, the study identified only 880 physicians in the entire country, most of them in private practice in Syria's four largest cities. The World Bank study indicated serious deficiencies in every possible category, and repeatedly noted a glaring disparity between the availability of services in urban and rural areas.[40] This disparity, along with other forms of "difference," made the inhabitants of the countryside natural objects of experts' developmental aspirations and anxieties.[41]

Given the demographic changes, expanded freedoms of assembly, and leftward political shifts described above, the public spaces of Damascus also became sites of contestation. Ba'thist, Nasserist, communist, and other "radical" forces employed new, more inclusive, and ideologically informed modes of political mobilization to stage large, noisy, and sometimes violent demonstrations, strikes, and marches in the city's streets, parks, and traffic circles. These and other manifestations of disorder frequently brought the increased numbers of military and security personnel now stationed in the capital into the streets as well.

The resulting anxieties experienced by the urbane, self-consciously modern inhabitants of this environment produced two interrelated phenomena. First, reformers with developmental aspirations now displayed a pronounced sensitivity to the Syrian countryside's moral and material "backwardness." Second, the valorization of recently established modes of "civilized" (*mutamaddin*) urban life would subsequently inspire nostalgic yearnings for an idealized urban environment that supported a lifestyle of leisure and consumption perceived to be under threat by disorder.[42]

THE MIRROR OF CITIZENS: SYRIAN EXPERT MEDIA IN CONTEXT

The military regimes of 1949–1954 sought, with varying degrees of success, to control the public discussion of politically sensitive issues. They promulgated a bewildering variety of communiqués, legislative decrees, and basic laws seeking to banish "corruption," "foreign influence," and "destabilizing forces" from the press.[43] They also displayed their interest in mass media by centralizing and expanding the country's national broadcasting service and by increasing the number and variety of state-owned publishing enterprises imbued with citizen-building and mass-mobilizing agendas.[44] Due to their developmental utility, these entities survived the transition to civilian government, retaining staple features like "Hurriyyat al-Muwatin" (The Citizen's Freedom) and "Thaqafat al-Muwatin" (The Education of the Citizen).[45]

Upon the restoration of civilian government in March 1954, a new page was turned in the tempestuous history of relations between state and press. With the restoration of the parliament and constitution of 1950, all subsequent press legislation was purged from the books. In the absence of any qualifying legislation for the press, the governing principles were embodied in Article 15 of the 1950 document, which granted remarkable press freedom and autonomy from government supervision.[46]

As a result, an astonishing number and variety of periodicals were published during the Democratic Years.[47] Along with a plethora of specialty journals published by Syrian government agencies, foreign embassies, private corporations, educational and religious institutions, and professional associations, literate Syrians could choose from a remarkable range of conventional news and entertainment periodicals. In Damascus alone, at least twenty-nine different titles appeared as daily newspapers between 1954 and 1958.[48] While many of these publications were marginal, ephemeral, duplicates (mergers and name changes were common), or vanity publications, at least twelve were genuine mass circulation dailies that appeared five to six times per week without interruption throughout the Democratic Years. In addition, more than forty weekly, biweekly, monthly, and bimonthly newspapers and magazines were published in the capital during this period.

These periodicals are significant for two main reasons. First, they comprise the largest body of primary sources from which we can reconstruct Syrians' lived experiences of momentous changes, as the archives of the post-independence Syrian state remain closed to researchers. Second, they constituted "cafées-in-print, places the reading public could frequent to pick up information and to entertain themselves," and performed the function of constructing and maintaining "a community of like-minded people."[49] The discourse in expert media outlets like *Your Doctor, The Soldier, The Journal of the Police and Public Security,* and the programs and publications of the Syrian Broadcasting Service presented this community with a menu of attitudes, perspectives, and behaviors that delimited and defined the citizen and his relationship to compatriots, the state, and the nation.

Thanks in large measure to the work of Benedict Anderson, the capacity of mass media ("print-capitalism") to disseminate ideas about politics, commerce, consumption, entertainment, sexuality, science, and law; to evoke collective dreams and anxieties; to "cement sociabilities, prescribe behavior," "establish new distinctions," and "give rise to belief, imagination, and action" is unquestioned by most scholars of the modern period.[50] In fact, mass media's centrality to the construction of various forms of collective identity is a theme of several recent case studies of Middle Eastern countries, including Syria.[51] Yet the massive and diverse body of texts produced in state- and privately owned periodicals published during the Democratic Years remains largely untapped by scholars. By focusing on the pedagogical discourse found in expert media sources, this study adds a new, previously overlooked dimension to the story.

Some methodological observations about these sources are in order. In the postwar Arab world, a business model prevailed that was very different from that commonly pursued by publishers in the West. Whereas the overwhelming majority of periodicals published during this period in Europe and the United States derived their revenue from advertisements, the cost of which was calculated according to paid circulation, in 1950s Syria, advertising and paid circulation were only two possible sources of revenue. Others included overt or covert financial support from (1) the Syrian government; (2) political parties and/or prominent members of these parties; (3) agencies of foreign governments dispensing subsidies or providing technical support to the publications with editorial policies deemed in accordance with those governments' policy objectives; or (4) business and/or political figures providing compensation, either in the form of cash or advertising contracts, in return for favorable stories camouflaged as hard news, or the suppression of scandalous stories about themselves and their associates.[52]

Given this frequent state-subsidization of ostensibly private media, we cannot treat state and private media as two discrete units of analysis. We can make no analytical distinctions between "top-down" (hegemonic) or "bottom-up" (popular) speech based on the nominal status of any specific publication. During the Democratic Years, Syrian mass media constituted one large, diverse landscape that was guided by the presumptions, aspirations, and anxieties of male, urban, educated elites. Yet expert media comprised more than a conversation between these elites. It spoke most frequently and earnestly to the public. When dissenting voices appeared, they rarely questioned the developmental ethos described above.[53]

As a result, my approach to these sources focuses on the texts addressed to the literate public rather than the responses of readers. But this approach is not exclusively informed by the theoretical or methodological dispositions of cultural history. Due to the business model described above, Syrian publishers routinely inflated the circulation figures they provided to potential advertisers and the public while jealously protecting the actual numbers from the eyes of these advertisers, their competitors, and the state.[54] Thus the available data on Syrian press circulation is unreliable. We cannot know—we can only infer—which media outlets reached the largest number of people.[55]

Furthermore, many of the readers' responses appearing in the Syrian press were fictitious, composed by the expert "replying" to them. Many other letters to the editor were the compositions of military and security personnel writing at the request of senior officers who supervised journals published by the Ministries of Defense and Interior. My approach to these sources uncovers the public articulation of an epistemic edifice, a discursive field that illuminates the expression of postcolonial knowledge and aspirations at the "critical juncture" of modern Syrian and Arab history.[56]

2   The Citizen and the Law

> During the fifties, the focus of our attention was the West. How
> do we become like the West? The conflict between modernism
> and the desire to hold on to the past, the direction toward mod-
> ernism and toward modern life and the imitation of the West, the
> fifties were like that exactly, and that was the kind of subject that
> Najat Qassab Hasan talked about. He and all of his colleagues
> were working for the construction of a modern state.
>
> —HANAN QASSAB HASAN, FEBRUARY 27, 2002

No SYRIAN "working for the construction of a modern state" through the
inculcation of citizenship enjoyed more enduring prominence than Najat
Qassab Hasan (c. 1920–1997), a social-reforming attorney who built a career
on such public education.[1] Using newly available technology and adapting
existing genres and structures of rhetorical authority, he sought to reform
laws that structure social relations and thereby to reform the individual, the
family, and the nation.

Najat Qassab Hasan (fig. 2.1) was a polymath who pursued an extraordinary number and variety of occupations: attorney, teacher, political activist, journalist, author, musician, composer, dramatist, satirist, screenwriter,
caricaturist, translator, grammarian, and media personality. In the process,
he became a pivotal figure in independent Syria's leftist/nationalist intellectual circles. Born in Damascus into a pious family of minor 'ulama' (religious
scholars), merchants, and craftsmen, Qassab Hasan studied the sciences and
philosophy at the Tajhiz, Damascus's most prestigious Arabic-language secondary school, where, in 1937, he joined the Syrian Communist Party. He later
attended the Syrian University, where he received bachelor's degrees in primary and secondary education from the Teachers' College[2] and later a J.D.
from the Faculty of Law in 1945.[3]

Qassab Hasan's family represents a classic example of upward mobility,
and by extension social progress, in modern Syria. His father, Sa'd al-Din, was

FIGURE 2.1 Najat Qassab Hasan. *Al-Idha'a al-Suriyya,* October 16, 1955, 10.

a member of a Sufi brotherhood and an "Arab carpenter," or skilled artisan who specialized in fashioning doors, windows, and wooden ornaments for the traditional houses of the Ottoman period. Thanks to the expansion of educational opportunities, from such humble origins the family produced, in Najat's and subsequent generations, physicians, attorneys, academics, high-ranking civil servants and military officers, and government ministers.[4]

Throughout his time at the university, Qassab Hasan worked as a secondary-school teacher and a journalist while also volunteering as an adult literacy teacher in rural villages around Damascus, which provided firsthand knowledge of lower standards of living, education, and healthcare in the countryside.[5] He continued his political activities, eventually becoming the Communist Party's Damascus secretary and a member of its Central Committee. For several years, the party was the focus of Qassab Hasan's life, the vehicle for much of his social activism, and the place where he met his future wife. General Secretary Khalid Bakdash engineered Qassab Hasan's expulsion from the party in 1951, ostensibly for the latter's bourgeois and Titoist proclivities. The real reason was almost certainly Qassab Hasan's opposition to Bakdash's dictatorial style of leadership and slavish adherence to Soviet policies, particularly his endorsement of the partition of Palestine.[6]

The expulsion was a turning point in Qassab Hasan's life as he lost his institutional base, as well as many former sources of employment, and was compelled to return with renewed vigor to journalism and the practice of law. Despising the daily realities of conventional legal practice, Qassab Hasan continued to provide pro bono legal services to peasants, unskilled workers, small businessmen, and abused women and children, while seeking ways to use his professional training to educate the average Syrian about the law as an instrument of social justice.

Eventually, Qassab Hasan hit upon the solution combining his skills as attorney, journalist, teacher, and polemicist. Joining others asserting various forms of developmental expertise, he employed print and broadcast media to dispense legal advice and knowledge to the masses. The most popular of these efforts during the 1950s was the radio program *al-Muwatin wa al-Qanun* (The Citizen and the Law; fig. 2.2), which was modeled on another expert's program: Sabri al-Qabbani's successful *Tabibak khalf al-Midhya'* (Your Doctor behind the Microphone).[7] Qassab Hasan's program provided a forum for dispensing factual information about civil and criminal law, and presented an idealized image of the modern, responsible citizen to a broad cross-section of Syrian society, making his a household name and earning him the moniker "the radio attorney."[8]

The main source for this and the following chapter is the column "The Citizen and the Law," which consisted of edited transcripts of the radio program of the same name.[9] These transcripts appeared in the Syrian National Broadcasting Service's official biweekly, illustrated magazine, *al-Idha'a al-Suriyya* (Syrian Broadcasting), which was imbued with the spirit of citizen-building and developmental mobilization. In his *The People's Stories: Two Hundred and Ninety Civil Cases That Appeared in the Column "The Citizen and the Law,"* Qassab Hasan enumerated the underlying principles of his approach to the law in response to a listener's query. In summary form, they are: (1) "I am with the law"; (2) "I am with the *shari'a*"; (3) "I am with custom"; (4) "morals are . . . superior to any text"; (5) "when I look to and focus my mind upon the past, I do so for the sake of the future"; (6) "I am with women because in most cases they are ill-treated and targets for the anger of men"; and (7) "I am . . . with progress."[10]

Thanks to his knowledge of the complexities of Syria's post-independence civil and criminal codes, rhetorical prowess, and careful selection of topics, Qassab Hasan was able to present his advice and judgments as both thoroughly modern and in keeping with a specific construction of Islamic tradition. This exercise was central to his broader agenda and a characteristic

FIGURE 2.2 "The Citizen and the Law." *Al-Idha'a al-Suriyya,* October 16, 1955, 10.

feature of much of the period's public discourse. Qassab Hasan's selective appropriation of the expertise of *'ulama'*—broad, deep knowledge of the *shari'a,* a legal construct equally complex as Syria's criminal and civil codes, and the special interpretive skills that are a hallmark of that scholarly tradition—enabled him to assert and substantiate his very specific brand of expertise, one intimately associated with the development of the modern bureaucratic state.

His privileged access to state-owned media gave Qassab Hasan's pronouncements the imprimatur of officialdom, endowing him with a particular kind of expert authority. This access also provided the means to engage in rhetorical sleight of hand, the invention of correspondents, letters, and issues to further his purpose, implanting specific legal or ethical principles in the popular consciousness. A highly educated man who was profoundly dissatisfied with the current state of his society, he employed—in alliance with the prestige and power of the state—the most modern technology available in an attempt to refashion that society according to an idealized image of his own conception. His formal ideological commitments and genuine sympathies for the poor aside, Qassab Hasan's idealized citizen invariably displayed the characteristics of the "enlightened" bourgeoisie. And Qassab Hasan's equally sincere advocacy of women's rights was frequently accompanied by the endorsement of patriarchal responsibilities and privileges.

Najat Qassab Hasan had an abiding contempt for the stereotypical attorney in private practice—the mercenary "shark" or "hired gun"—who had long been a popular figure of avarice, dishonesty, and the artful perversion of justice. He declared that he never wanted to be an attorney, and compared the profession to a "person who enters a shop full of coal wearing a white suit. He cannot avoid having his clothes soiled." Eschewing conventional legal practice that "involves disregarding the rights of another party," Qassab Hasan pursued what he deemed his profession's proper purpose, providing "assistance to the weak and the aggrieved party," in other words, the project of social reform.[11]

When Qassab Hasan spoke of the law, he meant both the cold theoretical abstraction and the Syrian state's synthetic legal system, which encompassed "secular" legislation; the shari'a, or "Islamic law"; and, finally, *'urfi* (customary) law, a body of "tribal" and other pre-Islamic practices that were still prevalent in the rural areas of 1950s Syria. Qassab Hasan's reliance on all three sources of legal thought and practice reflects his pragmatic embrace of the Syrian legal system's complexities. The list's hierarchy of systems bespeaks Qassab Hasan's developmental bent, which often led him to conflate the urban with modernity and rationality, and the rural with backwardness and ignorance, a perspective shared by many of his Arab nationalist predecessors and contemporaries.[12] Yet Qassab Hasan viewed all three legal systems as subordinate to "morals," by which he meant universal and transcendent principles inherently "superior to any text."[13]

As an arbiter endowed with the requisite knowledge and authority, he rendered legal opinions sanctioned by any, all, or none of the three systems. At the level of more specific ideological commitment, Qassab Hasan's empathy with women was in keeping with his lifelong advocacy on behalf of the exploited, abused, and marginalized.[14] It also expressed a central concern of both colonial and postcolonial epistemology, the "advancement" of women as an index of modernity and civilization.[15] Syria's prevailing social and economic arrangements had long condemned other groups, chief among them peasants and religious or ethnic minorities, to subordination and dependency. Yet these groups received no mention in Qassab Hasan's manifesto.

His conception of historical process is also telling. His assertion that the past's chief relevance lay in its capacity to inspire those attempting to shape a better future was in perfect accord with prevailing nationalist ideology. This forward-looking orientation was a characteristically modern attitude, as was Qassab Hasan's advocacy of progress. His declaration that opposition to progress constituted futile and self-destructive resistance to "the movement of history and the logic of things" neatly incorporated modernist, nationalist, and Marxist assertions about the inevitability of positive change.

Qassab Hasan understood law as the elaboration of rights and responsibilities that define and constitute the citizen, as the glue that binds citizens to nation, state, and society. Using mass media as a vehicle, he labored tirelessly to disseminate knowledge of the law and stimulate interest in it, because he believed it was only with such knowledge and interest that citizens could become "virtuous," by which he meant equipped to exercise their rights and discharge their various responsibilities to family, community, and nation. But Qassab Hasan also considered the law a living, evolving force, an eternal work in progress, subject to constant interpretation and modification. And he made it his life's work to play a significant role in legal education, interpretation, and modification.

THE POWER AND AUTHORITY OF THE MODERN MEDIA EXPERT

At first blush, Najat Qassab Hasan, an avowed communist with a secular law degree, seems unqualified to render judgments on fields of law closely identified with jurisprudents (*fuqaha'*) trained in the shari'a. This seeming incongruity, however, was obviated by local and regional trends in educational infrastructure and policy. The developmental imperatives of the region's modern states produced ever-increasing numbers of graduates from Western-style law (and other professional) schools throughout the first half of the twentieth century.[16] This fact, in conjunction with the distinctive characteristics of the Syrian legal system, ensured that by the 1950s, the secular Faculty of Law at the Syrian University had educated hundreds of attorneys versed in the Islamic and secular particularities of civil law.[17]

Moreover, Qassab Hasan's authority to render such legal judgments in the absence of a traditional education in Islamic jurisprudence (*fiqh*) is explicable given the inability of the *ulama* to achieve lasting consensus on anything but the most minimal qualifications of the *faqih* (jurisprudent) or *mufti*.[18] In fact, some of the most prominent "popular muftis" of the modern period acted as authoritative interpreters, issuing hundreds of legal opinions with no formal training at academies of Islamic law, establishing their authority through the enactment of their chosen identity rather than through scholastic accreditation.[19]

Qassab Hasan's rhetorical strategies also assumed elements of the Islamic jurisprudent's authority. By the 1950s, the terse question/response format had long been a conventional element of advice columns appearing in mass-circulation periodicals in the West and elsewhere. But it was an archetypal structural feature of a much more venerable and locally authentic genre of discourse, the *fatwa*, or nonbinding legal opinion issued by a scholar of Islamic law.[20] "The Citizen and the Law" was originally entitled "Legal Advice: General Answers to Specific Questions" (*Istisharat Huquqiyya: Ajwiba 'Amma 'ala As'ila Khassa*),[21] an unmistakable reference to the structure and purpose of the conventional fatwa.[22] In addition, Qassab Hasan often employed concepts and terminology specific to Islamic jurisprudence, invoked the name of God, concluded with disclaimers reminiscent of the mufti's *Allahu a'lam* or "God knows best," and cited Prophetic hadith in support of his opinions.

Methodological similarities accompanied these structural and instrumental congruences. Fatwas are most concisely defined as "determinations of law, assuming a set of facts," a definition that theoretically constrains the mufti's agency within the realm of interpretation, thereby denying him an actively investigative role.[23] Qassab Hasan nominally embraced this restriction, frequently appending to his judgments disclaimers like "I must believe [the facts of] every letter that arrives."[24] He devised, however, a method to escape from these methodological constraints.

Patrick Gaffney has observed that knowledge in the Islamic sciences must be "converted into authority" before it can be "socially effective."[25] Like the mosque preachers in Gaffney's study, Najat Qassab Hasan required an institutional site from which to demonstrate his expertise, establish his authority, and have some impact on Syrian society. Qassab Hasan had long been friendly with many of the most significant figures in Syrian mass media.[26] In the pre-television era of 1950s Syria, radio and print media were the only effective means of disseminating the ideologies informing a new, collective national identity. Initially, Qassab Hasan's most important media connection was Ahmad 'Isseh, Adib al-Shishakli's director-general of Syrian Broadcasting from late 1950 to early 1954, when Qassab Hasan made his initial contributions to Syrian Broadcasting's programming.[27]

Publisher and editor of the leftist, pro-Nasser, and anti-imperialist daily newspaper *al-Ra'y al-'Amm* (Public Opinion), 'Isseh provided Qassab Hasan with the opportunity to publish, under a pseudonym, the satirical and stridently political front-page editorial "Bil-'Arabi al-Fasih" (Plain Speaking).[28] This venue enabled Qassab Hasan to comment freely on issues of regional and international politics and to ridicule his conservative and "backward" domestic political opponents, in short, to say what he could not say in his role as an "objective" radio persona. These editorials help to clarify Qassab Hasan's ideological commitments and also contextualize his legal opinions.

Beginning in 1955, regular Saturday afternoon and evening time slots for "The Citizen and the Law" provided Qassab Hasan with access to the largest listening audience in Syria's major cities. Edited transcripts of (or supplements to) the program appeared in *al-Idha'a al-Suriyya*, expanding his radio audience to include highly educated and politically engaged readers interested in radio programming, broadcast journalism, technology, literature, music, and political and cultural affairs. *Al-Idha'a al-Suriyya* was the ideal print venue for Qassab Hasan's mission in other ways as well, for the journal's citizen-building agenda was manifest throughout its pages.[29]

In every issue of *al-Idha'a al-Suriyya,* the directors-general contributed introductory editorials expressing dreams of autarchic development, anti-imperialist sentiments, and chagrin at the Syrian people's underdeveloped conception of citizenship. These editorials also frankly declared the broad-

FIGURE 2.3 "The World Hears Damascus." *Al-Idha'a al-Suriyya,*
September 1, 1953, front cover.

casting authority's citizen-crafting agenda in terms that corresponded with and complemented Qassab Hasan's.[30] The most salient example was Director General Ratib al-Husami's editorial about the relationship between the citizen and the radio, which appeared in the journal's first issue (fig. 2.3).[31] Al-Husami, a former People's Party MP from Homs, was at the opposite end of the political spectrum from Qassab Hasan. Yet in post–World War II Syria, an almost universally held belief in the missions of citizen building and "civilizing" the rural poor eclipsed otherwise sharp ideological differences.

In 1987, Najat Qassab Hasan estimated that his listeners and viewers had sent him "tens of thousands of letters" over the course of his broadcasting career.[32] Given these numbers, some measure of discrimination was inevitable. Indeed, the nature of Qassab Hasan's radio program facilitated selectivity. Whether by choice or due to technological limitations, the host of "The Citizen and the Law" did not take listeners' questions live. Instead, Qassab Hasan solicited letters from his listeners and then read summaries of their missives on the air, followed by his carefully fashioned opinions. This format gave Qassab Hasan the authority and opportunity to select and edit letters, and tailor both questions and responses carefully to his citizen-crafting agenda. In editing questions, he followed traditional jurists' praxis, as by the Ottoman period, the reformulation of questions submitted to muftis had become commonplace. In one respect, however, Qassab Hasan appeared to break with accepted practice. Muftis are routinely cautioned to "answer questioners without preference and in the order in which they arrive."[33] Qassab Hasan habitually "picked up" or "set aside" letters, basing such decisions on his judgment about the questions' "general benefit to the listener."[34]

Even such careful selection and redaction were sometimes insufficient for Qassab Hasan's purpose. When his petitioners failed to raise an issue of sufficient novelty and/or interest, he would invent a question and attribute it to a notional correspondent. Apparently this was a frequent practice, particularly during the period of "The Citizen and the Law's" initial broadcasts. At the age of fifteen, Qassab Hasan's daughter Hanan discovered her father's technique and decided to join in the game. She composed and mailed him a letter, complete with an imaginary name and address, disguised handwriting, and a subject both dear to her heart and conforming to her father's interests. After Qassab Hasan read this letter on the air, Hanan proudly confessed her "crime," and he, with equal pride, acknowledged and congratulated his daughter on her success.[35]

The immediate purpose of Najat Qassab Hasan's fabrication of letters was one shared by reformist intellectuals throughout the developing world—

mounting a critique of existing social relations.[36] The ultimate objective was legislative reform. He would tell his fictitious correspondent that "the law prohibits what he or she sought, and that, in his opinion, it was inappropriate for the law to prohibit this, then he would discuss and criticize the law, as part of the effort to have it changed."[37] Here we see the practical application of Qassab Hasan's "first principle": "I am with the law, but I am not with it absolutely." For Qassab Hasan, the law was "like cold, heartless iron," conceived in relation to "abstract situations" and thus inapplicable to many real-world problems. Therefore he considered the law a mere starting point for the jurist, who must "render practical decisions and interpretations that . . . end with what is appropriate to the particularities of the problem."[38] Laws that failed to address persistent inequalities and injustices must be changed. In the meantime *all* laws are to be creatively interpreted and applied, a legal philosophy that affords enormous power to the jurist. Through the invention of correspondents and issues, Qassab Hasan constructed a seemingly real and objective context from which to wield his mass-media authority, selectively interpreting the law in order to critique Syrian social relations and the inadequacy of the country's legal system. By literally inventing Syrian citizens as both sources and subjects of public discussion, Qassab Hasan manipulated reality in the service of his ultimate goal, the comprehensive reform of Syrian society.

COMMERCE, PROPERTY, AND HONOR IN AN URBAN ENVIRONMENT

By the dawn of the twentieth century, Syria's capital, Damascus, and its most populous city, Aleppo, had been "urban" for many centuries.[39] During the 1950s, both cities experienced the consequences of unprecedented growth: the physical and conceptual restructuring of urban environments, increasing both a sense of anonymity as well as intimate contact with persons not bound by blood, marriage, or other long-term relationships of trust.[40] These new realities produced various real and perceived dangers, as well as more frequent interaction with functionaries of government institutions, and with modern professionals who served as intermediaries between citizen and state.

Qassab Hasan addressed these quintessentially urban issues in terms of relationships between merchants and their customers; the ownership, use, improvement, and sale of commercial and residential real estate; the accumulation and liquidation of debt; the problem of crime in densely populated neighborhoods; and the complexities of landlord-tenant relationships. Throughout, he argued that citizens are obliged to (1) know the law(s) governing their relationships, (2) obtain documentary evidence of all transactions, (3) make use of state institutions to resolve disputes, and (4) respect the rights and privileges of state officials as a prerequisite for effective governance and social stability.

In form and content, the following case is classic Qassab Hasan. A paraphrase of a much longer and more detailed presentation, it is an extremely concise summary of the factual circumstances, focusing attention on what the interpreter considered the crucial issues. It is classic in another sense, in that it also resembles, in almost every particular, the form and content of a traditional fatwa.

> Mr. M. D., a greengrocer, from the Upper Midan neighborhood of Damascus, complains of a man who, along with his young children, took from his shop goods exceeding 65 Syrian lira in value, then disputed the amount after a delay of two years, and swore under oath before a court that he was free of any debt. So what can he do under such circumstances?[41]

The greengrocer, from a neighborhood famous for the business acumen of its merchants and the fervor of its Arab nationalist politics, had extended credit to a customer, who, along with his children, took goods of not inconsiderable value, delayed payment for two years, and then swore under oath in court that he owed the greengrocer nothing.[42] Qassab Hasan began by chiding Mr. M. D. for not knowing the law and exercising his rights under it: "It was in the petitioner's power to assert his rights by making a sworn deposition in court" for a period of one year after the date of the "the last transaction on the account." Since that period had long since elapsed, Mr. M.D. was left with no legal recourse.[43]

The general conclusion Qassab Hasan drew from this specific case was the difficulty of establishing, to the satisfaction of a court, the validity of a debt that was accumulated over an extended period of time. Consequently, he counseled all shopkeepers to keep an account book in which, at the beginning of each month, they required all of their customers to affix their signatures next to their names and the amount they owe. "By this means they make the notebook an official document binding upon the signatories." Finally, Qassab Hasan advised shopkeepers not to extend credit to those customers they "trust least," "unless in exchange for a signed, dated receipt."[44]

So, what was Qassab Hasan saying? First, he was scolding Mr. M. D. (and, by extension, all shopkeepers) for his ignorance of the law. Knowledge of the legislation governing retailers' relationships with their customers empowered both parties to protect their rights through informed, rational practices. For the shopkeeper, a fundamental aspect of those practices was prudence, that is, dispensing one's trust with great care. Most critical, however, was maintaining an accurate documentary record. Oral agreements made in the absence of court or other state officials were unenforceable and therefore worthless. So, "let shopkeepers take heed!"

If a merchant leased his shop, he had to guard against the dishonesty of the property's owners. Another shopkeeper, "Mr. Muhammad from Aleppo," wrote of just such a problem. For more than three years he had rented a storefront jointly "owned by eight people," to each of whom he paid his respective share of the monthly rent. Nine months earlier, one of the landlords began refusing to accept his portion of the rent. Noting that "Mr. Muhammad" was understandably "confused" by this behavior, Qassab Hasan rhetorically asked, "What should he do?" Qassab Hasan's response provided a brief summary and explanation of the rights and responsibilities of both parties according to the legislation governing the rental of commercial property. He then warned "Mr. Muhammad" that the landlord in question might be preparing a common ploy: refusing to accept the rent at the established rate for a considerable period of time, letting the amount due accumulate, then mailing a "document to the tenant demanding the entire amount, which the tenant will be incapable of paying due to the size of the accumulated sum. At that time, the partner will demand evacuation from the entire shop, not just a portion comparable to his share alone."[45]

Qassab Hasan cautioned Mr. Muhammad to set aside the precise amount due each month, "and keep the accumulated rent in safekeeping near at hand," so that he might thwart the landlord's gambit and maintain his right of access to the property and thus the means of his livelihood. Again, we see Qassab Hasan insisting on adherence to a precise set of procedures as routine, habitual practices and prescribing a healthy measure of mistrust when others depart from them. Finally, in praising Mr. Muhammad for his extraordinary patience, Qassab Hasan provided another echo of the fatwa, invoking the assistance of the Almighty in the shopkeeper's struggle to remain in business: "Now I must say to the petitioner that I hope God will assist him!"[46]

Qassab Hasan's response to a question posed by "Mr. al-Hajj 'Abd al-Qadir al-Jabbas and his friends from Idlib" makes more extensive and pointed use of concepts and rhetorical devices traditionally associated with the interpreters of Islamic law. The gentlemen from Idlib, a medium-sized city near Syria's northwestern border with Turkey, inquired if the *furughiyya* (paying or accepting payment for the surrender of established tenancy rights) of a vacant store, house, or inn is "lawful [*halal*] or unlawful [*haram*]."[47] These two

Arabic terms indicate that the petitioners were requesting a ruling according to the shari'a, in other words that they were tacitly acknowledging Qassab Hasan's authority to issue fatwas.

Qassab Hasan began his reply, which certified *furughiyya*'s legality, by signaling that he understood and embraced the query's purpose and spirit: "In matters of business, Islam forbids usury and nothing else." His embrace of the role of *faqih* is in keeping with the essence of the "second principle" guiding his legal practice: "I am with the *shari'a*. I understand it, love it, and value its principles."[48] Yet Qassab Hasan elaborated on his ruling, not with references to the traditional sources—the Qur'an, hadith, and precedent—but by summarizing the logic underlying the practice of *furughiyya*:

> Every shop has an abstract value in addition to its material value, which derives from the quality of its location, the trust of its customers, and the fact that they are accustomed to good service. Therefore, the merchant relinquishes not just the shop, but simultaneously relinquishes all of its abstract qualities. So, let those who sought an answer to this question rest assured that it is not unlawful and not forbidden.[49]

Qassab Hasan issued a fatwa on a topic quite specific to Islamic law without a single explicit reference to either the shari'a or the massive body of texts it encompasses.[50]

By the time he began broadcasting "The Citizen and the Law," Qassab Hasan had formulated a very clear, nuanced position on the shari'a and its appropriate application in post–World War II Syria. Emphasizing the currents of flexibility, compassion, and independent judgment within the jurisprudential tradition, Qassab Hasan referenced a shari'a that was humanist, socially progressive, rational, and utterly compatible with modern society.[51] In the process, he implicitly argued for the viability of *ijtihad*, or independent reasoning, and asserted his authority to act as a *mujtahid*, or authoritative interpreter of issues related to the shari'a. Without access to mass media, the construction of this identity would have been impossible.

RESIDENTIAL REAL ESTATE: LANDLORDS, TENANTS, CITIZENS, AND REFUGEES

Qassab Hasan's exchange with "the citizen Mr. Hasan Salim" from Damascus, entitled "On Rental Law," warned that residential tenants in a modern city must insist on documentation in all transactions and avail themselves of the services offered by state institutions. Mr. Salim's landlord had refused to sign a lease in his own name, instead insisting on making it out in the name of an intermediary agent. Throughout his more than three-year tenancy in the property, Mr. Salim had periodically requested a change in this arrangement, and each time was rebuffed. Then, asserting the impact of his radio program, Qassab Hasan reported that, after hearing "The Citizen and the Law," "which advises people how to resolve their disputes in a legal manner," Mr. Salim returned to his landlord, again requesting a written lease and a receipt for all rent paid, which the landlord flatly refused, declaring that he would continue providing receipts to the aforementioned intermediary agent. Mr. Salim asked whether he should continue to pay the rent or withhold it until the landlord produced a lease in Mr. Salim's name and a receipt for all rent paid to date.[52]

In response, Qassab Hasan explained the intent and specific elements of the fraud the landlord had perpetrated against Mr. Salim in attempting to conceal the actual relationship between landlord and tenant. Whenever the tenant became sufficiently dissatisfied with any of the terms of his agreement with the landlord (or with the latter's failure to adhere to same) to file an official complaint, "the owner will deny that he is renting the property. Then he will ask the renter to vacate the property on the grounds that he [the renter] is illegally occupying it." After summarizing the civil and criminal penalties stipulated in Article 20 of Syria's rental law, Qassab Hasan advised Mr. Salim to pay the rent exclusively by postal money order, because the record of its receipt and of its exchange for currency or a deposit slip were "equivalent to an official receipt from the owner." Furthermore, the landlord's refusal to accept delivery of the postal money order, when coupled with evidence that Mr. Salim has resided "peacefully and openly" in the property for more than one year, was sufficient to send the landlord to prison.

Besides reiterating the necessity to document all transactions, the main practical lesson Qassab Hasan imparted through Mr. Salim's story was the utility of modern state institutions, in this case the Syrian postal service. Without the irrefutable official documentation that could only be provided by state institutions, Mr. Salim had no way to substantiate his claims and obtain protection from his landlord's fraud. Individual renters, often transients or strangers without known connections to family or patronage networks in a modern city, were at the mercy of dishonest property owners.

Qassab Hasan noted that many people equate deceptive business practices with "cleverness," a "notion" that will get them into legal trouble: "If deception succeeds once, it fails a thousand times, and exceeding cleverness will lead one into serious problems." Therefore, he urged all citizens, be they landlords or renters, to adopt a "reasonable" and "cooperative" approach to one another, envisioning a better world in which all such relationships are based on the virtues of "cordiality and friendship rather than being a cause for conflict or enmity."

Yet another case of tenant-landlord relations enabled Qassab Hasan to emphasize the indispensability of state institutions and the civil servants who staff them. "Mr. Sh. Sad, the Palestinian refugee," purchased a house already occupied by a tenant. For some time, he was happy to use the resulting income to cover his rental of a small apartment. As he was planning to marry, however, he needed a larger residence and sought a way to evict his tenant, a civil servant. The tenant's occupation was the critical point in this case. As Qassab Hasan explained, "The law affords someone who owns a particular house yet does not live in it the right to evict the person to whom it is rented. Yet this same law mandates that this order is not applicable to civil servants or other government employees, taking into consideration the fact that they perform a public service that must not be disrupted by the daily prospect of eviction."[53]

Most exceptions to this provision required criminal or otherwise grossly irresponsible behavior on the part of the tenant. The exceptions that Qassab Hasan emphasized, however, were those that came into effect if the *landlord* was also a civil servant. If he was employed in another city and "returns to the city in which the rented property is located due to a transfer or is relieved of his position or is pensioned off, or his family returns after his death," then the tenant might be evicted, whatever his status.[54] The efficient functioning of the young and fragile Syrian state's institutions was, for both Qassab Hasan and those who drafted the relevant legislation, the supreme consideration. The law Qassab Hasan cited, the Basic Personnel Law, was one of his favorites, as it forbade civil servants—who upheld state intervention in support of economic development—from practicing favoritism in regard to political affiliation, formalized evaluation and promotion based on merit, insulated senior bureaucrats from "political intervention," and acknowledged government employees' right to collective bargaining.[55] Qassab Hasan closed by counseling Mr. Sh. Sad that, in the absence of the above circumstances, his only option was to "pursue an amicable agreement" that resulted in the civil servant's voluntarily vacating the residence.[56]

Another aspect of this case merits discussion. Rather than "citizen," Mr. Sh. Sad received the appellation "Palestinian refugee." The ability of a refugee from the Palestinian "catastrophe" (*nakba*) of 1947–1949 to purchase a house in 1950s Damascus appears to have been unremarkable. Yet Mr. Sh. Sad's case highlights Palestinians' ambiguous legal condition in Syria. Afforded a status roughly equivalent to permanent residents in the United States, Palestinian refugees and their descendants had (and continue to have) the right to own property, operate businesses, marry Syrians, and work, even in Syrian government service. Yet they have been legally barred from acquiring citizenship, for this would be seen as acknowledgment that Palestinians would never return to their homeland and never reclaim their property, status, and rights within historic Palestine. Such a position was, and largely remains, unspeakable within the field of Syrian political discourse.

Equal to a Syrian citizen under the law in many respects, Mr. Sh. Sad's nationality was irrelevant to the case at hand. So, why was it mentioned, if only in passing? For Qassab Hasan and the overwhelming majority of his contemporaries, Palestine was the *cause célèbre* of the era. For politically engaged Arab intellectuals, the ongoing suffering of Palestinian exiles living in their midst was like an open wound and featured in the pseudonymous editorials Qassab Hasan contributed to the newspaper *al-Ra'y al-'Amm*. So, the repeated use of Mr. Sh. Sad's sobriquet was almost certainly Qassab Hasan's way of keeping the issue of the Palestinian diaspora before the public and of admonishing his fellow citizens to treat refugees with compassion.

Yet Qassab Hasan did not neglect the rights of property owners without such political credentials. His response to "the lady Wafiqat al-Katib from Damascus" provides a case in point. She sought to evict a tenant who had failed to pay the rent. In response, she had behaved rationally, sending him a note requesting immediate payment of three months' rent. Affirming that her tenant had received the note but had failed to respond after ten days, she asked if her request was legal and whether she had the right to start eviction proceedings.[57]

Qassab Hasan was careful to assert the rights of the tenant, seeking clarification on the precise terms of the demand for payment. Echoing once again the mufti's methodology, his response focused on the case's factual circumstances: "The lady did not clarify whether she requested payment for three previous months' rent or for three months in advance. If we assume that her request was for rent previously accumulated, the demand was legal. . . . If the request was for three months' rent in advance, the tenant is obligated to pay for only one month." In other words, the landlady could only evict her tenant if he had rejected or ignored a demand to pay accumulated debt. In closing, Qassab Hasan reasserted the sanctity of documentation and determined that even though the landlady's demand was excessive and therefore improper, this fact did not "render the document [that she sent him] legally invalid." The tenant was legally "obliged to pay the amount due."[58] Unfortunately, as the following case demonstrates, urban life presented some dilemmas for which documentation was not always useful or even obtainable.

GUESTS, STRANGERS, AND CRIME: IS HONOR PASSÉ?

> Mr. M. Sh. from Aleppo says: He had become acquainted with a group of people from Hama who were guests at his neighbor's home. Such friendship developed between him and the group from Hama that he invited them all to a soirée in their honor. When the neighbors returned to their home, they found the door open and their jewelry missing. The neighbors accused a servant of Mr. M. Sh., and then him, of theft. So, he asks, should he go to court to have his name cleared, or what should he do?[59]

Responding to this question, Qassab Hasan made a rare foray into the realm of criminal law.[60] Presuming (in the absence of evidence to the contrary) Mr. M. Sh.'s innocence, Qassab Hasan declared that he had nothing to fear from any legal proceedings stemming from this accusation and assured his readers that,

> indeed, he will be exonerated if he is innocent. For the legal principle is that if there is doubt, it will be interpreted to the benefit of the accused, because it is better to let a thousand criminals go free than to convict one innocent man. As long as this principle is in effect, it is difficult to convict an individual with weak evidence, and impossible under any circumstances to convict without evidence.[61]

Syrian law specified punitive provisions to discourage false or frivolous accusations of criminal activity. An accuser could be ordered to pay all of the defendant's court costs and to compensate the defendant for lost wages and other material injuries, according to the ruling of the presiding judge. These provisions, as Qassab Hasan noted, also made it very difficult to prove an allegation of slander. Any successful prosecution had to establish that the accusation originated with the alleged slanderer and "that he knew he was lying, and that he did so with malice." As a result, "few lawsuits for slander are successful." Nevertheless, Qassab Hasan advised Mr. M. Sh. that upon his acquittal, he should ask the judge who rendered this verdict to "apply Article 135 of the penal code, which requires the publication of a verdict of innocence in one or more newspapers at the personal expense of the accuser." Second, he should request from the same court "compensation for the moral and material damages that he has suffered."[62]

When recounting the events leading to the accusation against Mr. M. Sh., Qassab Hasan expressed no outrage over the crime of burglary and no surprise that the culprits were not immediately identified and apprehended. Despite his general privileging of the urban over the rural, Qassab Hasan clearly shared another characteristic with postcolonial intellectuals, the tendency to see the modern city as a "deeply profane place, corrupted by money and commerce."[63] Thus he considered these events so unremarkable for the residents of Damascus and Aleppo (if not Syria's other cities as well) that they required no such remarks.

As he did when issuing opinions on matters of civil law, Qassab Hasan drew upon sources of the shari'a and customary law in support of his legal advice. By citing a "celebrated hadith" that "urges people to avoid the realms of accusations and suspicion," he remained true to his "second principle."[64] And by citing elements of popular proverbs imparting similar admonitions, he adhered to his "third principle," which states, in part, "I respect . . . popular wisdom in common proverbs. And I do not scorn what the people learn from them."[65]

Qassab Hasan's comments on the concept of honor are also of interest. After securing his acquittal, Mr. M. Sh.'s chief desire was to "clear his name." Qassab Hasan attempted to lower his correspondent's expectations in this regard but eventually advised him how to proceed in court in order to "recover his honor before the people" and "receive just compensation for the harm that was done to him." He, however, could not resist expressing his exasperation with the "many questions, . . . both written and verbal," he continually received on the subject of "honor, *as people call it*" (emphasis mine).[66]

This dismissiveness derived from two sources. A preference for empirical processes caused Qassab Hasan to accord far less significance to public perception than to the opinion of the court, a state institution that produced "truth" by discovering, presenting, and evaluating evidence. Clearly, one who could declare it "impossible under any circumstances to convict without evidence" believed that these evidentiary procedures established one's status before the law *objectively.*[67] Honor, on the other hand, was merely a perception, a subjective effect of objective phenomena, in this case, virtuous character and conduct.

In addition, ideology almost certainly informed Qassab Hasan's position. At the very least, he considered honor to be somewhat quaint, an affectation for the practical, hardheaded urbanite and the citizen of a modern state. At worst, this anachronistic concept evoked images of dueling gentlemen settling their disputes on "the field of honor." It was a relic of the "feudal" past, and thus anathema to a progressively minded intellectual in the 1950s Arab world.

Najat Qassab Hasan's leftist ideological commitments and populist media persona notwithstanding, a sense of *noblesse oblige* suffused his invention of petitioners and their cases.[68] From his vantage point as a modern legal expert, Qassab Hasan would not disavow the superiority of his knowledge or the concomitant pedagogical responsibility. His objective in broadcasting fictive correspondence was legislative reform, specifically the modification of laws that he considered unwise in conception and/or unjust in effect. Yet his ultimate goal was far more ambitious: to change the relationship between the law and the individual in order to construct a particular political subject, one defined by an equally distinctive relationship with the state, "the virtuous citizen." Access to mass media provided the vehicle to construct his identity as a legal expert and to pursue his developmental ambitions.

In the meantime, Qassab Hasan rendered judgments according to existing laws, a delicate business requiring constant interpretation and reinterpretation in light of "what is appropriate to the particularities of the problem." Addressing such particularities also entailed exercising compassion, lest the "cold and heartless" nature of the law triumph over the "nobler and higher" principle of leniency.[69] Like his more traditional counterparts, Qassab Hasan sought to preserve or restore social stability and equilibrium, largely through the encouragement of the virtuous behavior underlying amicable relations among parties to commercial transactions and other legally defined relationships. Yet his modern vision of social peace and stability hinged on popular perceptions of the state and its laws. In his view, the system of rights and responsibilities structuring the citizen's daily life must *seem* to be just, rational, and beneficial to preserve the bond between the citizen and the law. If not, the citizen will cease to be a citizen and become something else, an agent of instability, and the law will cease to be the law and become a brute and mindless force.

Education was the only antidote to these dangers. The citizen must know the rights and responsibilities that define his or her status. This required the repetition of these rights and responsibilities in school, print, and broadcast media until they were as familiar as one's own name. More importantly, the citizen must be convinced of two seemingly contradictory postulates: He must believe that the law, in the generic sense, is eternal, a natural force that exists independently of human consciousness. And he must believe that the law, as a specific collection of sanctions and proscriptions, is inherently mutable, perpetually subject to human adaptation. In short, the citizen must believe that the law is an agent of progress. In order to make this argument, Qassab Hasan drew selectively from the heterogeneous collection of legal precepts contained in Syria's civil and criminal codes. Rejecting or ignoring reactionary and obscurantist currents within the Islamic jurisprudential tradition, he emphasized the flexibility and pragmatism of independent reasoning, which instructed the jurist to modify his judgments in accordance "with the changing times."[70]

Qassab Hasan's devotion to reason and rationality explains his emphasis on documentation, not as the fetishization of sacred texts but as an expression of his positivist faith in the infallibility of the empirical. Contracts and other documents underpinning commercial transactions clarified the particularities of mutually binding legal relationships, with the state acting as rational actor and arbitrator of dispute. After all, how could the civil servants of the weak, young Syrian state fulfill their duties—collect taxes, enforce of the law, render justice, and foster development—if citizens failed to keep accurate records?

3 Social Justice and the Patriarchal Citizen

> The Personal Status Code is useful to the citizen when he is a boy, so that he knows his relationship to his family, his rights, and his duties, and it is useful to him as a young man so that he knows how to raise his family. It is also useful to a married couple throughout their relationship, until they are compelled to separate by divorce or death. And it is useful to all the people when they must clarify the conditions of a will or a bequest. Therefore there is no citizen who is not in need of it.
>
> —NAJAT QASSAB HASAN, *Qanun al-Ahwal al-Shakhsiyya ma'a Sharh Qanuni wa Insani Kamil*

AMONG SYRIA'S ECLECTIC array of legal forms, codes, and genres, Najat Qassab Hasan afforded the Personal Status Code (PSC) particular significance for its role in codifying the features of the patriarchal citizen. Thus it was frequently featured in his radio broadcasts, journalism, and other publications. Governing the realm of family law (chiefly marriage, divorce, guardianship, and inheritance), the Code of Personal Status in effect during the Democratic Years drew on Islamic law for various sects of Muslims, canon law for Christians and Jews, and yet another corpus for Syria's sizeable and politically significant Druze minority.[1] The PSC of 1953 was one of military dictator Adib al-Shishakli's modernizing reforms. In this area, as in many others, the restoration of civilian government did not constitute the comprehensive repudiation of Syria's authoritarian legacy that so many Syrians and outside observers have imagined it did. This and previous codes were remnants of the Ottoman legal system, which subdivided civil law into the categories *ahwal 'ayniyya* (financial affairs) and *ahwal shakhsiyya* (personal affairs), and treated individuals first and foremost as members of a religious community.[2]

This body of civil legislation defined and codified the legal rights and responsibilities of individuals based on their status—for example, age, gen-

der, marital status, parentage, and so on—as well as the relationships among
these categories of person and among members of significant religious communities—Muslims, Jews, Christians, and Druze. The code offered a detailed, comprehensive guide to the management of all relationships defined
by blood or marriage, and offered principles and lessons that could be applied beyond the confines of the family. From Qassab Hasan's perspective,
the psc instructed citizens, at every stage of life, to respect the rights of others, zealously defend their own rights, discharge their various duties and responsibilities, and address the failure of others to fulfill such obligations. The
code inculcated positive norms that, when properly internalized, informed
an individual's daily thought and conduct. At this point they became the
"features of the virtuous citizen."[3]

Drawing upon the psc, Qassab Hasan presented the patriarchal citizen
as a paradigm distinguished by his capacity to discipline himself and those
around him (most particularly the members of his family) by his sense of responsibility and by his commitment to service. Although the family was the
primary site for expressing this commitment, the *pater familias* also stood
ready to serve his community, city, state, and nation. Self-discipline and stern
but benevolent guidance at home prepared him for service to these larger collectivities. This tutelage also made the patriarch the conduit through which
women and children were integrated into larger social institutions, guiding
their adoption of the features of the virtuous citizen, even if they did not
wield the agency of that idealized figure.

Service, defined as acknowledging and discharging duties to elders, dependents, and the greater (collective) good was the primary virtue underpinning all others. The willingness and capacity to make material sacrifices, submit to legitimate authority, and sublimate individual interests and desires to
the pursuit of nobler, sometimes abstract, goals—"the common weal"—constituted the essence of service. This conception of service informed Qassab
Hasan's decision to become an attorney and shaped the way in which he practiced the profession. Like other members of his generation who served their
country by opposing "the onslaught of French colonialism" in their youth,
after independence he turned to *the* project: "building a new state on sound
and ethical principles," a state that could achieve "complete unity" and assure
"social justice for all the people."[4]

PATRIARCHY AND CITIZENSHIP

To paraphrase George Orwell's oft-quoted truism, embedded within the Syrian psc was a message: "All citizens are equal, but some citizens are more equal

than others." This disparity of rights and responsibilities was most evident in Qassab Hasan's gender-inflected discussions of the family. The ultimate goal was another of the virtues that Qassab Hasan most frequently celebrated: amicable relations. Achieving and maintaining amity required that everyone knew and accepted his or her place, with all its attendant responsibilities. In other words, Qassab Hasan consistently upheld patriarchy and embraced a host of associated conventions defining manly behavior. Strengths of various kinds defined men's virtues. Among the most important were governing one's sexual desires, monitoring and correcting the behavior of dependents, and jealously guarding one's position as head of the household. Accordingly, Qassab Hasan most frequently identified the weakness or foolishness of husbands and fathers as the cause of familial discord.

Qassab Hasan practiced in his private life what he preached in public. He raised his daughters in a manner unique in post–World War II Syria, ensuring that they were highly educated and independently minded and imbued with the notion that they should not marry unless they knew their prospective husbands well enough to develop genuine respect and affection for them. Qassab Hasan's daughters also benefited from the practical application of his philosophy. As a result of the broad listenership of his radio program, Qassab Hasan's home became an unofficial shelter for women fleeing abusive husbands and fathers. These women often stayed under Qassab Hasan's protection for two months or more, sharing a bedroom with his imperturbable daughters while he explored their legal options on a pro bono basis.[5] In this way, Qassab Hasan enacted one of his legal principles, protecting women from the "anger of men" while also instructing his daughters in the need to make sacrifices on behalf of those less fortunate than themselves. By offering such protection, Qassab Hasan was also "uplifting" women so that they could better fulfill their responsibilities to their families and the nation.

Yet there were limits to Qassab Hasan's feminism. While he held the "measure" of Syria's development the degree to which the country's men "elevated" women's "worth and standing," respected them, and accepted that the "era of the slave girl and the harem" was over, he also advocated making women "equal with men" only to the extent that this equality did not "conflict with their human, biological role" as wives and mothers.[6] In valorizing women's roles as wives and mothers Qassab Hasan was in good company, for the overwhelming majority of Arab intellectuals in the modern period, whether nominally nationalist, Islamist, or socialist in ideological orientation, shared this developmentally informed position. Qassab Hasan's position on women's roles and rights harmonized with his belief in benevolent patriarchy. Although he declared it "impermissible" for men to "oppress" women, he advocated treating them "as God commands us, with correctness, justice, and benevolence."[7] Juristicially, women were minors; they had to be protected and uplifted by men, feats they were incapable of accomplishing on their own. Indeed, Qassab Hasan was certain that "normal" women viewed patriarchy as the natural order of gender relations. Questions of property ownership and inheritance most frequently threw these relations into stark relief.

LOVE AND MARRIAGE

Many of the cases that Qassab Hasan discussed touched on a "central argument of modernity" vis-à-vis marriage in Islamic societies: the proposition that the "reinvisioning of marriage from a procreative to a romantic contract" constitutes a paradigm shift characteristic of the modern period.[8] Qassab Hasan explored this subject in an exchange appearing under the title "On Harsh Preconditions for Marriage," the "emotional case" of two young people who were "compatible with one another" and had been contracted to marry through negotiations between their respective families.[9] The union was agreed upon, in principle, when the two parties were minors. By the time, however, that both parties had reached the age of legal maturity—eighteen for males and seventeen for females—the young woman's family had begun to raise obstacles, demanding a dowry far in excess of the fiancé's capacity to pay.

The young man informed Qassab Hasan of his intention to take his prospective bride before a shari'a court judge, where they would establish that both had achieved legal maturity, provide evidence of the valid marriage contract signed by their fathers, and the young woman would declare that "she wants to marry this particular person, is not willing to marry anyone else, and that her family has made excessive and unreasonable demands of him." He then asked Qassab Hasan what position the judge was likely to take and whether he, the fiancé, had behaved responsibly in this matter.

In reply, Qassab Hasan suggested that the girl's family was "attempting to reject the suitor indirectly," by resorting to a well-known and frequently employed stratagem, one best expressed by the formula, "If you don't want to marry off your daughter, raise her price!" He sided with the young couple, declaring that their positions appeared to be "sound" and that they "did nothing blameworthy," and advised the young man to do just as he planned: go with his betrothed "to consult the Islamic judge and request that he marry them," as both had enjoyed "this legal right" since reaching the age of majority.

This judgment, however, did not constitute an unqualified endorsement of the young couple's autonomy with regard to their families. When he shifted registers to address a more general audience, Qassab Hasan asserted that if the boy had not become engaged to the girl "with the agreement of her family and wanted to go over their heads," he would oppose the marriage, not on legal grounds, but on pragmatic ones rooted in social conventions. If a marriage, however legal, had been contracted under such conditions, the groom would "not live in accord with his wife" because he would be "an enemy of her family" from the outset.

"Likewise," Qassab Hasan continued, the girl could not "dispense with her family, no matter what she might say initially." As if to mollify readers inclined to side with the girl's family, Qassab Hasan reminded them that in such cases, "the judge will permit her legal guardian to express his opinion during a specified period of time. If the guardian does not object, or if his objection is not worthy of consideration, the judge will allow her to marry, provided that there is compatibility in the match." He further cautioned, "One should not resort to this course of action except in extreme circumstances, those in which the harshness of the family is unreasonable and without foundation." Qassab Hasan closed by assuring the reader that, "at any rate, this legal right presents no danger, so long as it is left to the wisdom and assessment of the judge, the legal guardian possesses the right to express his opinion, and his opinion is heard and discussed with wisdom and deliberation."[10]

Thus Qassab Hasan deftly balanced two of his abiding principles, maintaining patriarchally grounded social stability on the one hand, and upholding the rights of women on the other. The gist of his ruling was that Islamic law, when interpreted and implemented properly, empowered a woman to marry the man of her choice. Such a decision might have been based on practical considerations, romantic feelings, or a combination of these. Ultimately, though, the right was inviolate and, theoretically, the woman was the final authority on whether or not to marry. The only caveat Qassab Hasan specified was "reasonable" social conventions arising from pragmatism rather than adherence to tradition. Respect for the rights of all concerned parties must be observed in marriage contracts, he argued, for that would be the only way to restore amicable relations and social peace.

This case also highlights the relationship among marriage, the law, and social accord. A properly enacted marriage—one that is sanctioned by the law, mutual consent, and both parties' families—protects the rights of all concerned. It thus sets the stage for well-ordered social relations, defining the bride's and groom's relationships with their natal families, establishing amicable relationships with their spouses' families, and providing the social environment for their maturation into responsible adults and citizens. Conversely, an improperly enacted marriage—one that is conducted outside the shari'a court or in the face of family opposition—will produce lasting enmity, destabilize these elemental social relations, and ultimately fail.

THE SHARI'A COURT AND THE BACKWARDNESS OF THE COUNTRYSIDE

Such assertions of the shari'a courts' practical benefits are found in most of Qassab Hasan's rulings on marriage. These rulings depicted the shari'a courts as sites of the enlightened, rational thought and practice associated with modern civilization. One such case, characterized as "a strange type of story," was entitled "On the Shortcomings of *'Urfi* [Customary] Marriage." It related the story of a "miserable" man who had fallen victim to fraud when contracting a marriage agreement "according to custom" with a girl "from a village in a northern province." This man had paid the girl's guardians, her brother and uncle, an unspecified sum, a "sheikh" had led a simple prayer, "two words that sanction matrimony" were "exchanged between the parties," and the matter was concluded, all outside of the shari'a court. Shortly after the man moved his new wife into his residence, she abandoned him and "married another man with the approval of her brother and her uncle."[11]

Qassab Hasan first informed his petitioner that he had made himself "the prey of a conniving family that is more like a gang of criminals." Furthermore, even though the woman's subsequent marriage was null and void, in practical terms the "miserable" man had no effective legal recourse.[12] Chiding his petitioner for his foolishness, Qassab Hasan declared that "his first and greatest error, not registering his contract in the Islamic court," had sealed his fate. Then Qassab Hasan issued his ruling:

> The voice of the law has grown hoarse urging people to marry in the Islamic court, which guarantees the validity, integrity, and permanence of every marriage, and the rights of the parties to it. And the hand of the law has become tired meting out punishment to those who disobey its rulings and do not marry in a legal manner. Nevertheless, there are still simple people who are attracted to easy marriage. . . . Why do you run away from the Islamic courts, you simple souls? Is it because they guarantee your rights and leave no possibility of losing them?[13]

Qassab Hasan's argument in favor of the shari'a courts appears, at least superficially, to be exclusively functional. He did not contend that use of the shari'a courts was mandatory due to their underlying textual authority or centrality to Islamic culture. Rather, he entreated his readers to trust the courts for their contemporary utility. Perhaps doing otherwise was impious, but it was also unwise. Qassab Hasan repeatedly implored his listeners and readers to behave rationally—to safeguard their personal rights and their material wealth by making use of the shari'a courts' readily available and reliable services. While Qassab Hasan praised *'urfi* law for its adaptability and its provision of "popular wisdom," he placed it in a subsidiary and complementary role to secular law and the shari'a.[14]

Qassab Hasan's reference to "a village" as the site of "backward" practices and "criminal" behavior hints that he believed "lawful" and "advanced" life was, by definition, urban. The ambiguous designation of a "northern province" is equally telling. While it may have been a device to further obscure the "miserable" man's identity, it also elicits unavoidable associations. When this particular issue of *al-Idha'a al-Suriyya* was published, the three largest of Syria's four "northern" provinces bordered southeastern Turkey and northwestern Iraq, encompassing areas whose economies were overwhelming agricultural or pastoral, and whose populations featured nomadic peoples and disproportionately large numbers of minorities, including Kurds, Turcomans, Armenians, Assyrians, and Yazidis.[15]

The conflation of the countryside with backwardness also conveyed paternalism, as was evident in Qassab Hasan's characterization of those who "still" rely on customary law as "simple souls." This characterization is a facet of a larger modernist/nationalist narrative that locates all human societies on an interrelated set of spatial, temporal, and developmental continua. From this perspective, Syria was being held back by its own internal continuum— its urban populations were as "advanced" as many in Europe, while its rural populations still lived in the past. In their simplicity, these country people remained blissfully ignorant of their backward state. Qassab Hasan implicitly attributed disastrous marital decisions to such adverse socioeconomic conditions, belying a class perspective that also informed his jurisprudential philosophy, particularly his assertion that "socially downtrodden husbands" were more likely to tyrannize and abuse their wives.[16] In this case, these roles were reversed, as a man from the city surrendered to his desire for a younger woman and thus fell prey to criminal elements. Yet Qassab Hasan failed to note another gendered aspect of this tale, the way in which the young girl's guardians exercised propriety interest over her sexuality, profiting from the desire it elicited.

Qassab Hasan often used the PSC to educate the ignorant about their rights and chide the weak about responsibilities. The shari'a courts interpreted and applied the code's provisions to protect such people from each other and from the consequences of their ungoverned desires. Perceived character defects like foolishness and weakness were antithetical to the patriarchal citizen constructed by Qassab Hasan. Thus these conditions were leitmotifs of the cases he chose to present. The letter from a petitioner dubbed "another man who is more than weak" provides a classic example. Qassab Hasan introduced the case by informing his readers that the man in question, a civil servant, was thirty years of age, earned a monthly salary of 160 Syrian lira, owned his home, and had four children by a wife for whom he professed great affection and respect. Despite this enviable domestic situation, the man had taken another wife, the product of a "no-good" family, an older woman he loved "to the point of weakness," "suffering any indignity" at her hands, and about whom he felt unhealthily possessive, "jealous even of the breeze that touches her."[17]

This man's second wife deserted him soon after bearing his child. Despite his pleas, she refused to return unless he assented to a catalog of demands: transfer into her name sole ownership of his house, present her with a sizeable sum of money in cash, sign a new marriage contract granting her the right to divorce him without condition or cause, and permit her to maintain a separate residence near her family. Further, she threatened to take from him their child, for whom she would demand lavish support if he divorced her or failed to meet her demands in full. Finally, the man reported that he was suffering from a "nervous illness," which Qassab Hasan suggested was the probable source of his weakness and the reason he "destroyed his own life and that of his family" to "chase after a mirage."

In exasperation, Qassab Hasan asked his readers, "What can I do with such a sick person? If I scold him, I will be crueler than his illness. If I remain silent, the disease will devour him. He is indeed sick in mind, body, and soul." In the end, Qassab Hasan concluded that "cruelty" was the greater kindness, telling the man that he "must leave this new wife who has gone astray . . . otherwise he will find himself . . . confronting all of her evil deeds and their consequences." Qassab Hasan suggested that the "sympathy, affection, and care of his first wife" would help him on this difficult path. Admonishing the man for abandoning "true" love in favor of its exclusively carnal, and therefore "sinful," counterpart, he charged the civil servant with "contemptible weakness in the face of desire." For good measure, he cited "a hadith of the noble Arab prophet," which counseled believers to beware of "the greenery planted in dung," that is, "a beautiful woman of evil origin."

Addressing his readers, Qassab Hasan exclaimed, "How glorious will be the day when we see people so conscious of national and social welfare that they marry only after careful consideration. Then, if they marry, they stay with their spouses, feel close to them, and avoid polygamy, which is, in these conditions, contrary to the wisdom of the law and social welfare." Here, Qassab Hasan's explicitly stated preference for monogamy informed by "true," or "respectable," love seems perfectly in accord with modern, bourgeois sensibilities. Yet his attitude toward polygamy is also quite conventional from the viewpoint of Islamic law. He issued no condemnation of the desire to take a second wife or the act of doing so per se. Rather, he argued that in this particular case, the conditions under which these events occurred rendered the "more than weak" civil servant's behavior contemptible. His neglect of the first wife and their children to the point of jeopardizing their health, happiness, and material welfare is precisely the sort of circumstance that is deemed to preclude polygamy in Islamic law.

At the same time, Qassab Hasan cited the distinctly modern and secular concept of "national and social welfare" as the ultimate source of authority. Here we see the clearest expression of Qassab Hasan's view of the family as the microcosm of society. Just as the family demanded that "the welfare of the four children should come before the welfare of the father," society "requires putting the good of the many before the good of the few." Thus, the virtuous citizen suppressed carnal desires, marrying only when the union served (or at least did not harm) the broader interests of community and nation.

Qassab Hasan's depiction of the ideal husband and father made it clear that weak men could not fulfill their obligations. Furthermore, as a category of person deserving of sympathy and assistance, "the weak" did not include adult males. They simply were not permitted to experience, much less act on, weakness. This proscription applied even more severely to the civil servant, who was, almost by definition, male in 1950s Syria. The special privileges that accrued to state employees were accompanied by responsibilities Qassab Hasan deemed noble and weighty. In those bearing such responsibilities, weakness and foolishness were even more deplorable character flaws, for they could result in the abdication of responsibilities to the entire nation.

POOR JUDGMENT AND THE LIMITS OF THE LAW

Qassab Hasan battled a different form of male foolishness in a case he titled "Childrearing by a Mother of Bad Morals." "Mr. 'Ayn from Aleppo" reported that he tried to "rescue" a girl "living in a bad environment" by marrying her. Soon after she bore him a daughter, the young woman abandoned him and returned to her unspecified "past behavior." Mr. 'Ayn immediately sought and was granted a legal separation, but custody of the child was awarded to her mother. As he feared the consequences of his daughter's "absorbing the morals" of her mother's "sinister" environment, he asked Qassab Hasan for the legal means to effect another "rescue," this time of his daughter from his estranged wife's custody.[18]

Noting yet another example of the Syrian Civil Code's coincidence with the shari'a, Qassab Hasan informed Mr. 'Ayn that the custody and primary guardianship of boys under the age of seven and girls under the age of nine was automatically awarded to the mother, provided that she had reached the age of majority, was "of sound mind," and was capable of "preserving the health and moral character of the child." Mr. 'Ayn faced the prospect of a long, expensive, painful, and quite possibly fruitless legal battle. First, he would have to establish to the court's satisfaction, through witness testimony and documentary evidence, that the mother was not competent to "protect the health and moral character of his daughter." Even if he could do that, however, the court would be statutorily compelled to award the child's guardianship to her maternal grandmother. Then the father would have to mount a new legal action, demonstrating by the same means that the maternal grandmother was equally unfit, or that she was incapable of protecting the child from her mother's evil influence. Then, and only then, would the court appoint as guardian the child's paternal grandmother, Mr. 'Ayn's mother.

Qassab Hasan asserted that the issues in play could not be addressed exclusively within the legal realm, for the real problem originated with Mr. 'Ayn's decision to "marry a girl in dubious circumstances." Asserting that immoral environments corrupt most forced to live in them, Qassab Hasan argued that there was little hope for the "repentance" of Mr. 'Ayn's estranged wife. Whatever "nobility" informed Mr. 'Ayn's original rescue mission, it would bring him nothing but pain now, for "noble mindedness is no virtue when its toll is paid by innocent children."

Qassab Hasan closed by expressing the hope that all of his readers, "particularly the young people among them," would avoid becoming "victims of misplaced pity," lest they wind up "like he who nourishes a viper in his bosom." To illustrate this lesson, Qassab Hasan cited Prophetic precedent, declaring, "It is reported in the noble hadith, 'Choose for your semen!' That is, think carefully about selecting the woman who will be the mother of your children." He then enlisted "popular wisdom," recalling another proverb about the intractability of bad character: "Old habits do not change this side of the grave."[19]

All of this leads to an obvious question: What, precisely, were the estranged wife's transgressions? Qassab Hasan appears to have opted for decorum when discussing potentially indelicate topics. Yet, significantly, this observance of decorum was always gender-specific. In this case, the almost inescapable conclusion is that "bad morals," "sinister environment," and "dubious circumstances" suggest a gross violation of sexual norms, perhaps even prostitution. Although Qassab Hasan appeared to feel no constraints when discussing the most intimate manifestations of male sexuality—semen, for example—he refrained from naming the violation of cultural and social norms that rendered this young woman an unfit mother. This sensitivity raises questions about the acceptable limits of public speech, at least as perceived by Qassab Hasan and his colleagues at the Syrian Broadcasting Authority.

More significantly, this sad tale uncovered for Qassab Hasan the limits of the law to make virtuous citizens. Unhealthy environments often "corrupt" the morals of those residing in them, and a person's "bad character" could not be transformed by the "misplaced pity" of another. Virtuous citizens needed to exercise prudence when attempting to help others, for the application of the law could not reverse the consequences of poor judgment.

THE LAW HELPS THOSE WHO GOVERN THEMSELVES

The law's agency was circumscribed in other ways. It did not endorse the illicit acquisition of wealth, but it could serve that purpose if the injured party was too ignorant or credulous to detect and resist such fraud. These limitations were evident in two cases involving property ownership, inheritance, and patriarchal responsibility. In most societies, these issues are among the most complex and acrimonious. The situation in 1950s Syria was certainly no exception, for the majority of cases addressed on the program "The Citizen and the Law" concerned bitter disputes between real and/or potential legatees to estates. One of these cases chronicled the hostilities among the members of a family whose patriarch had died, leaving behind two widows, five children, an unmarried sister, and a limited inheritance consisting of a modest retirement income and half ownership of a house.[20]

The deceased was a civil servant, by all accounts a "good man" who had "toiled throughout a lifetime" to support his family, and been honest and blameless in his personal, professional, and financial dealings. Upon his death, two disputes emerged. First, one of his sons claimed more than the share of the house left to him by his father, demanding part of his mother's share, and attempted to seize the small share left to his half-sister, who was born after the civil servant died. Second, the deceased's sister, who was said to be wealthy in her own right, threatened a court action to retain an allowance that she had received for some time from her late brother, to which she was not formally entitled under the law.

To resolve the first issue, Qassab Hasan delved into the maddeningly complex provisions of Article 889 of the Syrian Civil Code, which addressed the inheritance of real estate when building and other improvements had been made by one party on property owned, in whole or in part, by another. In the end, Qassab Hasan ruled against the son, citing black-letter law that he had no right to "own anything that he did not acquire through . . . inheritance or purchase." Qassab Hasan's ruling adhered to both the letter of the law and the spirit of his jurisprudential philosophy, protecting the rights of "the weak and the aggrieved," in this case an elderly widow and a female infant. Once again, he reaffirmed the most venerable principles of Islamic ethics and jurisprudence, protecting the interests of widows and orphans.

As for the dispute over the deceased's sister's allowance, Qassab Hasan presented a lengthy elucidation of the Syrian Civil Code's articles governing financial support of relatives. The fundamental principle governing relations between adults related by blood or marriage was that "the financial support of each individual is his own responsibility, with the exception of the wife, whose sustenance is the responsibility of her husband." As Qassab Hasan pointed out, this patriarchal maxim was "stipulated by canonical Islamic law and the current legal code," the only exception being adult offspring who were incapable of earning a living or contracting a marriage "due to a physical or psychological defect." Since the sister was an adult, possessed assets, and did not suffer from a debilitating physical or mental illness, she was not entitled to material support of any kind nor could she even request it before her assets were "exhausted."

Here we see another example of the perfect concordance of Islamic and secular law in 1950s Syria. Qassab Hasan was careful to distinguish between "canonical Islamic law and the current legal code," when in fact the latter had merely adopted the precepts of the former. His injunction to the parties concerned encouraged amity by insisting that all outstanding issues "must be resolved with goodwill in an environment of familial accord." While acknowledging that the law could and did provide answers to disputes over the distribution of estate property, Qassab Hasan reminded the petitioner that legal resolution "will not restore the serenity that has been lost, and no solution will return the love that has been squandered." The answer to both problems, he argued, "rests on love, and on shame for every act that abuses this love."

Qassab Hasan therefore told the deceased civil servant's son that he must reach agreement with his mother and cease disputing the "inheritance while she is still alive." He further told the errant son that he and his siblings must "visit their aunt and comfort her," for perhaps she would have never threatened legal action had she ever "received any sympathy or affection" from her late brother's children. This idealization of the affectionate, mutually supportive family unit as the microcosm of the national community was accompanied by the idealization of parenthood, in the form of the mother's "love and selflessness" and the father's lifelong labor and sacrifice on behalf of his dependents. This conflation of family and society was also reflected in the other mode of this "good man's" noble sacrifice, his professional life as a civil servant. In this sense, the dedicated career civil servant, although not a party to the dispute, was presented as the quintessential citizen whose patriarchal rights and responsibilities transcended his death.

A similar case prompted a rather different response from Qassab Hasan, however, as it featured the good civil servant's polar opposite. A woman defrauded her elderly husband of his share of a piece of land that they had purchased jointly by registering it exclusively in her name. When the husband discovered and protested this deception, members of the wife's family "convinced him that if he built a house on the land, half of the property would be registered in his name." After he built the house at his own expense, the man's wife evicted and divorced him for what he called "trivial reasons," and their children unanimously took their mother's side in the conflict.[21]

First, Qassab Hasan presented his reasoning for finding the patriarch guilty of the mortal sin of weakness. An "indulgent" man, he explained, would of course trust his "life partner" and the mother of his children to register a piece of property in the correct and honest manner. Upon learning, however, that this trust had been betrayed, a merely indulgent husband would not succumb to a second and more transparent ruse, assume considerable expense, and place his remaining wealth at risk in order to regain what was rightfully his to begin with. Qassab Hasan concluded, this man was "oppressed" rather than indulgent, a condition inevitably resulting from his underlying shortcoming: weakness.

In support of this conclusion, Qassab Hasan posed a question that went to the heart of patriarchal privilege encoded in the shari'a and Syria's PSC: "How did the wife divorce her husband in a country where the law makes divorce the prerogative of the man?" Questioning his petitioner's account,

Qassab Hasan summarized the only two possible explanations. Either a judge granted his wife a separation, something that the law never sanctioned for "trivial reasons," or the man signed a marital contract granting her "special rights in the question of divorce." If the latter was the case, Qassab Hasan declared that the man "should not reproach her, for he is the one who gave her these rights."

The fact that all of the adult children had immediately taken their mother's side also raised suspicions in Qassab Hasan's mind. After repeating his oft-stated policy of taking "every letter that arrives" at face value, Qassab Hasan declared that even if the case was exactly as described, it was unlikely that a man's children would side with their mother and her relatives unless they had lost all respect for their father. He therefore advised the weak man to "reexamine his behavior," for only the persistent display of severe character defects could cause his wife and children to see the head of the household as "refuse" and expel him from his home so callously and "without regret." Clearly, he had failed in his patriarchal duties.

Qassab Hasan's final piece of advice repeated a classic theme. After noting that his petitioner's claims could never be independently substantiated without the legal "documents of ownership" that constitute "irrefutable evidence," he informed him of his only remaining option: call his wife into court, where she could be compelled to state "under oath whether he shares in the ownership of this property or not." Given her previous behavior, the outcome was almost certain.

"Perhaps," Qassab Hasan concluded, "in this man's story there is a lesson for him and for all." Actually, this story contained two overarching lessons for the citizen, both of which derived from family relations, but being gender inflected, were more broadly applicable. The first lesson was that "the law helps those who govern themselves." In other words, the citizen of the modern state, he argued, must be well informed about his legal rights and alert to their potential violation. If he voluntarily surrendered a right that the law deemed inalienable, he had no one else to blame when he suffered the resulting injury. Qassab Hasan considered the citizen equally at fault if he failed to document important transactions or displayed excessive credulity in his personal relations.

But, for Qassab Hasan, the greatest blame was attached to those who displayed weakness, especially when their social/familial role demanded strength. "The normal, reasonable father who possesses a sufficient degree of manliness [*rujula*] remains the head of the family. . . . No normal woman would be pleased if her man lost his manliness." If a man behaved "abnormally," and thereby caused others to lose or withhold the respect that was ordinarily his due, he must change his behavior or bear the awful consequences. Maintaining others' respect for one's manhood was the essential requirement of both patriarchy and citizenship.

Syria's PSC constituted a site for educating the Syrian population about the proper conduct of family relations and a guide for governing the self and others. As the family was an idealized representation of society in miniature, it was also the academy in which the proper conduct of the citizen was observed and emulated.[22] This conduct was acutely gendered, the stern but benevolent patriarch serving as the primary agent of amicable relations and, by extension, the template for the citizen. The patriarch was expected to govern his desires and the behavior of his wife, children, and other dependents.

Wives and children deferred to this authority figure as long as he adhered to the ideal model. Thus the most significant threat to family stability appeared when its *pater familias* abdicated his responsibilities and displayed weakness or foolishness before those who looked to him as an exemplar. Najat Qassab Hasan condemned such breakdowns of self-discipline—even when they were glossed as pity or nobility—as the willful sabotage of familial integrity and amity. Those who internalized the features of the virtuous citizen enjoyed a beneficial relationship with the law, for their lives were expressions of its principles. But there were limits to the law's civilizing beneficence: it could not help those who exercised poor judgment or allowed compassion, love, or sexual desire to blind them to the character flaws of others.

4 Punishing the Enemies of Arabism

On April 22, 1955, Colonel 'Adnan al-Malki, the deputy chief of staff of the Syrian Army, was shot to death while he attended a soccer match at Damascus's National Stadium by one of the military policemen assigned to protect him. Despite his elevated rank and significant responsibilities, al-Malki was not a high-profile public figure at the time of his death. Within a few months, however, his name and face were among the most familiar in Syria, as reconstructions of his life and death occupied center stage of a state-orchestrated drama.

Al-Malki's murder realigned political forces in Syria, and arguably in the entire region. The assassination inspired numerous conspiracy theories and provided both impetus and justification for eliminating opponents to a tenuous new coalition of Ba'thists, Nasserists, communists, and "independent" nationalists within Syria's parliament, armed forces, and security services. Not unlike the 1963 Kennedy assassination in the United States, al-Malki's murder attained mythic dimensions thanks to popular media attention.

The media-disseminated narratives of al-Malki's life and death transformed him into a "national" martyr while valorizing Syria's politically ambitious officer class and reifying their preeminent role in Syrian politics. The assassination narratives also constructed a model of modern, heroic Arab citizenship. The al-Malki model of citizenship exalted the ritual enactment of masculinity, asserted eternal vigilance against internal and external enemies, supported the display of moral probity in private life, lauded professional education and training, and, last but not least, celebrated the nobility and redemptive power of sacrifice.

A close reading of the Damascene press during the months before and after al-Malki's death reveals that prior to his murder, al-Malki scarcely figured in the popular consciousness. His public persona emerged in May and June 1955 with two nearly simultaneous and closely related developments.

First, the Defense Ministry's illustrated weekly, the mass circulation *al-Jundi* (The Soldier), launched a campaign to lionize al-Malki. This effort was soon taken up in the ministry's monthly publication, *al-Majalla al-'Askariyya* (The Military Journal), and spread to other state and privately owned press outlets, demonstrating the reach and influence of specialized publications. In a second, related phenomenon, sensational press accounts of the investigations into the so-called Malki Affair began to appear. These stories identified al-Malki's killer, a military policeman named Yunis 'Abd al-Rahim, as a member of the Syrian Social Nationalist Party (SSNP) and introduced the Syrian public to a cast of co-conspirators from the party and its alleged accomplices at home and abroad. The SSNP was resolutely anticommunist, and its members considered Baghdad—rather than Cairo—Syria's "natural" ally. With some reservations, the SSNP also looked on the role of the United States in the region favorably.[1] In sum, the SSNP's views were anathema to the coalition of Ba'thists, communists, and Nasserists who dominated the army's senior officer ranks.

Soon the first installments in what would become a vast body of hagiographic literature appeared. These interrelated collections of discourse depicted al-Malki as an Arab nationalist saint and those implicated in his murder as unspeakable monsters in league with foreign enemies of Syria and the Arabs. Continual ritualized performance of emotion (grief, remorse, anger) at public events and in the press affirmed and defined al-Malki's martyrdom. Initially, senior officers in the Syrian armed forces and prominent members of the country's political elite participated in this psychodrama. Gradually, though, the circle of public mourners widened to include prominent figures in the spheres of journalism, literature, the arts, and the sciences from throughout the Arab world. Ultimately, public lamentations of Syria's loss and the demonization of those allegedly responsible spread from specialized media to become a truly mass phenomenon: the government convened mass vigils and marches and myriad media outlets solicited and provided venues for non-commissioned officers, enlisted men, and cadets in the armed forces; representatives of various crafts and professions; factory workers; peasants; and primary, secondary, and university students to join in the mourning.

The special military tribunal tasked with investigating, trying, and sentencing those involved in the conspiracy to murder al-Malki began its public proceedings in June 1955. Under the direction of Deputy Chief of Staff for Intelligence Major (soon Colonel) 'Abd al-Hamid al-Sarraj, the tribunal was empowered to collect evidence on all aspects of the Malki Affair, as it was by then routinely called. This exercise was the first Soviet-style show-trial in

Syria, establishing a pattern that would last for a decade. At its first session, the tribunal declared the ssnp a clandestine, criminal organization inimical to public order and the Syrian constitution, and charged the party with conspiring to penetrate and take control of Syria's armed forces, and thereby stage a coup. It further charged the ssnp with a wide array of treasonous activities.

Alleged offenses included offering to serve as agents of Iraq's pro-British regime, maintaining covert contacts with various officials of the U.S. government, and operating a vast espionage network within the Syrian Army, the Defense Ministry, and numerous other government agencies. Ultimately, the court charged thirty-one defendants with capital crimes and nine others with offenses punishable by life imprisonment at hard labor.[2]

Thus commenced a propaganda onslaught as Syrian periodicals of every stripe began to provide daily coverage featuring the tearful testimony of al-Malki's relatives, friends, colleagues, superiors, and admirers, as well as lurid details from the confessions of the accused, which often detailed heinous criminal conspiracies never mentioned in the indictments.[3] Throughout, the court, state officials, and the press poured scorn on the defendants' claims of innocence and their attempts to justify their beliefs and actions. The pervasive and incessant discussion of al-Malki and his alleged killers threw into relief the critical relationship between access to mass media and power in a developing state, for such access provides venues for the "systematic, even Machiavellian, instilling of nationalist ideology."[4] By such means, Syrian media denied the ssnp's members, ideological fellow travelers, sympathizers, defenders, and associates a public voice. Rather, the press "othered" the accused, describing them in fiendish terms in opposition to the hero al-Malki, the paragon of all possible virtues, the possessor of almost superhuman qualities and abilities.

'Adnan al-Malki was thirty-six years old when he was murdered. According to the prevailing narrative, he was a charismatic, forceful, and highly visible figure among his generational cohort in the armed forces (fig. 4.1). He was reputed to be an avid sports fan and sportsman, which added to his hyper-masculine posthumous image.[5] Colonel al-Malki was also said to be a proponent of Nasser-style "positive neutrality," a stance endorsed by the Ba'th Party, in which his brother Riyad was a senior figure. The scion of an old, notable, Sunni Damascene family, he was the perfect exemplar of the self-image that the Syrian Army was seeking to construct—youthful and vigorous but sober and socially grounded, politically conscious but non-sectarian.

FIGURE 4.1 Colonel 'Adnan al-Malki. *Al-Jundi,* July 7, 1955, back cover.

Al-Malki's hagiography depicted him as heir to a noble family legacy of patriotism and public service, an opponent from infancy of Western imperialism, and a brilliant student who studied harder than his classmates because he comprehended the awesome responsibility he would bear in the future.[6] Upon entering the army, al-Malki became the perfect comrade, accepting the burdens of work while forever bearing a broad smile on his "radiant face," and always displaying the "right" political commitments. He risked his life and freedom to support the Palestinian cause, oppose dictatorship and oppression, and champion the Syrian people's legitimate yearning for dignity and sovereignty.[7] The dramatis personae of this mass-media morality play reads like a who's who of Syrian politics, commerce, journalism, arts, and letters. The gradual inclusion of humbler mourners soon provided all, great and small, rich and poor, from every corner of the republic, with the opportunity to construct social and cultural solidarity through the vicarious experience of al-Malki's assassination and identification with his selfless sacrifice.[8]

The urban notables who governed Syria for most of its first four decades of existence realized the power and utility of commemorating sacrifice by naming the capital's late-Ottoman-period geographical center Martyrs' Square, declaring the Iraqi soldier and politician Yasin al-Hashimi a martyr, exploiting his funeral for domestic political purposes, and dedicating the Mandate-period city center to the commemoration of General Yusuf al-'Azma, who died at the hands of French occupation forces.[9]

Thus the concept of the martyr's sacrifice, either secular or sacred, was quite familiar to the Syrian public in the 1950s. The Malki campaign, however, was unprecedented in its scope, duration, and intensity. It reconstituted the paradigm of martyrdom, institutionalizing the notion of blood sacrifice as the *sine qua non* of the modern state, nation, and community, and provided a new, thoroughly modern template for Arab heroism, an unusual form of personality cult, as well as indicating the way that modern media could be utilized to enact and substantiate such posthumous identities. One need look no further than the hagiography of Hafiz al-Asad's late son Basil in 1994 to see the refinement of this template on an even grander scale.[10]

What follows is not a study of the Malki assassination per se, or of the life of 'Adnan al-Malki. Rather, I examine the creation and management of the Malki Affair, the process by which the modern technology of mass media, specific forms of technical expertise, and the disciplinary power of the state were deployed in the service of the secular religion of nationalism to define the Syrian citizen, and the web of rights and obligations linking that figure to the nation and state.

The press coverage surrounding al-Malki's martyrdom and the subsequent military tribunals; the unlicensed, samizdat-style pamphlets circulated by opponents of the emerging new order in the aftermath of the assassination; the memoirs of prominent military officers, politicians, and journalists; the hagiographic journalism and literature published in the decades since the event; al-Malki's extant personal correspondence; the few available Syrian archival sources; and American diplomatic correspondence show how al-Malki and his presumed killers were constructed in the popular imagination.

ILLUMINATING TREASON

In July 1955, the magazine *al-Jundi* featured an article entitled "How They Received the News of the Disaster," which recounted the visceral reactions of both the famous and obscure to the news of 'Adnan al-Malki's murder. This presentation of Syrians' purportedly verbatim, first-person accounts of the circumstances in which they heard and responded to the news suggest that the event was the defining moment in an entire generation of Syrians' lives. Just one element of a larger press campaign, the article gave all Syrians the opportunity to construct social and cultural solidarity through vicarious experience of the assassination and identification with its victim.[11] This classic exercise in the politics of memory was designed to impose patriotic duty on Syrian citizens, and thereby maintain the internal cohesion of their imagined community.

While engendering solidarity, press coverage of al-Malki's murder also exacerbated citizens' "antagonism vis-à-vis others."[12] Martyr narratives easily lend themselves to demagoguery and fearmongering; they sharply demarcate boundaries between belief systems and communities that "may not have previously been apparent."[13] Indeed, they may actually bring these boundaries into existence. In other words, martyrologies illuminate the dark spaces in which treason abides, a process that the historian Peter Gay called "the cultivation of hatred."[14]

In arguing that 'Adnan al-Malki was the nation's iconic martyr, and thus deserving of the people's sacred love and adulation, the colonel's hagiographers also asserted that his killers and their allies were the objects of equally sanctified hatred, contempt, and violence. In the words of Jacques Derrida, the hagiographers "drew from the dead a supplementary force to be turned against the living" in an effort to "authorize and legitimate" their own leading role in national politics.[15]

The lionization of al-Malki in death required three ingredients to be effective: state power (and its corollary, the "legitimate" use of coercion), mass media, and the plausibility of foreign conspiracy. A faction of the army's high command energetically wielded the first, temporarily acquired effective control over the second, and exaggerated the third in an attempt to conflate army, state, and nation in the public imagination. After stirring up fears—some of which, to be sure, were valid—these officers presented themselves as the sole "source of protection" from ruthless, devious enemies.[16]

The process of elevating al-Malki to the status of national martyr began quickly. In his highly publicized funeral oration, Chief of Staff Shawkat Shuqayr solemnly pledged that the army would use all means necessary to avenge their brother officer.[17] Soon thereafter, Syria's civilian government granted the Ministry of Defense exclusive authority to investigate, try, and punish those responsible for al-Malki's assassination. The ministry's "extraordinary military tribunal" began by purging from the armed forces all members of the Syrian Socialist Nationalist Party.

"Cleansing" its ranks was both an acknowledgment of the army's central role in post–World War II Syria's political life and a manifestation of momentous long-term shifts in the larger region's ideological orientation. Given the army's centrality to politics, conflict over its ideological complexion was the most significant and decisive struggle of the era.[18] This ideological struggle also had a sectarian dimension. Members of the army high command were acutely aware that Christians, 'Alawis, and Isma'ilis were heavily represented in the SSNP, and that similar demographic trends were emerging within the army's own ranks.[19]

The post-independence instability of the officer corps only heightened these anxieties, and could account for the speed and thoroughness of the post-assassination purge. Yet the success of this project required forms of modern expertise not traditionally ascribed to military professionals. A tradition established during the reign of Syria's military dictators—the defense and security establishments' publication of mass-media outlets—persisted and expanded during the Democratic Years. The chief example was the Ministry of Defense publication *al-Jundi,* which played a critical role in the propaganda campaign against the SSNP. *Al-Jundi* was published under the supervision of the Third Division of the General Staff, or G-3, the office that 'Adnan al-Malki had directed until his murder. Since 1949, editorial responsibility for *al-Jundi* had resided with the Military Cultural Committee, the Defense Ministry's counterpart to the Ministry of the Interior's Directorate for the Spiritual Guidance of the Security Forces, a body that published its own glossy journal, *Sawt Suriya* (The Voice of Syria), during this period.[20]

Thus by 1955 the Syrian armed forces employed a cadre of experienced journalists, editors, polemicists, and propagandists with the requisite skills to produce crude but effective narratives of the treasonous conspiracies arrayed against Syria. The army's ranks also included many practitioners of "enhanced interrogation" techniques. Under the command of 'Abd al-Hamid al-Sarraj, these technicians of coercion were successful at "producing knowledge" in the form of damning confessions and reciprocal denunciations. Against such adepts in the darker arts of modernity, those wielding expertise in civilian jurisprudence were all but impotent.

WHO KILLED 'ADNAN AL-MALKI AND WHY?

The basic facts of the assassination are no longer in serious dispute. Al-Malki arrived at Damascus's National Stadium at approximately 4:00 PM on April 22, 1955, just as a soccer match between the Syrian Military Police and Egyptian Coast Guard teams was beginning. After greeting friends and colleagues, he took his seat in the VIP section near Chief of Staff Shawkat Shuqayr, Egyptian ambassador to Syria Mahmud Riyad, and other dignitaries.[21] Minutes later, military police sergeant and Syrian Social Nationalist Party member Yunis 'Abd al-Rahim shot al-Malki twice in the back of the head and then immediately shot and killed himself. Within hours, speculation was rife in the Syrian press about 'Abd al-Rahim's motives, the existence of co-conspirators, the latter's identities and motives, and the identity of the crime's ultimate author(s).[22] Leading suspects included the entire SSNP as a body, allegedly acting on behalf of foreign intelligence agencies (chiefly those of the United States and Israel); individual members of the party acting on a variety of political, personal, careerist, or even psychological motives; exiled former military dictator Adib al-Shishakli; or various combinations of the above.[23]

Less than a week after al-Malki's murder, the military prosecution's narrative of the crime was already set: Recently retired Lieutenant Colonel Ghassan Jadid and other members of the SSNP's senior leadership had collectively resolved to kill al-Malki because he was the most significant obstacle to their plans to seize control of Syria's armed forces and, ultimately, the state itself. Yunis 'Abd al-Rahim had accepted the mission, and his military police colleagues and fellow party members Fu'ad Jadid, Badi' Makhlouf, and 'Abd al-

Mun'im Dabbusi had served as auxiliaries, pledging to kill al-Malki if 'Abd al-Rahim failed, and to finish off the lead assassin if his suicide attempt was unsuccessful.[24] Once in control of Syria, the SSNP would divert the country from its "natural path" of neutrality, steering it instead toward alignment with the United States, membership in the Baghdad Pact, and appeasement of Israeli occupation and aggression.[25] The military prosecutors accused the SSNP of a crime that sought "not merely the elimination of one or more individuals," but "the elimination of Syria in its entirety."[26] — *nationalist discourse*

USING THE HARSHEST MEASURES AGAINST THE "ENEMIES OF ARABISM"

Rhetorically, 'Adnan al-Malki's status as a sacred national martyr hinged on the irredeemable evil of his killers. The army and its civilian allies exploited their newfound authority to shape mass-media coverage of the crime, its investigation, and the judicial proceedings that followed,[27] calling for vengeance against SSNP members and sympathizers depicted as subhuman, monstrous creatures displaying "repulsive" and terrifying defects of thought, deed, and character.[28]

In addition to the standard communiqués and press releases, "exclusive" interviews, coverage of court proceedings, and calculated leaks of "sensational" new discoveries, this campaign also featured a Greek chorus of voices from the general public endorsing the prosecution's extralegal impulses. Within two weeks of al-Malki's assassination, Syria's "intellectuals," embodied in the "professors and lecturers of the Syrian University," published their "sharp" condemnation of the crime and their "demand [that] the criminals and their supporters" be subjected to "the harshest measures."[29] "Man-in-the-street" interviews suggested that even the most underprivileged citizens supported the prosecution's narrative unquestioningly. For example, a "street peddler" neatly and poetically summarized the treasonous nature of the SSNP: "If the Israelis killed al-Malki, I would not cry for him. But if his death was at the hands of a Syrian, I would cry once for him and a thousand times for our condition." In this same article, a mechanic suggested the form that "harsh measures" might take: "If it were up to me, I would hang them in Marjeh!"[30] Marjeh is the popular name for Martyrs' Square, named in honor of the country's first "Arabist" martyrs, who were hanged on that spot by Ottoman provincial governor Jamal Pasha in 1916. The irony of proposing to hang the alleged murderers of Syria's newest Arab nationalist saint in the locale that officially commemorates the country's first went unremarked.

"TORMENTS NOT WITNESSED SINCE THE MIDDLE AGES": THE INVESTIGATION

From late April to mid-June, investigators seized documents and other evidentiary materials from SSNP offices and the homes of party members. These items served as the basis of suspect interrogation, the "cleansing" of the armed forces and the civil service, and the composition of inflammatory press leaks.[31] A month after al-Malki's assassination, the tribunal announced the dissolution of the SSNP and the confiscation of its assets. At the same time, Ba'thist and Leftist parliamentarians and army officers demanded the emendation of Syria's military penal code to expand the tribunal's powers, permitting it to conduct its investigation and subsequent judicial proceedings unhampered by niceties of civilian law like habeas corpus, prohibitions against the maltreatment of suspects, and strict rules of evidentiary procedure.[32]

In fact, soon after the tribunal began its efforts, clandestine SSNP publications, Lebanese newspapers beyond the reach of Syrian censors, and confidential sources reporting to foreign embassies began to circulate disturbing rumors about the mistreatment of detainees in the notorious Mezze Military Prison. Reports alleged that medical care and legal representation were systematically withheld, and that uncooperative suspects of both sexes and all ages were being subjected to "savage and barbaric" interrogation techniques such as electrical shocks, sleep deprivation, extraction of fingernails, simulated drowning (waterboarding), and repeated beatings.[33] These and other unspecified "torments not witnessed since the Middle Ages" were attributed to 'Abd al-Hamid al-Sarraj, who was said to be orchestrating the investigation from behind the scenes.[34]

While such information rarely appeared in the media, the extant documentary record offers a counter-history, providing considerable indirect evidence of ill treatment. Superficially, the transcripts of numerous depositions and pretrial interrogations suggest that proceedings followed proper, professional standards. The tone is generally dry and businesslike, the interrogators' questions only occasionally betraying hints of coercion.[35] But the detainees' responses tell a different story, referring to "off-the-record" sessions during which interrogators employed a variety of techniques to obtain confessions and statements incriminating codefendants.[36]

The records detailing the interrogation of three of the military police NCOs who would be sentenced to death at their first trial include accusations of torture. For example, Fu'ad Jadid declared himself "innocent of all the crimes" and repudiated his previous statements, as they were "extracted" after repeated beatings and electrical shocks. His colleague 'Abd al-Mun'im Dabbusi made a nearly identical declaration that his statements had been obtained via "every form of brutality."[37] Yet Badi' Makhlouf made the most moving recantation. He pleaded with "the esteemed court" to grant him permission to renounce his previous statements because of the "manner in which they were obtained," that is, after months of "unspeakable torture." He requested to stand before the court and describe these "torments not suffered by the early Christians at the hands of the Roman pagans," among them whippings, electrical shocks, and threats of "disgusting acts" committed against himself and his sisters. He then denied any role in al-Malki's murder and attempted to exonerate his comrades.[38]

Such brave gestures, however, had no impact on the military tribunal's indictments. The charges, published on June 29, accused over 140 members of the party with a remarkable array of crimes, chief among which were "incitement to murder," "murder and participation in its implementation," "inciting military personnel to disobey orders," "the commission of acts designed to incite armed insurrection," "communication with a foreign state," "exposing the country to the danger of hostile actions," "the acquisition of documents and information that must remain secret to preserve state security," the destruction of evidence by "burning the printing house" of the party's newspaper, "membership in a secret organization" deemed inimical to the constitution and public order, "encouraging military personnel to join a secret organization," the illegal possession of weapons, and "assisting a criminal to flee [from justice]."[39]

THE APPLICATION OF "ABSOLUTE AND PERFECT JUSTICE": THE TRIALS

The tribunal arose as a compromise solution to an ongoing crisis in civil-military relations. Immediately after al-Malki's funeral, leftist army officers and their ideological counterparts in parliament demanded the imposition of martial law. The government's counterproposal, a military tribunal with extraordinary authority, was accepted.[40] So, just one week after the assassination, the government announced that a special military tribunal with sweeping powers of investigation, arrest, and adjudication would hold open sessions examining all aspects of the Malki Affair.[41] Over the next sixteen months, this tribunal, composed of attorneys, civilian jurists, and army officers, supervised judicial proceedings that fell into three general categories: "trials of minor civilian and military SSNP members" charged only with membership in an "unauthorized underground organization"; "civilian hearings" on the "dissolution of the SSNP" and the disposition of its assets; and, most significant, a trial of civilian and military party members "suspected of complicity in al-Malki's murder."[42]

The army refurbished the villa of late military dictator Husni al-Za'im specifically for the tribunal's public sessions.[43] All of the proceedings convened in this space received extensive media coverage, but the trial of al-Malki's alleged killers was a grand piece of judicial theater unprecedented in Syrian history. The appointment of Badr al-Din 'Ulush as the tribunal's president provided a patina of legal expertise and propriety to the process. 'Ulush was, by all accounts, a jurist of distinguished reputation with extensive trial and appellate court experience throughout the Syrian judicial system.[44] His reputation, and his presence on the bench during the murder trial, permitted the Ministry of Defense to assert that, in keeping with its goal of "perfect justice," it had provided every possible "legal surety" and that it had done "more than the law required" in facilitating "all requirements of the defense," providing the accused with the "opportunity to defend themselves" under conditions of "complete and absolute justice."[45]

Yet, willingly or not, 'Ulush presided over a sham, a mass-media spectacle featuring the exposition of elaborate (and often contradictory) international conspiracy theories; coerced confessions; the condemnation of friends, relatives, and colleagues; and the berating and intimidation of defendants, witnesses, and attorneys. Unsurprisingly, the public sessions of the al-Malki murder trial have often been compared to the 1930s "show trials" held in Joseph Stalin's Soviet Union.[46]

Media attention was, of course, central to this spectacle. The need to court (or perhaps cow) the press was so acutely felt that some two months before the murder trial began, prominent journalists, editors, and publishers were summoned to the Damascus Officers Club where they received copies of the indictments and listened to remonstrations about the incontestable guilt of the accused and the sinister foreign forces guiding the defendants' actions.[47] The perceived significance of media participation became even more apparent shortly after the tribunal's initial session on August 26, 1955, when the court adjourned for twenty-four hours because the courtroom lacked sufficient "electrical equipment" to accommodate the many lights, newsreel cameras, microphones, and recording devices crowding the space.[48]

Other parallels with Soviet show trials included the obvious bias of some of the tribunal's members. For example, Lieutenant Colonel 'Afif al-Bizri, an ardent leftist with no legal training, was reported to have called for the immediate "liquidation" of the SSNP's leadership at the Damascus Officers Club just eight days after al-Malki's murder.[49] Furthermore, prominent Ba'thist attorneys like MP Khalil Kallas and the victim's own brother Riyad al-Malki served on the prosecution team and cross-examined defense witnesses in court.[50] Not surprisingly, several members of the defense team registered protests on the record, asserting that the trial was little more than one political party's exercise in vengeance against its chief ideological rival.[51]

The tribunal operated on the presumption of collective and associative guilt, as individuals were charged, tried, convicted, and sentenced on the basis of their individual actions, their tenuous association with other defendants, and their simple membership in a state-licensed political party that was retroactively designated a "secret" and illegal "apparatus." By adopting this principle, the tribunal made a significant departure from both major currents—Islamic and Western European—of Syria's legal tradition, and embraced a premise at the core of totalitarian systems of justice.[52]

This oppressive atmosphere was echoed and augmented by the Syrian press, which ridiculed the SSNP's ideology and its leaders' public protestations of innocence in the wake of the Malki Affair.[53] The testimony, physical appearance, and courtroom demeanor of party members were also subjected to mockery. As the most prominent party official in custody, the bespectacled 'Isam al-Mahayri was the most frequent object of this derision, said to have "foxlike" eyes that reflected the "devious cunning" required to "perpetrate the gravest crimes in the cruelest fashion" and then present himself in court as "a poor, innocent child."[54]

The tribunal's open sessions featured another distressing element of show-trial theatrics, self-preservation through the incrimination and repudiation of friends, colleagues, and relatives. Prominent politicians and journalists provided testimony helpful to the prosecution's case and thereby created welcome distance between themselves and erstwhile associates now on trial for their lives.[55] Families were not exempt from this treatment, as two of alleged assassin Yunis 'Abd al-Rahim's brothers were forced to provide testimony incriminating their late sibling and his colleagues.[56] The court even subpoenaed Muti'a Baghdadi, the teenage bride of defendant 'Abd al-Mun'im Dabbusi. When the defense objected on multiple and obvious grounds, the tribunal president waived the requirement of swearing in yet still insisted that the court, as well as the attending journalists, hear a frightened minor's "off-the-record" testimony about her husband's political opinions and association with the alleged assassin 'Abd al-Rahim.[57]

Not surprisingly, many of the defendants had initially provided lengthy, damning, and detailed confessions and testimony incriminating their party comrades, relatives, and friends.[58] Yet, as noted above, several then recanted their previous testimony in court, declaring that it had been obtained under torture.[59] This embarrassing phenomenon was usually met with refusals to amend previously entered testimony and stern lectures from 'Ulush about the legally mandated penalties for perjury.[60] When 'Isam al-Mahayri requested the amendment of his previous testimony, 'Ulush extracted the following statement from al-Mahayri before assenting: "I presented my testimony voluntarily and I was not subjected to beatings, torture, or pressure, but I was in a state of mind that has now caused me to reconsider this testimony."[61]

Throughout this travesty, several of Syria's more prominent attorneys, including Sayf al-Din al-Ma'mun, Munir al-'Ajlani, and Kamil al-Bunni, braved the potential consequences to represent the defendants, often making long, impassioned speeches asserting their clients' innocence and protesting the tribunal's many irregularities.[62] In fact, three weeks into the murder trial, the entire team of defense attorneys boycotted the proceedings for a period of two days, returning only after negotiations conducted by Zafir al-Qasimi, the president of the Syrian Lawyers Association and one of 'Adnan al-Malki's chief eulogists.[63] The details of the agreement that prompted their return to the courtroom were not disclosed, but we can infer them from subsequent events. Immediately after reaching this agreement, the lawyers proceeded en masse to the office of Tribunal President 'Ulush where they submitted a formal apology and a declaration of their immediate desire to "return to their duties." Al-Qasimi spoke at the beginning of the following session, declaring that "everyone in court is here to uphold the law," and that attorneys are "a family formed in service to justice and the law." 'Ulush then replied in kind, describing the law as the most "beautiful" of professions "because its purpose is the disclosure of the truth."[64]

These expressions of collegiality and positivism had no impact on the trial's outcome. On December 13, 1955, the tribunal announced that, "in the name of the Syrian people," it had sentenced to death seven of the defendants: George 'Abd al-Massih, Iskandar Shawi, Ghassan Jadid, Sami al-Khuri, Badi' Makhlouf, 'Abd al-Mun'im Dabbusi, and Fu'ad Jadid.[65] On January 10, 1956, Syria's Court of Cassation cited procedural irregularities and jurisdictional violations in overturning the original convictions and ordering a new trial.[66] Yet another presidential decree in April 1956 resolved this jurisdictional issue, and a second, much briefer trial produced the same convictions and sentences, which were then promptly upheld by the Court of Cassation.[67]

"DEATH WAS A MERCY": THE EXECUTION OF THE "CRIMINALS"

Ultimately, the military tribunal confirmed death sentences against only three of the seven defendants it had convicted of capital crimes.[68] President Shukri al-Quwwatli initially favored commuting these sentences to life imprisonment, but after being subjected to extraordinary pressure from Ba'thist parliamentarians and senior army officers of various leftist proclivities, al-Quwwatli agreed to abide by the decision of a review board constituted of three army officers and three jurists, which upheld two of the three sentences.[69]

Thus on the morning of September 3, 1956, Sergeants Badi' Makhlouf and 'Abd al-Mun'im Dabbusi were executed by firing squad.[70] An unsigned *al-Jundi* editorial appearing the following week depicted the "dreadful, still silence" pervading al-Mansura, the "place of death" at which the "suffering of the two villains ended." He then urged his readers to dispel any sympathetic feelings, as the chests shattered by the firing squad's bullets "were not those of citizens at all" but rather those of "enemies" who were excommunicated from their previously consecrated state the moment they "bound themselves to the colonialists." Given their wretched state, "death was a mercy for the two criminals," who had "shared in conspiracies" designed to "humiliate" their homeland's people, "tear apart its army," and expose its secrets to a host of foreign governments.[71]

Yet this measure of "merciful" justice was insufficient for the architects of the military tribunals. *Al-Jundi*'s readers were reminded that many other "villains" who had "escaped beyond the reach of justice" lurked "close at hand" in the "sewers of treachery," from which they continued to "spit their venom" and "spread their malice." The editorial asserted that the Malki Affair would not end until the "bullets of al-Mansura" were fired into all "remaining hearts . . . filled with hatred for truth and Arabism."[72]

Two weeks later, a similarly vindictive piece appearing under the pen name al-Muthanna urged Syrians to "rejoice in the reckoning," the "settling" of accounts, and the "destruction of injustice, treachery, and betrayal" signaled by the echo of the rifles' report. Asserting that "the news" of the executions was "on all lips and every tongue," al-Muthanna quoted a cleric, a judge, an intellectual, and an "average" man, woman, and boy all endorsing the executions. The "man of religion" cited the Qur'an to emphasize the enormity of the killers' crimes against God and all of humanity. A "daughter of the people" declared that, as a mother—"the maker" of the next generation and "the builder" of society—she had "the right" to demand executions and other measures that would protect her children from the "treacherous and evil claws of aggressive colonialism." Thus she longed for the "hand of justice" to seize the unnamed "mastermind" of al-Malki's assassination, the head of the "speckled serpent." A "neighborhood boy" joined in the dehumanization of SSNP members, declaring that Makhlouf and Dabbusi did not deserve dignity in death and recounting the "cries of joy" raised when the executioners' bullets entered the "loathsome bodies" of "the traitors."[73]

CAN THE ASSASSINS SPEAK? THE RESPONSE OF THE ACCUSED

Unlike the unfortunate Syrians accused of involvement in al-Malki's murder, the U.S. government was in a position to challenge the prosecution narrative. Embassy officials vigorously denied accusations of American complicity in meetings with Syrian officials and at press conferences. They persuaded Prime Minister Sabri al-'Asali to issue clarifications of his and others' inflammatory comments, and were even able to plant in the local press unattributed editorials composed by U.S. Information Service employees or "independent" writers following embassy guidelines.[74]

Those under the tribunal's jurisdiction enjoyed no such advantages, as the army and its civilian allies used every means at their disposal to silence dissident voices inside and outside the courtroom. Within a week of al-Malki's assassination, Hanna Kiswani, the SSNP's sole member of parliament, was stripped of his immunity and arrested, effectively cowing any of his colleagues who might have protested the extralegal measures to come.[75] Furthermore, a variety of means were employed to deny effective legal counsel to those who, like Kiswani, were caught in the army's dragnet. These included confinement and interrogation under harsh military rules and procedures, severely restricted and closely monitored communication with defense counsel, and the harassment, intimidation, and occasional prosecution of attorneys offering such services.[76] As a result, prosecutors at the Malki tribunals outnumbered defense counsel by a ratio of more than two to one, and many of the latter were Lebanese attorneys with little or no experience in the Syrian legal system.[77]

Defendants isolated and terrified by such arbitrary measures often implicated fellow party members in the conspiracy and echoed the prosecution line about foreign involvement. This phenomenon was most striking in the case of senior party official 'Isam al-Mahayri, former press baron and publisher of the party daily *al-Bina'* (The Structure). As the former co-proprietor of the Daily Press Corporation, al-Mahayri's effective control of five newspapers had once given him an unparalleled venue for his opinions. Now this public figure was reduced to groveling, making excuses, and implicating former comrades in court and in interviews and statements arranged, supervised, and censored by his army captors and interrogators.[78]

Other pressmen felt the wrath of the government, which highlighted the perceived significance of the media by pressuring the publishers of all major periodicals to print official releases about the Malki case and harassing those who persisted in presenting alternative views.[79] The most prominent example of the latter was the stridently anti-leftist Husni al-Barazi, whose daily newspaper *al-Nas* (The People) was shut down after he printed a sarcastic editorial that alleged the torture of SSNP defendants and featured the name of his archenemy, Ba'thist Speaker of Parliament Akram al-Hawrani.[80] Al-Barazi's editor-in-chief, Nazir Fansa, promptly established his own daily newspaper, *al-Anba'* (The News), whose editorial policy carefully toed the official line on the Malki Affair. Lebanese periodicals were, of course, beyond the reach of Syrian authorities and frequently smuggled into Damascus. Several continued to feature the SSNP counter-narrative, but the military tribunal bullied all attorneys for the defense into publicly denouncing and distancing their clients from these publications.[81]

Yet the most significant case of press suppression was the banning and destruction of the SSNP's official organ, *al-Bina'*. This destruction was literal, as within hours of al-Malki's murder, the paper's offices and printing press were sacked and burned. Insult was added to injury when party members were accused of burning their own facilities in order to destroy incriminating evidence, a charge that entered court proceedings and media accounts.[82] The SSNP, denied access to the modern media so readily available to its ideological opponents and the military prosecutors, had to rely on clandestine, samizdat-style leaflets and pamphlets. Risking arrest, torture, and prolonged imprisonment, SSNP members distributed these publications by hand in the streets or other public places like movie theaters by slipping them under doors or by sending them through the mail.[83] Unsurprisingly, these documents denied SSNP complicity in al-Malki's assassination. Several also asserted that the party was "the first victim of a Zionist-inspired Communist-ASRP [Ba'th] plot to destroy Syria," more generally equated communism with Zionism, and leveled frankly anti-Semitic accusations about Jewish "exploitation and fraud" in Syrian politics.[84]

Finally, SSNP members also sought to "speak" through acts of violence. Attempts on the lives of Chief Military Prosecutor Hamdi al-Salih and Chief Military Investigator Jalal 'Aqil, and threats against Shawkat Shuqayr, Akram al-Hawrani, 'Abd al-Hamid al-Sarraj, and Lieutenant Colonel Muhammad al-Jarrah were attributed to party members and their relatives, serving only to increase the scope and severity of the government's repression.[85]

WHAT WAS NOT SAID

Could a sordid tale of callous sexual exploitation be at the bottom of one of the most politically consequential events in Syria's post–World War II history? Throughout much of the modern period, many impoverished 'Alawi families contracted the labor of their young daughters to prosperous Sunni Arab families in Syria's cities. According to Patrick Seale, "As late as 1950 there were some ten thousand 'Alawi girls working as domestic drudges in Damascus."[86] In the summer of 1955, U.S. embassy communications cited persistent rumors that 'Adnan al-Malki's home was the workplace of one such unfortunate, the teenaged sister of his killer, Yunis 'Abd al-Rahim. According to the most lurid version of the story, al-Malki impregnated his young servant; Yunis demanded marriage and was rebuffed "derisively," an insult that provided the motive for the former's murder.[87]

This account has not been substantiated. Yet its significance lies not in its historicity but in its perceived plausibility. Actively spread by the SSNP in a vain attempt to discredit the hero-martyr and deflect blame for his assassination, such rumors acquired a measure of currency precisely because the conflation of class and sectarian identities bespoke real, long-term structural inequalities.[88] These rumors also echoed other undeniable realities: a majority of those publicly accused of complicity in the Malki Affair were members of religious minorities, while the architects and administrators of their prosecution and repression were almost exclusively Sunnis.[89]

Yet these issues rarely surfaced in public. The Syrian press either resolutely ignored the sectarian dimension of the al-Malki saga or referenced it obliquely.[90] For example, many daily newspaper updates on the investigation and trials repeatedly referred to suspects by their full (recognizably Christian) names or cited defendants' "home villages" in the 'Alawi heartland, even when the person in question had resided in Damascus for many years.[91] Another tactic was to compare al-Malki's accused killers with stock historical villains like the Shu'ubiyun, non-Arab converts to Islam who were routinely accused of secret adherence to pre-Islamic or heretical doctrines and practices and of clandestine opposition to the "rightful" political and social hegemony of Sunni Arabs during the 'Abbasid Empire's "Golden Age of Islamic Civilization."[92]

In nonpublic forums, such references were more frequent and explicit. Military Intelligence interrogators, for example, asked Orthodox Christian prisoners if their churches or parochial schools were sites of SSNP recruitment.[93] And, although he was a product of the minor Sunni notability, 'Isam al-Mahayri's interrogators questioned him closely about his writings, in which they detected the incitement of sectarian tensions and the promotion of ideas offensive to Sunni Muslim sensibilities.[94]

Furthermore, such attitudes and interests were not restricted to the lower ranks of the officer corps, as is evidenced by the memoranda of several private conversations between Chief of Staff Shawkat Shuqayr and U.S. embassy officials in the wake of al-Malki's murder. Shuqayr described the SSNP as "being composed primarily of members of minority groups" and "dominated by Christians" who sought the "improvement of their position" by effecting Syria's geographical reconfiguration and its political isolation from the "rest of the Arab world." Shuqayr further informed his American interlocutors that recent events had prompted the army high command to revise its academy admissions policies, which now excluded all applicants who were not "of Arab blood" and solid "pan-Arab ideals." For Shuqayr's American audience, these and other comments about the ongoing anti-SSNP purges conveyed the "unpleasant flavor of [the] persecution of a religious minority."[95]

This apparent paradox—the acute awareness of sectarian identity and nearly universal reticence to broach the subject publicly—is the legacy of centuries of Ottoman discrimination against heterodox Shi'i sects, and of French Mandate–era divide-and-rule policies favoring minorities in the Syrian Legion and Troupes Speciales du Levant, the institutional precursors of the Syrian armed forces. In this respect, the Malki Affair abounds with historical ironies: Two of the defendants sentenced to death, Ghassan and Fu'ad Jadid, were the brothers of Salah Jadid, Hafiz al-Asad's comrade in the secret Ba'thist Military Committee, which seized power in 1963. Furthermore, one of the two military police NCOs executed for al-Malki's murder, Badi' Makhlouf, was the first cousin of Anisa Makhlouf, the mother of current president Bashar al-Asad.[96]

"THE ECHO OF GUNSHOTS"

As Paul Silverstein and Ussama Makdisi have observed, "The violent enactment of communal identity is a decidedly modern phenomenon tied to the (colonial) formation of and (postcolonial) tensions within nation-states."[97] This was certainly the case in 1950s Syria, where political parties espousing revolutionary ideologies advocated extreme solutions to a host of problems attributed to the country's experience of imperialist state formation. The assassination of 'Adnan al-Malki and the savage response it provoked are just the most salient examples of this general resort to violent, absolutist, and antidemocratic measures.

The media discourse produced by this conflict was designed to cultivate hatred in "both senses of the term," that is, to both nurture and guide powerful emotions "within carefully staked out channels of approval."[98] In terms of regional politics, this tactic yielded remarkable short-term successes for the leftist army/parliament coalition mounting the media campaign against the Syrian Social Nationalist Party. The renunciation of Greater Syrian nationalism in favor of its pan-Arab variant, the abandonment of Iraq-centered Fertile Crescent Unity schemes in favor of consolidating a nascent alliance with Nasser's Egypt, and the adoption of the latter's neutralist stance vis-à-vis the Great Powers all evidenced a sea change in regional politics—the penultimate phase of the "struggle for Syria."

In the domestic sphere, the "echoes" produced by the gunshots fired at al-Mansura were equally momentous and decidedly less salutary, as Syrian politics increasingly "assumed a pathological character."[99] The SSNP's banishment from the sphere of "normal" politics in Syria only increased the country's instability, as the party became more desperate and reckless, adopting the features of a truly clandestine, paramilitary organization, and plotting with foreign intelligence agencies and other exiles to mount a number of unsuccessful coup attempts before fragmenting into rival entities.[100]

The campaign against the SSNP also gave the lie to one of the fundamental tenets of the post-Shishakli settlement that inaugurated the Democratic Years—the army's pledge to abstain from politics. As the officer corps' seemingly eternal fratricide erupted once again into the civilian sphere, all were forced to acknowledge that control of the armed forces remained "the deciding factor in Syrian politics."[101] Furthermore, 'Abd al-Hamid al-Sarraj's guiding role in the saga signaled the emerging hegemony of military intelligence and the normalization of that institution's brutal practices.[102] Finally, the relative ease with which the army and its civilian allies repeatedly compelled Syria's prime minister and president to dilute, share, or cede their offices' constitutional authority and prerogatives revealed the weakness and fragility of Syria's democratic institutions and presaged their ultimate demise.[103] The Ba'th and their allies would soon tire of their flirtation with bourgeois democracy, abrogating Syria's constitution to drag the country into a disastrous, experimental union with Egypt, the United Arab Republic. Ultimately, this fateful decision would return Syrian politics to the pre–Democratic Years pattern of coup and counter-coup, a series of contests increasingly more violent and vengeful.

Media coverage of the Malki Affair also reinforced other currents within Syrian (and Arab) political discourse: conspiracy theories and victimhood. The interrelated domestic, regional, and international political contexts in which al-Malki was murdered, as well as the attributes and affiliations ascribed to his presumed killers, sustained perceptions that Syria was the focus of a vast, sinister conspiracy, and that modern Syria's historical experience was best understood as a monochromatic morality play.

The rhetorical banishment of those holding opposing commitments from the sacred state of citizenship was also frequently accompanied by a more concrete one: in addition to all the other punitive measures it imposed, the extraordinary military tribunal also permanently stripped several of the defendants of their civil rights.[104] This practice, which became depressingly common under the post-1963 Ba'th regimes, transformed citizenship from an inalienable condition to a privilege enjoyed at the pleasure of the regime.

Finally, a primary victim of the Malki Affair was the rule of law. The previously quoted Ministry of Defense declaration that its extraordinary tribunal sought "perfect justice" included qualifying addenda: "in keeping with the patriotic traditions of Arab Syria, the policies of a democratic state . . . and the spirit of the army."[105] Clearly, the second of these qualifiers received short shrift, as the tribunal merely provided the legal expertise, framework, and facade for ideologically informed vengeance, subordinating one of the foundational principles of representative government to immediate political advantage.[106] In this way, the tribunal set a baleful precedent for future treason trials in Syria and perhaps for revolutionary "People's Courts" elsewhere in the region.[107]

5   Making the Martial Citizen

SCHOLARS OF NATIONALIST ideology have long noted that sacrifice, a nominally religious concept, is particularly "prone to migrate" into the political sphere, becoming an intrinsic element of collective identity.[1] The redemptive power of sacrifice at least partially explains why nationalist ideologues, acting as evangelists on behalf of their "civic religion," so often prefer the "dead to the living."[2] Given the perceived fragmentation and divisiveness of post–World War II Syrian society, the country's political elite was doubly receptive to martyr narratives that asserted and confirmed "group solidarity," thereby replacing ambiguity and uncertainty with "cohesion and substance."[3] Ideologically motivated sacrifice also makes the dead objects of commemoration, an act that enables others to rhetorically and symbolically partake of the martyrs' qualities, thereby instantiating their own identities as members of the political community. In the Syrian case, sacrifice was a core element of pan-Arabism, the revolutionary ideology most intimately linked with the country's modern history.[4]

It was in this context of a nationalist "cult of sacrifice" that 'Adnan al-Malki became a public figure in Syria and beyond.[5] The propaganda campaign surrounding al-Malki's life and death effaced the historical, flesh-and-blood mortal, replacing that fallible being with a sacralized, deathless archetype of manliness, selfless courage, joyful sacrifice, and the eternal guardianship of Arab sovereignty. Laden with religious imagery, this discursive transfiguration resembled nothing more than an inverse transubstantiation, the rendering of "flesh into Word." Much of this posthumous praise was mere cant, confirming the scholarly consensus that the historicity of martyrologies, whether sacred or secular, is largely irrelevant to their effectiveness.[6] In other words, 'Adnan al-Malki's story, like that of his predecessor Yasin al-Hashimi, constitutes "a classic example of defining a man's life by his death."[7] To complete the biblical metaphor, the verbiage resulting from this process "dwelt among" the Syrians for decades to come.[8]

The "revolutionary" rhetoric inspired by al-Malki's sacrifice also affirmed a particular conception of citizenship. First, it implied that the "features of the virtuous citizen" included a specific set of ideological orientations—non-alignment in the form of Nasser-style "positive" neutrality, ardent republicanism, and an accompanying conception of pan-Arab nationalism that was pro-Egyptian, anti-Hashemite, resolutely opposed to Zionism and Western imperialism, and committed to the struggle against "traitors" within Syrian society.[9]

Unsurprisingly, this conception of citizenship was also avowedly militaristic. Another intellectual trend of the postwar period facilitated the Syrian armed forces' construction of this martial citizen. Processes of state development, and the social science theories (e.g., modernization theory) developed to explain them, caused many Western scholars and policy analysts to perceive the military as the only "modern," "efficient," and "rational" institution in most developing states. Many Middle Eastern elites adopted this same view, placing their hopes in the professional military officer as the agent best equipped to "pull the country out of 'backwardness' and underdevelopment."[10] Two generations of Syrian officers shared this perspective, deeming the politically conscious soldier educated in the modern military arts and sciences to be the embodiment of the "model citizen,"[11] a view that underlay their repeated interventions into politics to "rescue" the nation from the bondage of its "incompetent and corrupt" hereditary class of civilian politicians.[12]

The successful narration of the martyr/model citizen's story to a wider audience through a suitable "communicative agent" is "perhaps even more crucial than the actual suffering and martyrdom itself."[13] As few people actually witnessed al-Malki's murder, a wider audience had to be created through the use of print and broadcast media. Al-Malki's champions in the army and their civilian allies used state media—initially, the magazines *al-Jundi* (The Soldier) and *al-Idha'a al-Suriyya* (Syrian Broadcasting)—to disseminate and refine al-Malki's martyrology, which became the core of a new, "emotionally powerful" national narrative of trauma, heroism, and defiance.[14] Eventually, this militarization of citizenship eliminated any pretense of the citizen's status as sovereign subject of politics, rendering that figure the object of authoritarian mobilization.

A HEART NOURISHED WITH HATRED FOR THE IMPERIALIST USURPER: AL-MALKI'S LINEAGE AND CHILDHOOD

'Adnan al-Malki was born into a very wealthy and prestigious old Damascene family in 1918. Originally North African *'ulama'* trained in the Maliki school of jurisprudence, 'Adnan's ancestors had established themselves as respected midlevel officials in the religious bureaucracy of Ottoman Damascus by the early eighteenth century.[15] Unable to penetrate the highest reaches of the empire's religious administration, they took advantage of transformative nineteenth-century political and administrative reforms to secure posts in the expanding secular bureaucracy, establish various commercial enterprises, and acquire large tracts of choice agricultural land.[16] By the late nineteenth century, the Malkis were well-established Sunni "urban notables," that is, "full-fledged members" of Ottoman Syria's political and economic elite.[17] Throughout the early twentieth century, the family expanded and diversified its influence in the domains of government service, the modern professions, and nationalist politics.[18]

Among the most prominent members of the clan was 'Adnan's father, Muhammad Shams al-Din al-Malki. One of Damascus's great landowners, the elder al-Malki was a longtime member of Syria's Chamber of Agriculture and one of the directors of the country's Agricultural Bank. He had been politically committed and active from his youth, joining several nationalist secret societies during the late Ottoman period and volunteering in 1920 to fight against the French alongside the doomed hero Yusuf al-'Azma at the Battle of Maysaloun.[19] Muhammad Shams al-Din's nationalist sentiments and knowledge of clandestine Arab nationalist organizations almost certainly informed the choice of his son's name—'Adnan was one of the two legendary progenitors of the Arab peoples.[20]

In keeping with this distinguished heritage, 'Adnan spent his childhood in the presence of many leaders of the Great Syrian Revolt against French occupation (1925–1927), and witnessed much of the wanton destruction wrought by the French Army's furious response. According to his martyr legend, these experiences "nourished this child's heart with hatred for the imperialist usurper" and, by extension, for all opponents of Syria's sovereignty, dignity, and unity with its Arab neighbors.[21]

AN EXEMPLAR OF MANLINESS, MORALITY, AND HONOR: AL-MALKI AS SOLDIER

MUHAMMAD SHAMS AL-DIN: "What do you want to be, 'Adnan?"

'ADNAN: "What is your wish, Father?"

MUHAMMAD SHAMS AL-DIN: (Pause)

'ADNAN: "I am a soldier!"

'Adnan al-Malki was just four years old when this exchange with his father is said to have occurred. In fact, as the official narrative would have it, 'Adnan was a child prodigy of ideologically inflected patriotism, spending his tender early years grappling with momentous questions such as "How did imperialism come to Syria . . . and to every part of our Arab homeland?"[22] According to this legend, al-Malki's role as a politically engaged military professional was all but inevitable.

Graduating from the Homs Military Academy in 1939, 'Adnan ascended rapidly through the ranks because of his talent, energy, charm, deft political maneuvering, and cultivation of senior-officer patrons, particularly Syria's two most significant post–World War II military dictators, General Husni al-Za'im and Colonel Adib al-Shishakli. Surviving and ultimately benefiting from the downfall of these officers, he became, at the age of thirty-five, a full colonel and the G-3, or chief of operations, of the Syrian Army, second in influence only to Chief of Staff Brigadier General Shawkat Shuqayr.[23]

Virtually all of the posthumous accounts of al-Malki's military career attribute his influence, in part, to his distinctive physical appearance and charismatic personality. This "exemplar of manliness, morality, and honor" is routinely described as tall, broad-shouldered, and athletic.[24] Interestingly, given the centrality of Arab "authenticity" to al-Malki's legend, many of the sources also frequently note the green eyes, pale skin tone, and light-brown hair that allegedly made him resemble a European or Russian.[25] Stories of al-Malki's bonhomie and resulting popularity "with his brother officers" abound. The published accounts consistently depict him as youthful, confident, energetic, and exuberant, perpetually flashing a broad smile and frequently erupting in fits of "explosive" laughter.[26] The photographs most frequently accompanying al-Malki's martyrology confirm these descriptions.

Yet, however well known the living 'Adnan might have been among army officers and politicians, he was virtually unknown to the Syrian public.[27] On the rare occasions when al-Malki's name or image appeared in the press during his lifetime, it was almost exclusively in Defense or Interior Ministry publications, which invariably depicted him as but one of several officers trailing in the wake of Chief of Staff Shawkat Shuqayr at academy graduation ceremonies, inspection tours of military facilities, public-relations events sponsored by the Ministry of Defense, or celebrations at the Damascus Officers' Club.[28] Most tellingly, despite his impeccable pedigree and personal charm, al-Malki did not rate an entry in Syria's standard biographical dictionary during his lifetime, although more than two dozen other military, security, and police officers did.[29]

Nevertheless, all the sources agree that al-Malki played a significant role in Syrian Army politics,[30] establishing his Arab nationalist credentials by volunteering to serve with the Arab League's ill-fated "Army of Salvation" in the 1948 Arab-Israeli War,[31] and increasing his influence by initially supporting the modernizing reform agendas of military dictators al-Za'im and al-Shishakli.[32] The post-Shishakli sources also document al-Malki's politicking in the civilian sphere: he was allegedly involved in several threatened coups.[33] In sum, many of al-Malki's colleagues appear to have considered him "a natural leader" of the officer corps. Yet the posthumous narrative scrupulously omitted the fact that many senior officers, including Shuqayr, privately questioned al-Malki's suitability for further promotion, deeming him "intemperate," "unstable," and indiscreet.[34]

A "SHINING STAR IN THE SYRIAN FIRMAMENT IS EXTINGUISHED": AL-MALKI AS MARTYR

> Long live the memory of the immortal martyr! And long may the Arab Nation live free and united! And [long live] the glory and immortality of its righteous martyrs![35]

This panegyric, composed by Riyad al-Malki, encapsulates several salient features of his brother 'Adnan's martyrology.[36] The reference to memory highlights how politically useful martyrs are for the business of constructing an official historical memory of a nation or state, which is precisely what Riyad was attempting to accomplish.[37] Designating the Arab nation, rather than Islam, as the repository of righteousness and the sacred ideal for whose freedom and unity 'Adnan sacrificed his life, emphasizes the secular current within his modern martyrology. The repeated claims of immortality reveal the extent to which religious concepts, symbols, and tropes were interwoven into this putatively secular story.[38] Finally, the shift from the singular to the plural—from 'Adnan "the immortal martyr" to the Arab nation's multiple equally "immortal" and "righteous" martyrs—associates the former with the latter, both past and future.

Al-Malki's murder, and its subsequent construction as martyrdom, did not occur in a vacuum. In order to produce meaning and achieve the "pedagogical aim" of moral and ideological guidance, martyr narratives, whether nominally secular or religious, must reach an audience.[39] And the propagation of any narrative requires access to media. Al-Malki's martyrology was initially disseminated through Ministry of Defense and other state-owned journals, subsequently spreading to private media like daily newspapers and

politico - religious
act of "martyring" someone

popular weekly magazines, and ultimately spawning a veritable subfield of book publishing.[40]

The narrative propagated via these media displayed several kinds of hybridity. Chief among these was the voluntary nature of sacrifice. The true martyr makes an informed choice: he foresees and embraces his death as a necessary act of sacrificial love on behalf of his imperiled community, however it is defined.[41] Most tellings of al-Malki's martyr narrative included assertions that he had, by a variety of means, acquired foreknowledge of the plot against him yet resolutely persisted in the beliefs and practices that motivated his murder. Such assertions confirmed both al-Malki's status as a prescient, and therefore "true," martyr, as well as the premeditation of his killers.[42]

Another rhetorical strategy central to al-Malki's martyr narrative was its placement within the larger martyrology of the modern Levant. This location was accomplished by purposefully associating al-Malki with his "righteous" predecessors, particularly the Arab nationalist activists hanged by Young Turk triumvir Jamal Pasha in 1916 and General Yusuf al-'Azma, who died charging the French lines at the Battle of Maysaloun in 1920.[43] Throughout the late 1950s and 1960s, this roster of martyrs expanded, and al-Malki's qualities served as touchstones for his successors.[44]

SOLEMN RITUALS OF NATION AND STATE: FUNERALS AND OTHER COMMEMORATIVE CEREMONIES

A variety of discursive, performative, and material forms of commemoration transfigured 'Adnan al-Malki into a national martyr by drawing on, adapting, and augmenting antecedents in Syrian history informed by a rich, syncretic tradition of mourning and elegy.[45] All of these reworked commemorative practices employed modern technologies and communicative media in the attempt to instruct and mobilize a mass audience. Thus, in both content and context, these commemorative forms were necessarily and inescapably political.

The public commemoration of the dead is always a political act. This is even truer of large state funerals and memorials, which are "ceremonies of power" whose shared objective is "to imprint the glorious past of the deceased, and of the regime that he had fought for, upon the national memory."[46] The ultimate goal is the mobilization and/or shaping of public opinion and emotion in a manner congenial to the regime, or at least to the faction within it acting as "funeral director."[47] As Lucia Volk has observed, public commemoration accomplishes this and other "political work" in multiple

FIGURE 5.1 'Adnan al-Malki's Funeral Procession, April 23, 1955.
Riyad al-Malki, *Sirat al-Shahid 'Adnan al-Malki,* 139.

ways: It creates "rhetorical spaces" in which "symbols, values, and identities" are negotiated. As "real physical spaces," monuments provide a setting for collective, ritualized commemoration. Finally, media coverage of these real and rhetorical spaces gives them a "second life as texts."[48]

In the short term, this rhetorical space is a site for the public performance of emotion—grief, sorrow, and anger. A rapidly assembled coalition of political parties with then marginal representation in Parliament (Ba'thists, Nasserists, and communists) joined forces with politically ambitious army officers to proclaim al-Malki's status as a national martyr on par with his predecessors. The old notables at the helm of the civilian government, "criticized by many for not taking the necessary measures" to protect al-Malki, soon realized that this "martyr coalition" represented a nascent new order that could mobilize public support and, perhaps, sweep them from power. Consequently, the notables' regime authorized the use of state funds and facilities for the solemn rituals commemorating al-Malki, and its senior figures participated, if sometimes grudgingly, in these rites.[49]

Al-Malki's hastily organized memorial service and funeral on April 23, 1955—one day after his murder—were, by all accounts, somber and impressive affairs. Lengthy ceremonial processions to and from the Umayyad Mosque drew large, respectfully silent crowds lining the streets (fig. 5.1).[50] The mass spectatorship of these events was critical, as it substantiated the martyrologists' claims of al-Malki's significance while also providing Damascenes with their first opportunity to participate in this reaffirmation of national community, defined by blood sacrifice and sorrow.[51]

On June 30, the Syrian state mounted the first of its publicly advertised "al-Malki Day" commemorations at the National Stadium, site of the colonel's assassination.[52] Under the watchful eyes of omnipresent security men, approximately ten thousand attendees (billed as "all of Arabism"),[53] including several hundred dignitaries representing foreign (Arab) embassies, the government of Syria, all its major political parties, religious sects, professional associations, and its "social strata," sat or stood through a three-hour program of prayers, elegies, and eulogies by nine featured speakers that "caused tears to flow."[54] The speakers included Army Chief of Staff Shawkat Shuqayr; the martyr's brother Riyad; the poet, former parliamentarian, and future diplomat 'Omar Abu Risha;[55] president of the Syrian Lawyer's Union Zafir al-Qasimi; Lebanese Sheikh 'Abdallah al-'Alayli; and Ignatius, the Greek Orthodox Metropolitan of "Hama and Its Dependencies" (i.e., the remainder of Syria).[56]

The participation of prominent Muslim and Christian clerics foreshadowed a significant theme of al-Malki's hagiography: his status as the martyr of "all the Arabs."[57] This message was also expressed in the syncretic content and style of the eulogies, which often featured the use of Islamic vocabulary and imagery to illustrate ostensibly secular concepts. Sheikh al-'Alayli, for example, lauded al-Malki's "eternal revolution against oppression" *fi sabil al-hurriya* (for the sake of freedom) rather than the traditional *fi sabil Allah* (for the sake of God).[58]

Attendance at these commemorative events increased in subsequent years, and the roster of speakers became progressively more international.[59] Yet the major themes remained consistent: 'Adnan's secure place in the pantheon of martyr-heroes, and the Arab, anti-colonialist, and nonsectarian mission for which he shed his sanctifying blood. The events of 'Adnan Day in 1957 succinctly illustrate the commemorative theater of nationalist martyrology. Prominent clerics led prayers; luminaries of Arabic arts and letters like

Iraq's Muhammad Mahdi al-Jawahiri and the "dean of Arab letters," Egypt's Taha Husayn, read eulogies; and officiating Syrian military personnel set the rhetorical tone: "In the name of God and in the name of Arabism, I open this great commemoration celebrating the eternal memory of our martyr ʿAdnan, who irrigated the soil of the Arabs with his blood."[60]

"THIS I PROMISE, OH MARTYR HERO":
THE MASS PRODUCTION OF ENCOMIA

Although poetic and other genres of martyr-encomia were familiar in 1950s Syria, the scope, scale, and variety of such literature produced in commemoration of ʿAdnan al-Malki were unprecedented.[61] Paeans to al-Malki's memory, in the form of poetry, essays,[62] and public addresses, bearing titles such as "This I Promise, Oh Martyr Hero," appeared in virtually every Damascus periodical of the era.[63] The most common elements of these efforts make familiar reading.[64] Yet the most prominent themes of this discourse were assertions of (1) the martyr's "immortality," (2) the transformative properties of his blood, and (3) his preternatural strength, all attributes that lie at the boundaries between the literal and the metaphorical, and the natural and supernatural.[65]

Many of Syria's most prominent cultural figures participated in this exercise, publishing poems, eulogistic letters, and essays in commemoration of al-Malki. These contributors included the novelist, translator, and Baʿthist political theorist Mutaʿ Safadi;[66] philosopher and founding member of the Arab Socialist Party and the Arab Writer's Union Antun Makdisi;[67] Professor of Arabic at the Syrian University and member of the Arab Academy ʿIzz al-Din ʿIlm al-Din al-Tanukhi;[68] poet, short story writer, and founding member of the Syrian Writers' Union Shawqi Baghdadi;[69] Dean of the Faculty of Arts at the Syrian University Amjad al-Tarabulsi;[70] prominent journalist, editor, and administrator of state media Yahya al-Shihabi;[71] and "unofficial spokesman" of the Baʿth Party Sulayman al-ʿIsa.[72]

Yahya al-Shihabi contributed an essay that, like the pronouncements of Najat Qassab Hasan, exemplified the glorification of strength and its cognate, the denigration of weakness in all possible forms. Al-Shihabi began by acknowledging that he was "not the first citizen" affected by the "painful news" of al-Malki's murder. He reviewed his decades-long friendship with al-Malki, citing examples of ʿAdnan's alleged fixation on the concept of strength, beginning with "naïve" utterances on the primary-school playground and eventually evolving into a philosophy of life: "What was there in the departed's life except for strength? On what besides strength did he focus his efforts? Strength in labor and in thought, in conviction, and in execution. Strength in everything there is." Yet, according to al-Shihabi, this strength was not manifested in "brute or deadly force" but, rather, constituted a "secret strength" quietly and modestly exercised in service to homeland and nation.[73]

The discourse repeatedly emphasized the concepts of selfless service and sacrifice. The martyr's exemplary attributes were most frequently explicated through the celebration of one element of his narrative, lifelong dedication to the Arab cause. For al-Malki's generation, the litmus test of this commitment, support for Palestinian resistance to the Zionist project, was voluntary service with the Arab League's Army of Salvation (*jaysh al-inqaadh al-'arabi*) in the 1948 Arab-Israeli War. Sulayman al-'Isa's lengthy poem cited this service as evidence of al-Malki's rightful place in the peerage of martyrs whose bloodshed in service to the nation was endowed with mystical properties.[74]

Yet the contributions of the intelligentsia constituted a relatively small part of this massive body of literature. Instead, professional soldiers' tributes appearing in "letters to the editor" and "readers' comments" columns dedicated exclusively to al-Malki's life and death comprised the overwhelming majority.[75] Many authors recounted service with al-Malki in the Army of Salvation and presented eyewitness testimony of his martyrly qualities. A classic example came from Retired Major Salim al-Safadi. Entitled "From the Pages of Immortality: The Tree That Was Watered with al-Malki's Blood," it recounts al-Malki's skill, courage, and coolness under fire during a military operation that began on the night of July 8–9, 1948.[76]

The tree in the title was a rendezvous point from which al-Malki, although wounded, led his men to safety. Yet in al-Safadi's coda, it becomes a "young [little] tree," a metaphor for the Arab nation that has been nourished by al-Malki's "pure, innocent blood." The sapling mourns 'Adnan in "its trunk and its roots," offers silent prayers on his behalf, stays in place to shelter his "brother soldiers," and preserves the memory of their "faithfulness, courage, boldness, and sacrifice in the fulfillment of duty."[77]

To illustrate the relationship between al-Malki's martyrdom and the Arab nation, al-Safadi also conflated the colonel's murderers with the force that had failed to kill him in Palestine: "oppressive Zionism."[78] A similarly inspired contribution was provided by Iraqi Flight Officer Khalil Hamdi al-Dabbagh, who declared that his love for al-Malki as a comrade in battle had prompted him to purchase a photograph of the martyr in order to "preserve his memory for the rest of my life." Al-Dabbagh expressed a longing for permanence in his closing lines: "'Adnan did not die, and his name will not be forgotten. Rather, it will remain eternal and immortal."[79]

But by far the most prolific and fulsome composer of al-Malki encomia was Sergeant Major Muhammad al-Yamani, who composed a series of stories about his service under al-Malki's command in Palestine. Al-Yamani's "With the Hero Martyr" column appeared as a semi-regular feature from June to October 1955, and featured vivid, emotional accounts of the Army of Salvation's "freedom fighters" struggling to survive while grossly outnumbered by the "Zionist criminals" surrounding them.[80] The most prevalent theme of these essays is al-Malki's remarkable leadership. Then a mere captain, he cheerfully and effortlessly assumed the responsibilities of much higher rank and won the devotion and admiration of all who encountered him, according to al-Yamani. Al-Malki's friendliness, graciousness, and inspirational speeches in camp and on the march, and his resolution, toughness, coolness, and bravery under fire raised the soldiers' spirits and pushed them to accomplish things they had previously thought impossible. In concluding these accounts, Sergeant al-Yamani declared that 'Adnan was like the "the rain for which barren land yearns" and "the light that radiates into the remotest parts of our lives."[81]

"I REGRET THAT I HAVE BUT ONE LIFE TO GIVE FOR MY COUNTRY": THE MARTYR SPEAKS FROM BEYOND THE GRAVE

> What better means of evoking feeling for the brotherhood of the living and the dead than by hearing them speak again?
>
> —JAY WINTER, *Sites of Memory, Sites of Mourning*

In addition to such hyperbole, Sergeant al-Yamani also employed more subtle rhetorical devices, like prosopopoeia, a "figure of speech in which an imaginary, absent, or deceased person is represented as speaking or acting."[82] Well-established in theatrical and political rhetoric since classical times, prosopopoeia figures prominently in both the sacred and secular varieties of al-Malki martyrologies.[83] Prosopopoeia permits the author to define the cause and principles for which the martyr sacrificed his life, and to attribute specific meanings to that sacrifice, even if this requires a measure of "political ventriloquism."[84] As the written word enjoys greater longevity than mere mortals, prosopopoeia also holds out hope that the martyr's "words and principles," whatever their historicity, will prove eternal.[85] In sum, in the political

techniques for rationalist creating discourse

sphere, prosopopoeia enables the representation of the past for the purpose of contemporary advantage.

As 'Adnan al-Malki left no published writings at the time of his death, his martyrologists were compelled to rely on three sources for prosopopoeial quotes. First were the reports of witnesses to al-Malki's utterances. As in the case of Sergeant al-Yamani above, the author was often the witness as well.[86] The second tactic was to present another historical figure's quote without attribution and in a manner suggesting it was al-Malki's. One of the more ironic examples was the translation of American Revolutionary War spy Nathan Hale's declaration (itself a classic piece of prosopopoeia), "I regret that I have but one life to give for my country," placed at the end of a story about al-Malki.[87]

The third source was al-Malki's extant private correspondence. This category was predominant, with most of the "martyr quotes" published in the press being selective excerpts from letters 'Adnan sent to his family while he was incarcerated (December 1952 – February 1954) in Mezze Military Prison for conspiring against Adib al-Shishakli.[88] Given the highly politicized environment in which they were written, it is not surprising that these missives often expressed anger, bitterness, and a degree of hopelessness. Yet the painful context in which they were composed also offered rich veins of material for martyrologists to mine. Al-Malki's letters often struck a grandiose tone: "We in prison are exemplary in our patriotic joy, our morals, the nobility of our principles, and our courage, and one day history will undoubtedly record this."[89] For al-Malki's martyrologists, this statement was nothing short of prophecy, for were they not doing precisely what he had foretold—documenting for posterity his courage and the nobility of his principles?

By definition, such courage entailed the absolute repudiation of weakness in any form. Thus al-Malki's missives are laden with references to the strength that can only be acquired through the endurance of prolonged suffering, specifically the kinds of trials and torments that are an integral part of sacrifice and martyrdom narratives in the pagan, Jewish, Christian, and Muslim traditions.[90] As a result of enduring these unspecified "tests" and "misfortunes" in prison, al-Malki and his colleagues strengthened their "patriotism," their "spirit," and their "nerve," thereby demonstrating the nobility of their principles. In this narrative, political prison is the crucible of patience, virtue, and strength, producing "nerves like iron and steel," the very characteristics required to achieve ultimate "freedom and victory" over oppression.[91]

Consequently, another leitmotif of this narrative was victimhood, both individual and collective. Al-Malki's letters are replete with references to unnamed "criminal oppressors," "enemies," and "traitors."[92] This calculated imprecision was almost certainly a function of self-censorship, as naming traitors and enemies—Adib al-Shishakli and his close confederates—in letters screened by the dictator's Military Intelligence censors could have had grave consequences. Yet al-Malki's circumspection was a boon to his martyrologists, who presented these quotes in the context of an ongoing inquisition against al-Malki's more recently identified enemies: the SSNP and other opponents of the "new order," that is, the tenuous coalition of Ba'thists, Nasserists, and communists in the Syrian parliament and army.

Ironically, several of the army officers executing this discursive legerdemain were, like al-Malki, former protégés of al-Shishakli, some of whom did not break with the dictator until it was clear that the February 1954 coup against him would succeed. They owed their reinstatement at previous rank and pay to the good offices of the martyr, former Deputy Chief of Staff for Operations and Personnel 'Adnan al-Malki, who, to his credit, did not seem to share their propensity for nursing grudges or their agile opportunism.

"ARABISM IS TAUGHT THROUGH THE REMEMBRANCE OF AL-MALKI": NATIONAL SPACE, TIME, AND ARTIFACTS

In addition to this torrent of praise for al-Malki, more "concrete" efforts were made to "render the hero's memory immortal"; give permanent, public expression to "the civic religion of nationalism"; and fulfill the pan-Arabist pedagogical mission summarized by the above quotation.[93] Such forms of commemoration included the mundane (e.g., the posthumous award of military decorations) and the inane, as in the naming of an antiquated battle tank after al-Malki.[94] Yet other physical manifestations of remembrance were imbued with dreadful solemnity, notably the reverent display of the blood-soaked uniform in which al-Malki died in a shrine at the Homs Military Academy.[95] Such practices were in keeping with Islamic (and Christian) traditions, which "spiritualized" the body as well as artifacts like the blood and clothing of martyrs.[96] Eliciting sympathy and guilt by "waving the bloody shirt" also had its more secular and republican antecedents dating back to Rome.[97]

Physically substantial public artifacts also commemorated al-Malki. Exactly two months after his murder, the Damascus municipal authority announced the naming of a major north-south thoroughfare bisecting the city's newest and most stylish residential neighborhood in al-Malki's honor.[98] Two years later, the traffic circle at the northern terminus of this boulevard was

FIGURE 5.2 'Adnan al-Malki's Memorial. *Al-Jundi,* May 1, 1958, front cover.

designated 'Adnan al-Malki Square and redesigned to accommodate the martyr's final resting place, a massive memorial complete with plaza, peristyle, eternal flame, and honor guard (fig. 5.2).[99]

A pictorial in *al-Jundi* describing the ceremonies surrounding al-Malki's reinterment and the dedication of his memorial deemed it appropriate that these events had occurred immediately after the Muslim holiday 'Id al-Adha, the festival commemorating the patriarch Abraham's willingness to sacrifice his son to God.[100] The article's placement also associated al-Malki's sacrifice with the Arab struggle against Western imperialism; it followed an editorial entitled "July 14" that laid bare French hypocrisy by juxtaposing a massacre of Algerians occurring on this date in 1957 with Parisians' celebration of Bastille Day. Finally, the same issue further linked resistance to imperialism with national space, time, and artifacts by reminding readers that July 20 was Maysaloun Day, the holiday commemorating the martyrdom of Yusuf al-'Azma, whose name and statue had graced another Damascus traffic circle and public square for many years.[101]

Al-'Azma's holiday was the penultimate event in a militaristic commemorative calendar that the Syrian state had observed each spring and summer since independence. The major dates in this calendar were Independence Day (April 17), Martyrs' Day (May 6), Maysaloun Day (July 20), and Army Day (August 1).[102] The commemoration of al-Malki's sacrifice was gradually incorporated into all of these celebrations, the most publicly visible means by which the Syrian state "instrumentalized the martyr and the practice of remembering him."[103]

Immediately after al-Malki's death, the state also began inserting holidays devoted exclusively to his remembrance into the commemorative calendar. First known as al-Malki Day (April 30, 1955), then 'Adnan Day (April 22, 1956–1957), and sometimes the Day of *the* Martyr (emphasis mine), these commemorations included the open-air memorial services discussed above; silent vigils and processionals through the streets of Damascus; rallies for students, workers, and professional organizations; and lengthy, in-depth coverage of these events in state and private media.[104]

Ultimately, these remembrance events became so pervasive that, by 1958, the Syrian Army began calling the commemorative calendar the Festivals of 'Adnan.[105] The number and regularity of these "festivals," along with the deceased's physical and metaphorical presence in the urban geography of Syria's capital city, expressed the concurrence of nationalist and religious imaginings in the realm of death and immortality.[106] The rhetorical objective of these commemorative forms, the apotheosis of the martyr hero, echoes rituals of the French Revolution that have been characterized as elements of "a new secular religion."[107] The secular worship of nation and state through the exaltation and transfiguration of the hero, servant, victim, and ideal citizen would also provide templates for more enduring and consequential projects of mobilization and domination.

THE ENDURING LEGACY OF 'ADNAN AL-MALKI'S TRANSFIGURATION

> The right way to look at the political uses of the past is not to wonder whether historical references are "true" or "false.". . . The question is rather: are they *useful* or not? And to whom?
>
> —VALÉRIE ROSOUX, "The Politics of Martyrdom"

FIGURE 5.3 Dedication of 'Adnan al-Malki's Statue.
Riyad al-Malki, *Sirat al-Shahid 'Adnan al-Malki,* 163.

'Adnan al-Malki's life constituted a "sacrificial offering" on the altar of that curiously compelling modern abstraction, the nation, imbuing his sacrifice with what Benedict Anderson has called "moral grandeur."[108] Conversely, a comparable offering on behalf of Syria's Chamber of Agriculture, Army Officers' Club, or military police soccer team would have lacked the same aura of sanctity. Unlike the nation-state, such mundane institutions do not produce citizens or the consecrated, defining condition of citizenship. Nor do they inspire martyrdom.[109] Commemorations of 'Adnan al-Malki's service and sacrifice were conceived as "vital acts" of citizenship, rituals that would "sustain particular myths of belonging" to the Syrian state and to the more expansive, if as yet disembodied, Arab nation.[110]

As martyrs are "particularly useful" during periods of crisis and instability, perhaps the enduring fragility and vulnerability of the Syrian polity, combined with its failure to realize its stated objective—the sovereign political unity of the Arabs—best explains the persistence of 'Adnan al-Malki's commemoration in the decade after his death.[111] Today, the most visible products of this process are the addition of a large bronze statue to the square already bearing al-Malki's name (fig. 5.3) and the renaming of the adjacent upscale neighborhood that is home to senior government officials and foreign diplomats in his memory.[112] In addition, the sense of political instability referenced above almost certainly motivated regime efforts to present an image of continuity with the past and evoke nationalist "traditions," even those of quite recent vintage.

The most common genre in the Malki-memory corpus has been the memoir asserting the author's professional, ideological, or emotional proximity to al-Malki and/or physical proximity to the assassination, and its status as one of the most significant events in the region's history. A classic example of this "I knew him" or "I was there" genre is Hani al-Sham'a's *Awraq Sahafi* (A Journalist's Papers). Al-Sham'a devoted a sizeable portion of his book, which covers the period 1955–1975, to a detailed description of the assassination and its immediate aftermath, which he said he witnessed due to al-Malki's personal invitation to attend the fated soccer match.[113] In lamenting the nation's grievous loss, such accounts celebrate al-Malki's leadership qualities and soldierly expertise, and thus confirm his representation as the ideal "martial" citizen. In the process, the authors assert and enact their own expertise as chroniclers, interpreters, and participant-observers of Syria's turbulent modern history, thereby enacting their own status as citizens.

Yet the narrative that these experts preserved and perpetuated has affected more than journalists' careers and self-images. 'Adnan al-Malki's martyrologists effectively redefined the concept of martyr in the popular imagination. Once a massive, prolonged state-sponsored propaganda campaign demonstrated that al-Malki, a relatively obscure professional soldier of few documented ideological pronouncements, could be ensconced in official memory as "*the* martyr of Arabism," other possibilities arose.[114]

This new, more expansive and malleable concept of martyrdom could, it appears, accommodate any regime-friendly figure of martial bearing, sportive reputation, and dynamic personality, no matter how he actually met his end. When Hafiz al-Asad's eldest son, Basil, died as a result of reckless driving on Damascus's Airport Highway in 1994, he was almost immediately declared "the martyr of the nation." In rapid succession, an opulent mausoleum was constructed over his final resting place, adulatory epithets were permanently affixed to his name, equestrian statues were erected in Syria *and* Lebanon, and dozens of streets, public squares, schools, hospitals, riding clubs, sports complexes, and humble gymnasiums soon bore "the Golden Knight's" name and/or visage. Given Basil's centrality to the future plans of his father's regime, lavish and prolonged ceremonies of official mourning were inevitable on his demise.

Yet the specific form and content of these commemorations, as well as the scale of hyperbole surrounding them, would have been unthinkable without the Malki template so conveniently at hand and so vivid in the memory of Hafiz al-Asad's generation. In this sense, al-Malki's "cult of the dead" almost certainly provided pointers for the mass mobilization of emotion (or its simulation), which was at the core of the live Hafiz al-Asad's personality cult in the 1980s, an enterprise that ultimately rendered the concept of citizenship as voluntary political participation a grotesque absurdity.[115]

Finally, the state-sponsored martyrology of 'Adnan al-Malki bore several related, and more ominous, long-term consequences for Syria's political culture. Many have observed that the process of transfiguring martyrs from dead individuals to living myths legitimizes "whoever may claim them."[116] As al-Malki was first and foremost "the army's martyr," his martyrology's representation of the "model citizen" was necessarily a professional soldier. The narratives of al-Malki's life and death sanctified army officers' ambitions to act as an autonomous political force in opposition to Syria's traditional political class, thereby valorizing and providing powerful institutional support for long-present authoritarian and antidemocratic impulses in Syrian politics.[117] Over the next decade, this "militarization of citizenship" would gradually displace the civilian from any meaningful role in Syrian politics.

6 The Magic of Modern Pharmaceuticals

THERE WAS NO more prominent exponent of scientific progress in the Arab East than Sabri al-Qabbani (1908–1973), whose public advocacy of development and citizen-building through the application of modern science and medicine spanned the most turbulent and transformative period in independent Syria's history, from the era of military dictators, the brief experiment with democracy, the abortive union with Egypt, and Syria's eventual domination by the Ba'th Party and Hafiz al-Asad.

Al-Qabbani explicitly stated his journalistic mission in the first issue of his magazine *Tabibak* (Your Doctor):

> Our guiding principle when we decided to publish this journal, *Your Doctor*, was simply to disseminate scientific culture, and in particular, medical culture, to the largest number of Arab readers possible. We do this because scientific advance never ceases, not even for a moment. Every day, previously mysterious aspects of nature and of human life are revealed, yielding knowledge and understanding that prompt yet new discoveries. And the pioneers of science and civilization are all connected in a historical procession, one in which there is no break between those at the head and those following behind. These pioneers are constantly achieving the most astounding triumphs of human endeavor, opening ever wider a window onto the secrets and mysteries of nature.
>
> Yet this glorious aperture remains closed to most Arab readers. Submerged by the crush of the base culture that fills our libraries and corrupts the current generation, they are hardly aware of its existence. That is why we felt the urge to publish this magazine, selecting for it all those topics that produce enjoyment, knowledge, and utility, printed on the maximum number of pages and at minimal cost.[1]

In this manifesto, al-Qabbani denigrated the Arab present, as opposed to a glorious, idealized past and a future of limitless promise. This conception

FIGURE 6.1 Cover of *Tabibak*, November 1956. (*facing*)

● العدد الثالث ●

تشرين الثاني ١٩٥٦

طبيبك

مجلة صحية علمية اجتماعية

of time is a paradigmatic feature of nationalist discourse, and one that was especially salient in the predominant forms of pan-Arabist ideology circulating in al-Qabbani's world.[2] In this vein, the glorious past of the Arabs and Muslims featured prominently in the early issues of *Your Doctor,* in the form of a recurring essay entitled "The History of Medicine" and its accompanying images.[3]

The most interesting of such attempts appeared on the cover of issue 3 (November 1956; fig. 6.1). The illustration portrays a medical school class in session during the Golden Age of Islamic Civilization (c. 750–1258 CE). Al-Qabbani's accompanying comments repeated the tale of "Arab scholars" conveying, along with "the banner of Islam," medical and other scientific knowledge, philosophical wisdom, and development to the Caucasus, to North Africa, and to the very heart of a Europe mired in the Dark Ages. Al-Qabbani concluded his reiteration of this Arab nationalist trope by declaring that the Arabs earned praise and glory "not only for saving and preserving medicine" but also for "inventing chemistry and establishing the fundamental principles of hygiene."[4]

Al-Qabbani clearly believed that modern science, as the ultimate instrument of developmental progress, could recover the glories of the past and realize a future of wondrous potential.[5] In this respect, his scientific *pronunciamento* encapsulates modern medicine's quintessential quality, its tendency to instantiate "the western tradition's idea of progress."[6] It also indicates the way in which scientific expertise asserted its exclusive possession of "special truth," serving as a surrogate for all forms of expertise.[7] One of the predominant themes in the Arabic-language media of the post–World War II period was the seemingly limitless potential of modern medical science to prevent, diagnose, and cure disease; improve nutrition and prenatal health; extend longevity; combat ignorance and superstition; and eradicate poverty—in short, to transform human societies.

This was the context in which Sabri al-Qabbani pursued his developmental dreams, asserting a new, thoroughly modern type of authority grounded in science, specialized education, and the revolutionary promise of technological advance. For al-Qabbani, the most significant of these new technologies was the mass production of pharmaceuticals. An affinity for powerful new chemical compounds and faith in their capacity to treat previously intractable or poorly understood conditions were characteristic of clinicians in the 1950s, the acme of the era of "wonder drugs."[8] This practice is evidence of al-Qabbani's avid reading of Western medical literature and his keen interest in the latest experimental drug therapies, those "most astounding triumphs of human endeavor" that he strove to share with his audience.[9]

In order for medical science to realize its transformative potential, it needed to reach a mass audience. It is for this reason that al-Qabbani pledged to provide in *Your Doctor* "the maximum number of pages" at "minimal cost," thereby disseminating knowledge to the largest possible number of citizens. His realization of that goal through the sale of extensive advertising space to multinational pharmaceutical companies is central to the story.

These "astounding triumphs of human endeavor" were critical to al-Qabbani's mission in a number of ways. Advertising from multinational pharmaceutical companies facilitated the publication of al-Qabbani's journal and thus the mass circulation of the latest scientific and medical knowledge in which he had such ardent faith. These advertisements were themselves visual and discursive expressions of this faith, touting the capacity of new chemical compounds to prolong, improve, and transform human lives.

THE PHYSICIAN, SABRI AL-QABBANI

Employing all available forms of print and electronic media, al-Qabbani spread the twin gospels of science and progress throughout the region. Like the attorney Najat Qassab Hasan, al-Qabbani operated within established traditions of authoritative discourse, promulgating his message of redemption through science while using the very same rhetorical styles, structures, and tactics that exegetes of the Islamic sciences had used for centuries. In the process, he highlighted the Arab subject's responsibility to consume the "true" knowledge of science, including the role that scientific advance played in his noble history, and the progress possible when scientific principles are applied in the present. Al-Qabbani's rhetoric also suggested that the citizen's duty of looking after his health and hygiene entailed consuming modern medications and other pharmaceutical products, which thereby contributed to the enactment of his identity.

Sabri al-Qabbani (fig. 6.2) was born into a relatively poor branch of the huge clan that produced, among other luminaries, the poet Nizar Qabbani.[10] After receiving his M.D. from the Syrian University's Faculty of Medicine (Kulliyat al-Tibb) in 1931, he served as a physician in the Iraqi Army for nine years. Returning to Damascus, al-Qabbani opened a private practice and clinic that offered free medical care to the indigent, and also began to explore the fields of journalism and politics. After experiencing press censorship and the corruption and incompetence of government officials, al-Qabbani ran as

FIGURE 6.2 Dr. Sabri al-Qabbani. 'Abd al-Ghani al-'Itri, *Hadith al-'Abqariyyat,* back cover.

an independent candidate in Syria's first post-independence parliamentary elections (July 1947). Upon his defeat, he announced that he was "finished" with politics and with Syria's political parties.

Al-Qabbani then focused exclusively on his medical practice until accepting appointment to the Faculty of Sciences at the Syrian University in 1948. Despite his earlier declarations, he continued to dabble in politics and contributed to journals that satirized Syria's notable class. In 1949, al-Qabbani also served Syria's first military dictator, General Husni al-Za'im, as personal adviser and interlocutor. After breaking with al-Za'im, al-Qabbani's interests turned to medical journalism, writing general advice columns and articles on more specific medical issues for various mass-circulation periodicals.

The first such outlet was Nash'at al-Tighilbi's weekly magazine *al-Jami'a* (The Community),[11] to which al-Qabbani contributed a regular column, "Tabib al-Jami'a" (The Community's Doctor), which usually focused on a single ailment common among the journal's readers.[12] Subsequently, al-Qabbani began to publish two features in each issue of a similar publication, 'Abd al-Ghani al-'Itri's *al-Dunya* (The World).[13] The first of these, "Hadhihi Nasihati"

(This Is My Advice), was very similar to the earlier "Community's Doctor." The second, "'Iyadat al-Qurra'" (The Readers' Clinic), represented a dramatic innovation and set the pattern for al-Qabbani's future success.[14] "The Readers' Clinic" consisted of questions from *al-Dunya*'s readers throughout the Arab world, and the doctor's frank, sometimes explicit, discussion of extremely delicate subjects. The column's success confirmed al-Qabbani's belief that people throughout the region were desperate for solutions to a host of individual, family, and social problems, and that they sought these answers from specialists possessing expertise in the modern sciences. During this period, al-Qabbani also appeared on a weekly radio program, "Tabibak khalf al-Midhya'" (Your Doctor behind the Microphone). Summaries of the program's episodes occasionally appeared as thematic articles in the monthly government journal *al-Idha'a al-Suriyya* (Syrian Broadcasting).

TABIBAK

By late 1955, al-Qabbani's success in medical journalism and broadcasting permitted him to retire from the Faculty of Medicine, return to private practice, and begin planning the publication of his own "popular medical and scientific" journal, *Tabibak*.[15] Launched in September 1956, *Tabibak* was so successful that al-Qabbani soon closed his practice and focused exclusively on medical publishing, producing his magazine, writing numerous books, and contributing the occasional article to daily Damascene newspapers until his retirement in 1970.[16]

In content and style, *Your Doctor* was a cross between the *Journal of the American Medical Association* and *Popular Science*. It soon reached an audience far beyond Syria's cities, a fact confirmed by the addresses of those writing to al-Qabbani for advice, which included Lebanon, Iraq, Saudi Arabia, Jordan, Egypt, Palestine, and the Sudan. *Your Doctor* contained translations of articles from Western medical and scientific journals in the regular features "Mawakib al-'Ilm wa al-Hadara" (The Triumphs of Science and Civilization) and "Tarikh al-Tibb" (The History of Medicine), a feature for the modern Arab woman entitled "Jamaluki Sayyidati" (Your Beauty, My Lady), and several semi-regular features dealing with newly available surgical and diagnostic practices, nutrition, exercise, and that host of issues Western readers would now associate with the concept of "wellness."[17]

For historians, however, the real jewel in *Your Doctor* is the monthly column "Tabibak fi Khidmatak" (Your Doctor Is at Your Service), in which al-Qabbani answered questions from his readers (fig. 6.3). This column reveals

FIGURE 6.3 "Your Doctor Is at Your Service." *Tabibak,* October 1956, 88.

much about general perceptions and knowledge (or lack thereof) of human anatomy, disease etiology, sexuality, reproduction, personal hygiene, obstetrics, and child-rearing in midcentury Arab society. The doctor consistently attempted to educate his audience, validating and naturalizing his answers by grounding them in the norms of modern science, which he contrasted to the ignorant beliefs and practices of the past, or those that were still prevalent in rural areas and among the uneducated. The criteria informing al-Qabbani's definitions of backwardness, superstition, and other normative concepts shed light on the interdependence of developmental discourse, mass media, and the development of the subjectivity underlying citizenship. In al-Qabbani's lexicon, "progressive," "advanced," and "civilized" are almost always synonyms for "urban" and "literate," and are also laden with gender implications.

Al-Qabbani's correspondence with the "youth of the Arab East" in the columns "The Readers' Clinic" and "Your Doctor Is at Your Service" constituted a classic example of expert appropriation of another figure's authority, the parent.[18] By publicly dispensing information and advice that would normally be provided—if at all—in the home, he enabled unmarried young men and women to bypass their parents, religious authorities, *and* their family doctors, and thus, in some measure, take responsibility for their own bodies, sexuality, and general health, both physical and psychological.

MODERN PHARMACEUTICALS AND GLOBAL CAPITALISM

> This was the message to the people when Sabri al-Qabbani used to talk about how one could get beyond magic and superstition and work with effective drugs and scientific medicine.
>
> —HANAN QASSAB HASAN, February 27, 2002

One of Sabri al-Qabbani's signature practices, dating from the beginning of his journalistic career, was the long-distance formulation and presentation of diagnoses, often followed by the dispensation of prescriptions by mail.[19] This was, in fact, a principal function of his two most popular columns. For example, "Mr. Nasir Bushi from Hama" wrote complaining of symptoms that suggested tonsillitis. Al-Qabbani appeared to accept Mr. Bushi's self-diagnosis, for without further comment he immediately summarized the contemporary debate within the medical community about the efficacy and wisdom of tonsillectomy, and then stated that he recommended "in any event" injections of penicillin *and* streptomycin "provided that they are administered for ten consecutive days."[20]

Here we encounter another characteristic feature of al-Qabbani's correspondence with his readers, endorsing courses of treatment including powerful and potentially dangerous drugs. In addition to strong antibiotics, al-Qabbani also recommended various hormones, appetite suppressants, intestinal parasiticides, anabolic steroids, anticonvulsants, barbiturates, amphetamines, and analgesics containing opiates, to name but a few.[21] In both his columns and his exchanges with readers, al-Qabbani frequently recommended specific medications identified by brand name. This tendency found perfect expression in an article entitled "How to Set Up Your Home Pharmacy." Therein al-Qabbani advised homemakers to stock their medicine cabinets with sixteen brand-name products, including analgesics, laxatives, antacids, sedatives, antidiarrheals, orally and topically administered antibiotics, antihistamines, and cough suppressants.[22] This practice became more prevalent with the appearance of "Your Doctor Is at Your Service." For example, in one of the earliest issues of *Your Doctor,* "H. H. from Jabla" wrote complaining of "the smallness of her breasts." After describing a home remedy involving the frequent application of hot compresses, al-Qabbani recommended a compound "manufactured by Séréno," available in the form of "pills or injections that contain the hormones of the mammary glands and the ovaries" that can "facilitate the enlargement of the bosom."[23]

The most frequent beneficiaries of such "name-checking" were Europe's postwar pharmaceutical giants: Schering, Wander, Bayer, Hoffman–La Roche, Pfizer, Glaxo, Parke-Davis, and Roussel.[24] Al-Qabbani's frequent punctuation of his diagnoses with exhortations to use the products of specific manufacturers raises the larger issue of his relationship to global economic forces. The significance of this concern is accentuated by many of the same manufacturers' repeated purchase of advertising space in *Your Doctor.*

On average, 15 percent of the pages in each issue featured at least one advertisement for a multinational drug manufacturer or distributor, its prescription or nonprescription medications, or various internationally marketed "health" products like Ovomaltine (marketed as Ovaltine in the United States), Eno Fruit Salts, Evian mineral water, and Johnson and Johnson's Baby Powder.[25] Furthermore, many of these advertisements appeared as inserts printed on thick, glossy paper featuring multicolor processes. Such expensive reproductions rarely appeared in Syrian periodicals during this period.[26] Conversely, *Your Doctor* rarely featured the smaller, more crudely executed, and less visually arresting advertisements for locally manufactured or licensed products routinely found in less specialized periodicals.[27]

Tabibak's near monopoly on advertising for foreign pharmaceutical and health products in 1950s Syria can be attributed, at least in part, to the journal's uniqueness. Its "wonders of modern science" ethos, combined with al-Qabbani's endorsement of specific name-brand products from a position of clinical detachment, made it the ideal marketing vehicle from the perspective of pharmaceutical manufacturers. All the available evidence suggests that the economic survival of al-Qabbani's journal was dependent on its relationship with these pharmaceutical manufacturers.[28] Expertise does not exist in a vacuum. It requires a platform from which to mount pedagogical projects. Like Najat Qassab Hasan and the mourners of 'Adnan al-Malki, Sabri al-Qabbani required access to mass media. In this case, global capitalism, rather than the state, facilitated this access. Capitalism also provided al-Qabbani's readers with injunctions to consume on a global scale.

Al-Qabbani's relationships with pharmaceutical manufacturers also informed the advice he dispensed to patients, a fact most obvious in the common elements between the various forms of this discourse (feature articles and advice columns) and the advertising that shared the pages of *Your Doctor*. Among the medications most frequently advertised in *Your Doctor* were the cold remedy Apragon and the choleretic Felicur, manufactured by Schering;[29] the Pfizer decongestant Tyzine;[30] and the antidiarrheal Chlorostrep, manufactured by Parke-Davis.[31] Al-Qabbani regularly recommended these products in "Your Doctor Is at Your Service." In fact, many of the advertisements referenced above appeared most commonly in the final pages of al-Qabbani's journal, adjacent to or within his advice column. This proximity of prescriptions and advertisements constituted a not-so-subtle reinforcement of the "message" summarized by Professor Hanan Qassab Hasan in the quotation above: if you want to be modern, rational, and free of "magic and superstition," then embrace "science" by taking the recommended medications.

Furthermore, this message was reinforced via several additional means, which can be explicated through an examination of the full-page advertisement for Armonil, a concoction of protein, vitamins, and muscle relaxants formulated for and marketed to bodybuilders (fig. 6.4). Beneath a photograph of bodybuilders displaying their prizewinning assets to admiring spectators, the copy reads, "A powerful therapy and restorer of the body that combats weakness of the blood and fills the body with vitamin B12."[32] Each appearance of this advertisement in *Your Doctor* was in the middle of the advice column "Your Doctor Is at Your Service."[33]

The use of images from these advertisements to illustrate articles on related topics penned by al-Qabbani or "renowned" specialists in Syria, Europe, and the United States enhanced the effect of strategic product placement in *Your Doctor*. The relevant example here is al-Qabbani's lengthy article "al-'Adalat: Kayfa Ta'mal wa Kayfa Nusta'miluha" (Muscles: How They Function and How We Use Them). This piece listed and described the primary chemical agents driving the metabolic processes underlying muscle growth, accompanied by the same photograph of bodybuilders appearing in the Armonil advertisement.[34] This tactic, the visual and discursive reinforcement of the relationship among medical "condition," modern science, pharmaceutical product, and desired outcome was frequently on display in *Your Doctor*.[35]

Another case in point is the presentation of Noludar (methyprylon), a sedative manufactured by Hoffman–La Roche. The most regularly appear-

ARMONIL

الارمونيل

علاج مقو ومرمم للجسم يعطى لمكافحة فقر الدم
وشحن الجسم بالفيتامين (ب ١٢)

FIGURE 6.4 Advertisement for Armonil. *Tabibak,* February 1957, 90.

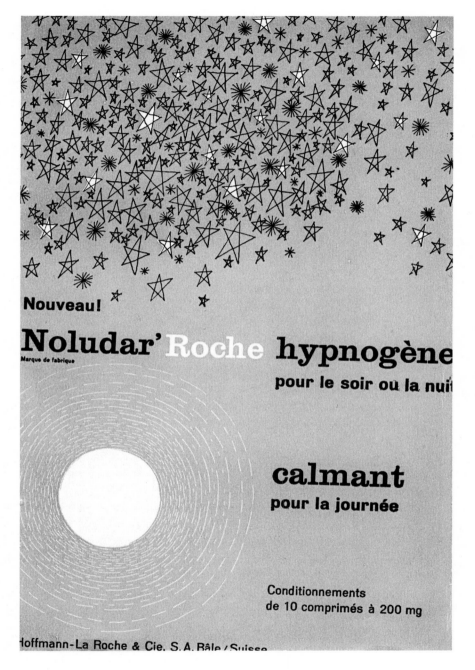

FIGURE 6.5 Advertisement for Noludar. *Tabibak*, October 1957, 52–53.

ing version of this product's advertisement is a full-page, multicolor insert (fig. 6.5).[36] The French text of this advertisement, which promises "sleep by night" and "serenity by day," echoes the "wonder drug" discourses advanced by most practitioners of Western medicine in the 1950s, the era when modern advertising found its true purpose: the identification (and some would argue, the invention) of a host of ailments and anxieties that the product on offer was specifically designed to remedy. And in this case, the effect of "product placement" outside the context of advertising is even more striking. One of the earliest issues of *Your Doctor* featured an "article" entitled "Noludar: Munawwim Jadid 'Ajib" (Noludar: A Wondrous New Sleep Aid), written by "Doctor Schmidt from the Hospital for Nervous and Psychological Diseases in Heidelberg, Germany."[37] This article, probably commissioned and distributed by Hoffman–La Roche, provided a seemingly disinterested, and therefore more persuasive, endorsement of a new state-of-the-art medication's properties, further enhanced by the cachet of Western expertise.

Many of Sabri al-Qabbani's brand-name endorsements addressed more serious issues that were central to national development: personal hygiene and public health. By the time al-Qabbani began practicing medical journalism, the eradication of communicable diseases and their underlying causes was fundamental to the Syrian government's asserted identity as the primary agent of the country's modernization and development, as well as a central element of an older, European discourse about the "hygienic citizen" and his role in the nation's future.[38]

Yet in 1950s Syria, as in much of the developing world, many illnesses treatable or preventable through simple hygienic practices remained widespread. Evidence of these conditions' persistence appears throughout the advice columns, advertising, and feature articles of *Your Doctor*.[39] For example, many of al-Qabbani's readers complained of intestinal worms acquired from contaminated meat or water,[40] some sought the means to eliminate the facial scars caused by smallpox,[41] those bitten by feral animals inquired about the symptoms of and treatment for rabies,[42] and yet others suffering from scabies sought expert advice on appropriate hygienic regimens.[43] One such exchange occurred with the "poor tormented one from Aleppo," who was experiencing "tiredness in his chest" and inquired about the "symptoms of tuberculosis." In response, al-Qabbani succinctly described the "signs of the disease" and then concluded by declaring, "consulting a doctor is a duty."[44]

When a petitioner's symptoms indicated a potential public health hazard, al-Qabbani always declared that every citizen was obliged to seek immediate, professional medical advice. Most of these injunctions were directed to readers residing outside Syria's four largest cities. This is particularly telling, for it not only reflects the relative absence of medical services in the country-side but also betrays the urbanite's assumption that people living outside the Arab world's major metropolitan areas were less healthy, educated, and civic-minded than their urban counterparts.[45]

Such issues made frequent appearance in al-Qabbani's feature articles. A classic early example is found in "'Ilaj hadith li mu'alajat al-qur'a" (Modern Therapy for Treatment of the Scalp), which identified, described, and provided photographic illustrations of several diseases of the scalp caused by bacteria and parasites commonly afflicting those living or working in un-hygienic conditions. After stressing that these ailments have very different causes and symptoms, al-Qabbani recommended the topical antibiotic and fungicide Asterol, manufactured by Hoffman–La Roche.[46]

CAN THE PATIENT SPEAK? THE DOCTOR AND HIS READERS

Several characteristics of al-Qabbani's discourse are present in his response to Mr. Samir al-Hajj in Beirut, who inquired about the "effects of [illegal] drugs and wine on the individual and society":

> Drugs and wine weaken all mental faculties and the person who is addicted to them is incapable of carrying out either mathematical operations or tasks that depend on memory. Numerous studies have demonstrated that wine has never made a worker or an artisan more productive or facilitated his work. Wine can cause ulcers and it weakens the intellect, causing the individual to lose self-control. But it is a mistake to think that a small glass of wine can cause any serious harm. What causes damage to the liver is the constant drinking associated with addiction.[47]

His declaration that a "small glass of wine" can cause no "serious harm" adopted a clinical perspective that ignored Islam's absolute prohibition against the consumption of alcohol.[48] Thus it highlights the relationship between the doctor's project and the epistemology and rhetoric of the Islamic sciences. Like his legal counterpart, Najat Qassab Hasan, al-Qabbani's responses to his petitioners were presented in the specific question/general answer structure of the fatwa. And like Qassab Hasan, the doctor frequently employed elements of fatwas, for instance, invoking the name of God, quoting the Qur'an or the hadith, citing a tenant of *fiqh* (Islamic jurisprudence), and affixing a formulaic codicil to his replies.[49]

Al-Qabbani embraced the very modern concept of addiction, a pathology that displaces its sufferers from the moral economy of divine proscriptions, effectively transforming sinners into patients whose redemption is the exclusive responsibility of medical specialists. Most importantly, al-Qabbani's immediate objection to the consumption of wine was strictly utilitarian in nature. Wine, like "drugs," inhibits the productivity of those who perform intellectual labor and does not increase the capacity of those who work with their hands. Such assertions betrayed an attitude that was both self-consciously modern and informed by contemporary conceptions of development, productivity, nation, and class.

These features were present in Sabri al-Qabbani's responses to inquiries about a remarkably broad range of medical and scientific issues. While some appeared to be motivated by sheer curiosity,[50] most were from readers seeking relief from symptoms of ailments distressingly common in every society, such as chronic headaches, hemorrhoids, allergies, arteriosclerosis, cancer, irregular heartbeats, epilepsy, and a wide variety of digestive/intestinal maladies.[51] In addition to inquiries about such physical conditions, al-Qabbani received a comparable number of letters describing problems more overtly psychological or interpersonal in nature.[52] These included stuttering, insomnia,[53] the recurrence of obsessive negative thoughts, persistent self-doubts, the social alienation wrought by retirement,[54] talking in one's sleep, a wide variety of "nervous disorders," disturbing dreams, and occasional oddities, like stomach cramps caused by viewing "love scenes on the cinema screen" and fear that reading crime stories—the petitioner's hobby—could be detrimental to one's health.[55]

A nearly equal number of letters were concerned with issues of mental or physical "self-improvement."[56] For example, several of al-Qabbani's readers requested non-dietary methods to reduce their waistlines.[57] Others sought to identify and minimize the potential health risks of repeated exposure to the sun, the means to make their voices more pleasing to the ear, and remedies, solicited by both young and old, for acne.[58] Many of these queries were informed by strictly aesthetic concerns, that is, the cultivation of masculine or feminine beauty. These included desires to eliminate the appearance of facial "lines,"[59] increase or reduce breast size,[60] straighten wavy hair, eliminate gray hair, stop or reverse male pattern baldness, and remove unwanted facial or body hair.[61]

In this same vein, a number of men inquired about the positive or negative effects of bodybuilding and weight training, while others sought medications or procedures that would increase their height.[62] Al-Qabbani's default reply to this final request was that "we have mentioned many times" that the "extract of the pituitary gland increases height if taken under medical supervision and prior to the age of eighteen."[63] Eventually al-Qabbani declined to address this issue in his column, declaring, "For fear of becoming boring, this journal cannot answer the same questions in every issue." He then referred readers to previous issues of *Your Doctor* and to his most popular book, *Tabibak Ma'ak* (Your Doctor Is with You), in which could be found "a detailed description of the research and the name of the remedy."[64]

Al-Qabbani had been providing this information to readers for several years before the debut of *Your Doctor*. In the process, he often recommended novel surgical procedures. An example of this is found in al-Qabbani's response to the "female student 'Ayn S. from Damascus," who expressed displeasure with the appearance of her nose and asked about the "possibility of beautifying" it without leaving visible evidence like scars. Al-Qabbani's terse response was, "Operations for beautifying the nose are conducted from inside the nostrils, and therefore, do not leave any trace. It is possible to have this procedure in Europe or in Beirut."[65] This reply implies that, for al-Qabbani and at least some of his readers, submitting to novel and invasive cosmetic procedures, despite their concomitant risks, was perfectly acceptable and even unremarkable.

A comparable exchange ensued when "Mr. 'Ayn S. from Baghdad" wrote complaining of a white film occluding his vision, presumably, he stated, "the result of a suddenly acquired infection." Al-Qabbani replied,

> Modern medicine has acquired the capacity to remove the damaged cornea and to replace it with another healthy cornea removed from the eyes of a recently deceased person, and in this way to restore vision to the sightless eye, provided that the other cornea was healthy. Although this operation is still in the experimental stage in the Arab East, it is the best method to treat your condition. So, be patient! Perhaps the specialists in Baghdad will be able to help you in the coming days.[66]

Implicit in al-Qabbani's advice is his assumption that "Mr. 'Ayn S. from Baghdad," like the "female student 'Ayn S. from Damascus," could possibly afford such a procedure when it became available locally, or that they would have the freedom to travel for such purposes.[67] While the ultimate targets of al-Qabbani's pedagogical project were "citizens to be," the project (and the journal's success) also entailed the identification of an ideal audience—those already inculcated with the outlook and practices of modern citizenship—and the cultivation of their material and cultural aspirations, frequently enacted through the purchase and use of the international pharmaceutical industry's products and services.

Al-Qabbani's responses also provide additional evidence of his self-iden-tification as a man of modern science. Until the nineteenth century, practi-tioners of Arab-Islamic medicine shared with their Christian counterparts a general abhorrence of dismembering the human corpse, fearing the post–Judgment Day consequences (for themselves, the donor, and the recipient) of defying "the Creator's will."[68] But al-Qabbani precisely delineated the "divi-sion of labor" between those wielding expertise in the secular and Islamic sciences. He clearly considered corneas and all potentially useful tissues har-vested from cadavers to be at the disposal of surgeons and their patients, their medical and scientific utility in this world outweighing any speculative con-siderations of their purpose in the next.[69]

Al-Qabbani's exchanges with his readers are notable for the delicate and deeply personal nature of the issues they raised. To his credit, al-Qabbani un-derstood from the outset that the potential for embarrassment could deter many of his readers from making such inquiries in a public forum. Thus it was often necessary to conceal their identities by substituting names with initials (as in the previous examples),[70] pseudonyms,[71] or both.[72] In this, al-Qabbani adopted another of the traditional mufti's practices: the use of "generic de-scriptions and fictional names" to distance "the query from the particular evidential circumstances of the questioner."[73]

In *Your Doctor*, al-Qabbani maintained this distance by providing a cou-pon (*qasima*), or form, that the reader could clip out (in some issues, the page on which the form appeared was perforated), complete according to specific instructions, and send through the mail (fig. 6.6). Readers were instructed to submit their "scientific, medical, or sexual question" with the qasima "in order to receive a correct answer." The coupon also provided a space for the petitioner's "complete name" and another for his or her chosen pseudonym. It then imposed a limit of one question per mailing and pledged to "maintain the confidentiality of the real names, addresses, and questions."[74] Thus al-Qabbani's correspondents had the option of concealing their true identities when inquiring about issues they considered too intimate and embarrassing. When petitioners failed to exercise this precaution, al-Qabbani would efface their identities entirely, designating them simply as "a gentleman," "a lady," or "a reader."[75]

The reader's coupon served another purpose as well. In an early issue of *Your Doctor*, al-Qabbani cautioned his readers that, due to the enormous vol-ume of letters he was receiving ("tens per day"), he would henceforth respond only to questions submitted with the coupon, thereby limiting his replies to queries from readers who had actually purchased the magazine. Al-Qabbani

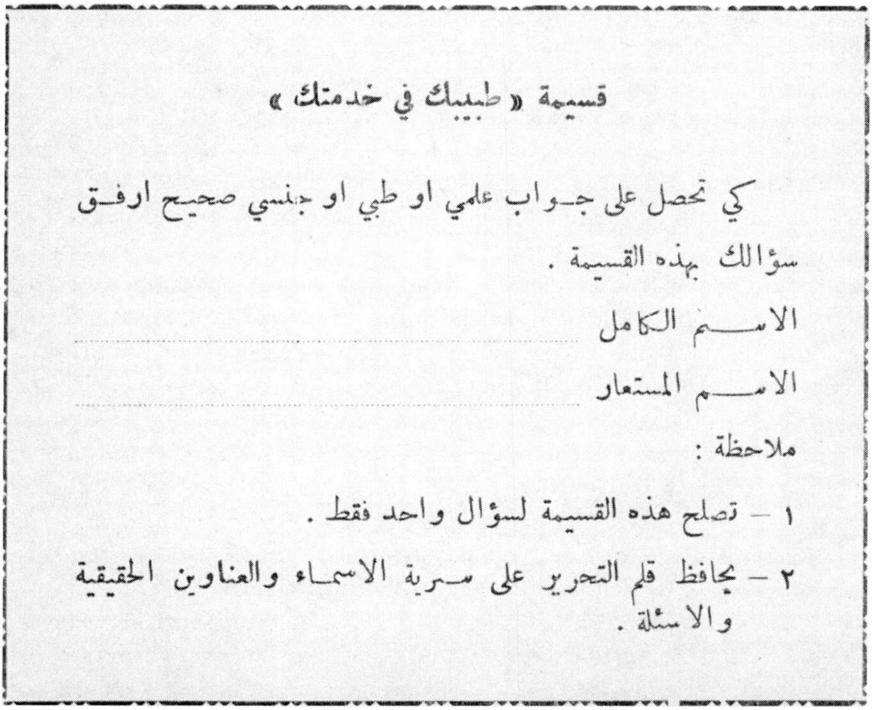

قسيمة « طبيبك في خدمتك »

كي تحصل على جــواب علمي او طبي او جنسي صحيح ارفـق
سؤالك بهذه القسيمة .

الاســـم الكامل

الاســـم المستعار

ملاحظة :

١ ‑ تصلح هذه القسيمة لسؤال واحد فقط .

٢ ‑ يحافظ قلم التحرير على سـرية الاسمـاء والعناوين الحقيقية
والاسئلة .

FIGURE 6.6 Reader's Coupon (*qasima*). *Tabibak*, September 1956, 1.

justified this change in policy by asserting that it was "only fair to favor those who actually own the issue." And, true to his word, he subsequently admonished by name petitioners who sought to evade this requirement, refusing to answer their questions because they "did not meet the magazine's requirement to accompany [their] questions with the special coupon."[76] In this way, the citizen was again encouraged to consume, that is, to purchase and read the journal rather than send a postcard or letter to al-Qabbani's office address. The *qasima* also expressed the unequal power relations between the expert and his interlocutors, a disparity that the historians of Islamic legal discourse have also identified as intrinsic to the fatwa genre.[77]

FOR DOCTORS ONLY: THE DOCTOR AND HIS COLLEAGUES

Many of the practices outlined above prompted criticism from al-Qabbani's fellow physicians in Syria. Discussing sexual and other sensitive topics of-

fended many of his more conservative colleagues. More significantly, prescribing powerful medications for patients he had never examined exposed
al-Qabbani to charges of abandoning the fundamental precepts of clinical
practice, violating basic professional standards, and placing the public at risk.

According to 'Abd al-Ghani al-'Itri, al-Qabbani's lifelong friend and
the publisher of *al-Dunya,* the magazine in which "The Readers' Clinic" appeared, such sniping stemmed from envy of al-Qabbani's unprecedented success.[78] Nevertheless, al-Qabbani did alter his customary practices in ways that
seemed calculated to allay such criticisms. In an apparent attempt to assuage
accusations of careless diagnoses and prescriptions, al-Qabbani lengthened
his responses to readers' questions, adding considerable detail and the occasional qualifier.[79] Al-Qabbani also made a series of changes to the content of
Your Doctor—a series of articles celebrating certain of his colleagues' educational and professional accomplishments, public service, and institutional affiliations;[80] feature articles written by prominent physicians from throughout
the region; and the column "Li al-Atibba' Faqat" (For Doctors Only),[81] which
usually discussed new research, procedures, medications—that deepened the
journal's integration with Syria's medical establishment.[82]

Finally, al-Qabbani hired a team of Syrian medical specialists bearing
"notable" family names to join him in answering questions submitted to
"Your Doctor Is at Your Service."[83] He announced this innovation in the January 1958 issue of *Your Doctor,* providing a list of these physicians and their
respective fields of specialization. At this time, the reader's coupon was also
amended to reflect the new policy. An additional line, bearing the instruction
"Cite the name of the physician to whom you want to address your question," was added.[84] In the subsequent issue, "Your Doctor Is at Your Service"
displayed this new division of labor, with the specialists answering approximately 35 percent of the questions and al-Qabbani fielding the remainder.[85]
Thereby al-Qabbani reduced his considerable workload and expanded the
volume and scope of medical expertise on display in his journal.[86]

This initiative was not out of keeping with al-Qabbani's long-term position. He had, in fact, always tacitly acknowledged the limitations of his expertise as a general practitioner, and when he deemed it necessary, he advised consulting a specialist.[87] Deference to more specialized expertise was
an acknowledgment that "experts aggregate knowledge from various sources;
they are not solitary geniuses."[88] It was also another example of convergence
between conventions of the secular and Islamic sciences. Scholars have noted
that Abu 'Abdullah al-Shafi'i, Ahmad bin Hanbal, and Malik Ibn Anas,
founders of three of the major schools of Islamic jurisprudence, routinely ac-

knowledged the limitations of their knowledge when issuing fatwas. In such cases, they declined to answer, referring the petitioners to noted specialists in the relevant fields. In this way, "reticence on the part of the jurist became a mark of qualification and integrity."[89]

Sabri al-Qabbani's medical journalism reveals, first and foremost, a general presumption that the necessary but insufficient indices of citizenship were modern education and "Arab" consciousness, phenomena that were increasingly prevalent in the region's urban areas and virtually unknown outside of them. Al-Qabbani used mass media to wage war on the ignorance and backwardness that ignored the "fundamental principles of hygiene," for he believed that the citizen who was equipped with the knowledge and the means to maintain his own health and vitality increased his capacity to fulfill the virtuous citizen's duties in the realms of consumption, production, and reproduction.

Al-Qabbani's publications also illuminate the modern media expert's relationship to the institutions and forces that make his mission possible, and, to varying degrees, inform its style and content. The most obvious of these forces was foreign capital in the form of advertising revenue provided by multinational pharmaceutical companies. The content of al-Qabbani's advice, coupled with his editorial practice, highlights the relationship among capital, technology, and culture. Multinational pharmaceutical manufacturers possessed the largest advertising budgets and were actively seeking a foothold in emerging markets. These same corporations were also among the world leaders in the manufacture of both new wonder drugs that were transforming public health in the developed world and the most popular and reliable nonprescription medications.

As is the case today, such companies used their local agents to distribute free samples of their latest products to prominent and influential physicians, accompanied by copious literature attesting to those products' efficacy at treating heretofore-intractable maladies. Thus, it is likely that al-Qabbani recommended what he sincerely believed were the most effective remedies for his readers' ailments. Precisely because he was thoroughly incorporated into a global network of economic interests, it was a matter of course that the products of al-Qabbani's multinational advertisers came most easily to mind.

Most importantly, al-Qabbani's relationships with pharmaceutical giants, and with various individuals mentioned elsewhere in this study, augmented his authority as an expert and power to speak through mass media. Al-Qabbani used this power not just to promote his advertisers' products but also to instill in his "Arab readers" a new kind of subjectivity, one that refused superstition and embraced science by consuming modern pharmaceuticals. This observation is key to understanding the function of advertising in a broader sense. According to productionist readings, advertising's purpose is to stimulate consumption and thereby increase the profits of manufacturers. While this assessment accurately describes the intent of advertising, consumptionist readings provide another perspective, stressing the consumer's agency in this dialectical process. Such readings assume that a given product's consumers might be motivated by the desire to transform themselves through its purchase and use. This transformative potential is often an integral, if somewhat subliminal, element of advertising's message.[90] The content of *Your Doctor* encouraged al-Qabbani's readers, and particularly his correspondents, to do just that.

7   Sex and the Conjugal Citizen

> In an effort to enable every citizen to read this journal, and in
> view of the fact that some readers send to this column ques-
> tions requiring frank answers inappropriate for circulation
> among children and adolescents, we have decided to observe
> discretion in answers concerning sexual matters. It is possible
> for the reader who wants a frank answer to enclose with the
> question an envelope with return postage so that we can send
> a private answer in it.
>
> —*TABIBAK*, MAY 1957

SEXUAL AND REPRODUCTIVE issues occupied pride of place in Sabri al-Qabbani's exchanges with his readers.[1] The earnestness with which these readers
sought the most rudimentary information is often quite touching, simultaneously reflecting a general state of ignorance and displaying a host of proto-
typically modern aspirations and anxieties. Gender was a particularly salient
feature of these exchanges, in which forms of female sexuality not inextricably linked to reproduction were often occluded or even pathologized. This
tendency was in keeping with a construction of the ideal citizen as masculine subject. One consequence of this construction was the reconfiguration
and problematization of male sexuality. If the success of the postcolonial,
state-building project depended on the service of its patriarchal, rational,
and martial citizens, these citizens' ungoverned sexual desire threatened that
project.

Sabri al-Qabbani's discussion of sexual matters echoed such concerns in
its treatment of masturbation and homosexuality, deeming these expressions
of male sexuality inimical to social stability, productivity, and reproduction.
Accordingly, al-Qabbani sought to confine male sexual desires within the
bounds of marriage, and thereby to transform the potentially destabilizing
and destructive sexual citizen into the conjugal citizen, whose expression of
sexual desires contributed to social stability and progress.[2]

Al-Qabbani's predominantly male correspondents displayed these and other anxieties about sexuality and wrote to the doctor about nocturnal emissions and other signs and effects of puberty. Young adults confessed fears about "addiction" to masturbation, while older adults expressed concerns about sexually transmitted diseases and various forms of sexual "inadequacy" like premature ejaculation, erectile dysfunction, and small or otherwise "abnormal" genitalia.

In dispensing his conceptions of gender and sexual norms, al-Qabbani rhetorically poached on the turf of sociologists and criminologists, asserting the medical expert's authority to describe, define, and proscribe solutions for a plethora of libidinally related "social problems," even when acknowledging medical science's relative incapacity to effect their cure. In al-Qabbani's advice columns, another kind of modern expertise is also on display. As the publisher of a journal supported by abundant advertising revenue, al-Qabbani was free to edit his correspondence with readers at will. Like the attorney Najat Qassab Hasan, al-Qabbani enjoyed the power to speak in his own voice *and* in the voices of his correspondents, editing questions in order to obscure identities, emphasize particular issues, and remain within the bounds of decorum. This final imperative required skill and subtlety, for one of the foundations of al-Qabbani's success was his willingness to discuss in a frank and open manner subjects commonly considered excessively sensitive or indelicate. This signal characteristic, apparent at the outset of the doctor's journalistic career, was sustained throughout his public life.[3]

Given the sensitivity of its subject matter, discourse about sexuality is perhaps the ideal site in which to observe the construction and reification of cultural norms in the modern period. Like his contemporaries in the West, al-Qabbani's claims of scientific objectivity and detachment were often accompanied by homiletic pronouncements that employed clinical-sounding but highly normative euphemisms translated directly from the psychoanalytical lexicon of the Victorian period.[4] The norm al-Qabbani most consistently advocated as the only healthy outlet for sexual desire—conjugality, or loving, (potentially) procreative, genital intercourse within the confines of marriage—was an ideal of modernizing pedagogues in the West, who saw marriage and reproduction "not as a right, but as a duty."[5]

All other forms of sexual gratification were either silenced or situated within a hierarchy of deviance, and were thereby defined as abdications of responsibility to a variety of collectivities. This discourse displayed several products of the modern transformation: (1) a new conception of certain sexual practices as social/psychological phenomena and problems; (2) a new lexicon to articulate this reconceptualization; and (3) an equally novel course of recommended treatments for such "afflictions." Incorporating all of the above, al-Qabbani's engagements with sexuality represent an attempt to delineate the postwar Arab world's "libidinal imaginary" by demarcating the boundaries of the citizen's normal, healthy sexual desire and practice.[6]

SEXUAL HYGIENE

Issues of sexual hygiene loomed large in al-Qabbani's correspondence. From the earliest days, his advice columns featured letters from readers experiencing symptoms of sexually transmitted diseases. The doctor's responses to such queries were usually clinical, dispassionate, and devoid of censure.[7] Some of these exchanges, however, reveal much about the construction of citizenship in the nationalist mode. Responding to "Miss R. F. from Latakiyya," who appears to have contracted syphilis, al-Qabbani summarized the disease's etiology and current treatment regimen (penicillin and bismuth), and reassured his reader that the prognosis for her cure was excellent. But the doctor could not resist imparting a history lesson informed by nationalist ideology, tracing the malady's initial appearance in "the East" to both the pre-Columbian Crusades *and* the modern period of Western imperialism.[8]

A comparable complaint from a male reader, which mentioned a discharge from the penis and "from around the foreskin," prompted a reference to the forthcoming publication of al-Qabbani's book, *Our Sexual Life,* which included "healthy advice" about "sexual diseases accompanied by detailed illustrations" and, for good measure, an extended discussion of the merits of circumcision.[9] The latter subject was apparently of great interest to al-Qabbani, for a lengthier article on it subsequently appeared in *Your Doctor.* The article presented a selective historical overview of the practice of male circumcision through the ages, noting that it has been advocated for reasons of hygiene, religion, and fertility, contrasting it favorably to the admittedly dangerous practice of female circumcision, and endorsing the practice as one whose benefits outweigh its risks.[10] While male circumcision is almost universal among Muslims, al-Qabbani was also in perfect accord with his American contemporaries, who by the 1950s were routinely practicing neonatal male circumcision as a "sanitary precaution" expressing several "moral, social, and cultural values."[11]

SEXUAL ANXIETIES

As part of his goal of providing "all the friendly advice and necessary instructions for young men and women,"[12] al-Qabbani devoted considerable space in his columns and books to the anxieties that the physical indicators of puberty stimulated in his readers.[13] More space, however, was devoted to the sexual anxieties of the adult male than any other topic. Large numbers of the doctor's readers suffered from some form of perceived inadequacy, chief among them impotence, premature ejaculation, and insufficient penis size. Equally common was frustration over the scarcity of culturally sanctioned outlets for sexual desire. These exchanges conformed to broader patterns of the doctor's correspondence in two notable ways. First, many of al-Qabbani's male readers lacked basic knowledge of sexuality and reproduction, a general ignorance that apparently could not be alleviated through other easily accessible sources. Second, not a single letter from a female petitioner complaining of "inadequacy" (her own or her partner's) appeared in any of the doctor's columns.

A common malady afflicting al-Qabbani's male petitioners was "sexual weakness," that is, impotence or, in today's parlance, erectile dysfunction.[14] The doctor sometimes attributed these symptoms to an underlying metabolic condition,[15] but he more frequently referred readers to his latest publications,[16] and recommended courses of powerful pharmaceutical agents and/or marriage.[17] Occasionally, however, al-Qabbani ventured into the realm of the psychological. A classic case is provided by the exchange with "Mr. Nizar N. from Aleppo," who asked about the "degree of the effect of intellectual activity on sexual prowess." The doctor noted that some of "the most important causes of impotence and of sexual debility" are "intellectual concerns." He advised Mr. Nizar N. to flee from the sources of stress and anxiety, to take "his rest at the seaside or in the country," far away from "the problems of the world and from what preoccupies his mind."[18] The most interesting aspect of al-Qabbani's answer is its implicit assumptions. The first is a quintessentially modern one: that many health problems are merely symptoms of an excessively fast-paced and stress-ridden urban environment. The second, and more interesting, assumption was that his interlocutor could afford such a holiday from work and the "problems of the world." As we saw earlier in his response to the Iraqi in need of corneal transplants, this exchange displays al-Qabbani's assumptions about the social class of his ideal citizen-interlocutor.

The doctor also received many letters from men experiencing "rapid," that is, premature, ejaculation, so many, in fact, that he frequently referred them en masse to the advice previously tendered in *Your Doctor*.[19] The gist of this advice—take powerful medications and get married—is by now familiar and, at first blush, unremarkable.[20] Yet in this specific context, the exhortation to marry indicates that the "patients" experiencing premature ejaculation were single, a fact that would have only increased the urgency of al-Qabbani's routine injunctions on behalf of conjugality.[21] But the larger, unanswered question is the prevailing definition of "rapid": too rapid for what or for whom? In other words, does this anxiety over the rapidity of ejaculation reflect a concern for women's pleasure or men's egos? Unfortunately, this issue is not addressed, an omission that confirms men's sexual subjectivity.[22]

Finally, al-Qabbani received a considerable number of letters from men displeased with the proportions and/or appearance of their genitalia. These included concerns over the relative sizes and shapes of testicles and scrota.[23] Not surprisingly, however, the primary focus of anxiety was the penis. A considerable number of petitioners complained of its "curvature," fearing that this constituted an impediment to marriage and procreation.[24]

Most, however, expressed dissatisfaction with the dimensions of their "members" (the preferred euphemism) and sometimes sought methods to "extend" them.[25] As the age of Internet miracles was far in the future, al-Qabbani offered no pharmaceutical or surgical solutions.[26] Instead, he relied on encouragement, assuring one petitioner after another, "you are a well-proportioned man," your size is "very close to the normal dimensions," and so on.[27] The key to this confidence by proxy appears to have been a firm belief in the irrelevance of penis size for mutually satisfying marital relations. Al-Qabbani's most explicit statement of this proposition appears in his exchange with "'Ayn. K. Dh. from A'zaz [Syria]," in which the doctor asserted that "large size is not a fundamental condition for a successful marriage, for women are attracted by kind words and gentle, amorous affection."[28] This declaration confirms that al-Qabbani conceived of the sexes as mutually exclusive, complementary opposites: men's "nature" is primarily carnal, deriving satisfaction from sensory gratification, while women's is at once more "delicate," "emotional," and "sentimental," an interpretation he shared with the sexual experts of late nineteenth-century France.[29]

Given this dichotomous conception, it should be no surprise that all complaints of sexual frustration appearing in the doctor's columns came from males. Whatever the cause of this female silence, the effect was, once again, to acknowledge male subjectivity and to render women as the objects of sexual desire, another tendency al-Qabbani shared with the "doctors of the law," or *'ulama'*, of the Ottoman period and social reformers in nineteenth-century Europe.[30]

In this exclusively male discourse, al-Qabbani drew on a familiar menu of treatments. The most frequent prescription was marriage.[31] Typical in this regard was the response to "N. S.," who complained of "pain in his testicles immediately after each amorous dalliance." The precise meaning of an "amorous dalliance" was not provided, yet the doctor's answer made clear that it did not include ejaculation: "This is an indication of congestion of the testicles and the need to empty them. Because of this, you'll find sticky secretions that emerge after urination. These are substances that the prostate discharges after a dalliance and the substances that have collected, accumulated, and piled up in the *vasa deferentia*." This clinical description of the condition is followed by the reassuring news that "there is no danger from this flow, and it will go away after marriage."[32]

Other favorite remedies for sexual frustration were the avoidance of potentially troublesome stimuli and the sublimation of potentially destructive sexual energies into more benign or ennobling pursuits. Both were suggested to "Mr. Muhammad 'Alim from Aamatour in Lebanon," who was plagued by "untamable sexual desire." Al-Qabbani advised him to "avoid stimulating situations, attending licentious films, reading amorous stories, and ingesting stimulants." He also urged Mr. 'Alim to make a hobby of physical exercise in order to "achieve mastery over" his urges and distract him "from thinking of sex."[33] All three treatments were prescribed for "Mr. K. from Hama," who sought a "soothing remedy" for the constant "sexual excitement and elongation" he was experiencing. Mr. K was advised to "exercise patience until marriage," an effort that would be eased by "prayer, fasting, sports, cold showers," and adopting a hobby that "distracts your mind from sex."[34]

Al-Qabbani, while quite frankly discussing the physiological and psychological consequences of male sexual frustration, did not (for reasons addressed below) recommend one obvious solution: masturbation. Instead, he cautioned patience and promised relief in the sexual intercourse that marriage licenses necessarily provide. This position was in keeping with the prevailing view of Western medicine. It also resonated powerfully with Islamic conventions, which, some analysts have argued, elevated intercourse within marriage to the level of worship.[35]

A rather poignant missive prompted al-Qabbani to add an interesting twist to his "marriage is the cure for all that ails you" prescription. "Mr. S. K. from Damascus" wrote complaining that he "gets flustered every time he sees a girl." Al-Qabbani began conventionally enough, observing that Mr. S. K.'s symptoms were "signs of . . . spiritual and sexual thirst" that would pass after marriage. This was unremarkable. The doctor then noted, however, that another remedy was in sight: "After you move to the West to pursue your studies, you will get accustomed to being in the company of women."[36]

The second prescription betrays the uncritical adoption of one of the leitmotifs of Arabic intellectual discourse in the twentieth century. Many modernist reformers posited an essentialist dichotomy of West and East as two mutually exclusive cultural spheres, the former being characterized by a "healthy" environment in which males and females learn to interact "naturally" from early childhood, and the latter constituting an "unnatural" environment in which rigid gender segregation warps "normal" development and cripples social relations. This "sexual segregation" thesis was often adduced to explain a host of perceived ills, chief among them same-sex desire and "excessive" masturbation.

In sum, the essence of al-Qabbani's counsel was abstinence outside of marriage. Yet he was aware that this ideal was not always attainable and that its pursuit could bear a heavy price. This is clear in the article "al-Inqita' al-Jinsi wa Athrat al-Nafsiyya" (Sexual Inactivity and Its Psychological Impact) and in his response to "Iskandar Ma'luf from Zahle," who inquired about the "danger of sexual abstinence."[37] In addition to his customary exhortation to embrace the citizen's "lofty aspirations," that is, to "serve" family and homeland by resisting surrender to the "animal nature" that threatens to "destroy" both body and spirit, al-Qabbani acknowledged that prolonged sexual abstinence could sometimes endanger emotional or psychological health.[38] For those experiencing such torments, this secular vow of chastity was not a viable option. In such cases, the attempt to satisfy sexual desire almost inevitably led to the violation of norms.

THE ISSUE OF FEMALE SEXUALITY

Men and male sexuality were the focus of al-Qabbani's concerns, but he did not ignore female sexuality. Not only were conjugal citizens partnered with women, but al-Qabbani, like Qassab Hasan, also positioned himself as an advocate of "modern" women's rights, asserting that he was a man who, more than most of his contemporaries, empathized with women and was capable of seeing sexual and reproductive issues from their perspective.[39]

This empathy for women did not, however, mean challenging the prevailing notion that female sexuality, even more than its male counterpart, could not exist independently of normative social relations, particularly those surrounding marriage and reproduction. Whenever issues arose at the intersection of sexuality and prevailing norms, the doctor's interventions were invariably "conservative": they acknowledged, accommodated, or even upheld the status quo. Furthermore, al-Qabbani frequently essentialized women's "nature" as the eternal and ineffable antithesis of men's. This characterization is most blatant in the primer *Our Sexual Life,* in which the chapter introducing female sexuality and reproduction is entitled "Woman! That Unknown" and is prefaced by a translated passage of Lord Byron's epic satirical poem *Don Juan:* "Man's love is of man's life a thing apart, 'tis woman's whole existence."[40]

This perspective is most obvious in al-Qabbani's focus on "feminine aesthetics." Despite the fact that men generated the majority of inquiries about personal "beautification" appearing in the doctor's advice columns, al-Qabbani dedicated space in every issue of *Your Doctor* to lengthy articles about the cultivation and maintenance of female, rather than male, beauty. The most significant of these features, "Jamaluki Sayyidati" (Your Beauty, My Lady), which stressed the importance of diet, exercise, hygiene, and cosmetics, appeared in eight of *Your Doctor*'s first twelve issues.[41] This reality was juxtaposed with the complete absence of letters from women inquiring about the medical science underlying their sexual pleasure or lack thereof. This served to reify women's status as objects, rather than subjects, of sexual desire.

Two of the above characteristics, empathy and conservatism, are apparent in *Your Doctor*'s treatment of virginity and marriage. Many unmarried women submitted letters expressing anxiety about losing the ultimate symbol of virginity, the intact hymen. In response, al-Qabbani and his specialist collaborators provided detailed information in a consistently sympathetic tone but never questioned female virginity's status as the *sine qua non* of "normal" marriage.[42] In fact, al-Qabbani actually endorsed premarital screening for virginity, provided that a physician conducted the "assessment . . . according to the correct [unspecified] procedure."[43]

Even when al-Qabbani's empathy with women was expressed in unambiguous terms, it served to reify gender norms. Such was the case in his exchange with "Mr. A. S. D. from Aleppo," who wrote seeking advice on his wedding night. Al-Qabbani sternly instructed him to consider what many husbands do not, "the wife's pain and . . . the consequences of repeated intercourse." The doctor prescribed the total abstention from intercourse for the subsequent seven days, giving his wife's "wounds" time to heal.[44] The message from "Your Doctor" was clear: the wedding night would necessarily bring pleasure for men, pain for women. This is just one of many examples in which al-Qabbani depicted female sexuality as fundamentally different from male sexuality.

In cases of real or suspected sexual contact outside the bounds of marriage, al-Qabbani was invariably solicitous, attempting to assuage his female correspondents' evident emotional distress. Ultimately, however, he advised these women to accept the social and legal inequity mandated by their gender. In one such case, al-Qabbani dissuaded a woman who had been unjustly divorced and abandoned for "non-virginity" from pursuing legal action, even though he claimed to accept the justice of her case.[45] In another deeply troubling exchange, al-Qabbani told a married woman who had been raped that, in order to retain the trust of her husband and preserve her marriage, she "must forget the event completely and not mention it to any living soul."[46] In essence, the doctor advised his female correspondents to abandon their rights as citizens, that is, as sovereign individuals who were equal before the law, in order to preserve their culturally sanctified roles as wives and mothers. For al-Qabbani, these identities offered the only possible sites of female agency, and thus the most logical place to employ the reform-minded medical expert's agency.

"ALL THE MEANS OF PREVENTING PREGNANCY": REPRODUCTION AND FAMILY PLANNING

Many young women wrote to Sabri al-Qabbani seeking information about fundamental issues related to reproduction, such as the definition of pregnancy, the distinction between human spermatozoa and eggs, and explanations of the menstrual cycle.[47] Such inquiries were so common that they usually prompted references to one of al-Qabbani's books. A significant number of the doctor's interlocutors, however, were women seeking precise information about effective methods of contraception.[48] While al-Qabbani invariably prefaced or closed his responses to these queries with the recommendation of his primer on family planning, *Atfal taht al-Talab wa Man' al-Haml* (Children upon Demand and the Prevention of Pregnancy), he also devoted considerable time and effort to providing detailed advice in his columns.

A classic example is the exchange with "Mrs. 'B. B.' from Damascus," who wrote seeking a "method of contraception after having given birth seven times." Al-Qabbani explained the fundamentals of the rhythm method, counseled Mrs. B. B. to "first read a great deal" before selecting the most appropriate method, and then directed her to *Children upon Demand,* which, he declared, listed and described all "safe, sound methods to limit concep-tion, and the names of the devices that are designed for the prevention of pregnancy."[49]

The book in question was just the latest and most comprehensive expres-sion of al-Qabbani's career-long interest in family planning, much of its con-tent having previously appeared in the pages of *Your Doctor* and other peri-odicals.[50] A remarkable document in its own right, *Children upon Demand* contained, among other things, a cylindrical calendar for calculating fertile and nonfertile days in the menstrual cycle, very graphic descriptions and il-lustrations of how pregnancy occurs, and instructions for the safe and proper insertion of a diaphragm and for the effective use of condoms.[51]

Here we see the clearest expression of Sabri al-Qabbani's mission. By utilizing multiple media to make contraceptive information available to lit-erate women without reference to their husbands or other male relatives, al-Qabbani provided them with the requisite means to control their own re-productive systems while publicly asserting their right to do so. The doctor's reformist position constituted a subtle twist on nationalist conceptualizations of family and nation, for it promoted an idealized, reified conception of moth-erhood while simultaneously equipping women with the means to forego ex-periencing that culturally sanctified state. This intervention acknowledged that, despite the male gendering of the conjugal citizen, the stability and sus-tenance of conjugality as a system structuring sexual and reproductive rela-tions required the cooperative agency of women.

Al-Qabbani's general advocacy of contraceptive choice was also in keep-ing with the broader Islamic tradition, that is, the historical consensus of the jurisprudents (*fuqaha'*) that contraception is a perfectly acceptable practice.[52] Yet this tradition sanctioned the practice only *at the instigation* of the hus-band and *with the consent* of the wife.[53] Herein lies the fundamental differ-ence, for al-Qabbani seemed to invert that relationship, equipping the wife with the means to practice birth control, presumably, but not necessarily, with the knowledge and consent of the husband.

While equally informative about the science underlying fertility, impreg-nation, and contraception, the doctor's pronouncements on men's reproduc-tive issues differed markedly in tone.[54] Al-Qabbani was frequently unsympa-thetic or scornful when he detected the operation of conventional masculine egos or attitudes. For example, he brusquely deflected one reader's suspicions about the paternity of his children by asserting the complexity of genetics, and dismissed another's fears that his wife had employed arcane methods to "deprive" him of his fertility as belief in "fairy tales."[55]

"PERVERTED FORMS" OF PLEASURE:
VIOLATIONS OF THE NORM

Conjugality required that male sexual desire be expressed exclusively through legally sanctioned and potentially procreative intercourse. Masturbation and same-sex relations were considered the most threatening deviations from this norm. Masturbation was deemed a shameful expression of self-indulgence, a diversion of sexual energy from reproductivity, and a rejection of normative sociality, as it bred seclusion and the abandonment of commitments to family, state, and nation. Same-sex relations bore the same threats but added another even more frightening—the inversion of gender norms. As in the contemporaneous West, men "playing the role" of women during sexual relations was thought a perversion of unparalleled potential to destabilize, hence its "unnatural" designation.

Masturbation frequently occupied the minds of Sabri al-Qabbani and his readers.[56] Featured in more than forty-five letters addressed to the doctor's various advice columns,[57] masturbation was also the topic of a chapter in al-Qabbani's *Our Sexual Life*.[58] The doctor nominally addressed masturbation as a ubiquitous natural phenomenon, a common means of expressing sexual desire that is grounded in physiological processes. Of greater significance for this study, he also frequently treated the practice as a "social problem," that is, the potentially destructive diversion of the conjugal citizen's procreative energies. Al-Qabbani's writings neatly embodied the modern period's transformation in prevailing perceptions of masturbation.

Intellectual discourse about masturbation in the Arab-Islamic world had always been primarily medical in nature. Until the late nineteenth century, the doctrines of Galenic, or "humoral," medicine prevailed. Given this system's conception of health as maintaining the proper balance of various substances (manifested as bodily fluids), its practitioners considered the occasional discharge of sperm necessary for the prevention of imbalances that would result in various types of illness. Therefore they accepted masturbation as an alternative to genital intercourse when the latter was unavailable or deemed unsafe.[59]

Beginning in the nineteenth century, this system was gradually eclipsed by Western medical discourse, which featured distinctive new conceptual frameworks, vocabularies, and treatment regimens. All of the above are on display in the doctor's reply to "M. N. from Homs," who complained of "dizziness and blurred vision" whenever he moved his head. Al-Qabbani's diagnosis of low blood pressure in the brain as the proximate cause is unremarkable, as are two of the possible underlying causes he adduced, deficient liver function, and anemia. The third possible cause, the "wasting of essential bodily fluids" through the regular practice of "the secret habit," is of greater interest, for it highlights the lexical change noted above.[60]

As others have documented, prior to the modern period, medical practitioners used the classical term *al-istimna*, the act of producing sperm, to denote the autoerotic practices of both men and women.[61] Al-Qabbani, on the other hand, almost always employed the euphemism "the secret habit" (*al-'ada al-sirriyya*).[62] A literal translation of the popular Victorian-era term "the solitary vice,"[63] the phrase had become "the operative expression in Arab medical terminology" by the time al-Qabbani attended medical school.[64]

This change transcended the merely semantic, for it signified the modern emphasis on masturbation's potential social, moral, and psychological consequences.[65] Like his predecessors, al-Qabbani occasionally cited putative physiological and metabolic contraindications, for example, permanent injury to the penis (usually in the form of "curvature"), "weakness of the nerves," "poverty of the blood" (as in the exchange cited above), and the proliferation of facial acne.[66] Such concerns, however, paled in comparison to potential social and psychological consequences of masturbation:

> QUESTION: 'Isam al-Hamawi from Hama and Shakir Muhammad from Mosul in Iraq ask about the danger of the secret habit.
>
> ANSWER: One becomes a prisoner of a habit that gains mastery over him, that makes him lonely and averse to social gatherings and to people, and leaves the signs of hopelessness and melancholia visible on his face.[67]

Similar responses employing tropes of mastery, slavery, surrender, helplessness, bondage, alienation, and melancholia abound in the doctor's columns.[68] The critical issue appeared to be the modern scourge of addiction, which entailed the surrender to narcissism, self-indulgence, and the attendant erosion of self-respect. For al-Qabbani, such surrender yielded the dreaded conditions "solitude," "melancholia," and social alienation, soon followed by the abdication of critical responsibilities to a variety of collectivities including family, homeland, and nation.[69]

This perception appears to have been shared by many of al-Qabbani's interlocutors, who frequently sought a "cure" for their socially destructive addictions. Occasionally al-Qabbani's treatments focused exclusively on the metabolic: various herbal and prescription "tranquilizers," dietary adjustments, and seasonal regimens of cold and warm baths.[70] Not surprisingly, however, social (as opposed to exclusively medical) concerns predominated in the doctor's designated treatments. Thus the cure that he most frequently prescribed was a simple one, marriage:

> QUESTION: The student 'Ayn. S. from Damascus complains of . . . the secret habit.
>
> ANSWER: Marriage is the best treatment to liberate you from that cursed devil lurking in the hearts of all young people.[71]

Al-Qabbani's response assumed the natural and universal nature of sexual desire. It also posited an equally natural and universal outlet, sexual intercourse within the confines of marriage. Furthermore, al-Qabbani ascribed redemptive properties to this sanctioned expression of sexuality, asserting that it would permit the former "addict" to "return to being a proper man," one who is no longer a "slave" to the habit, a citizen.[72] Al-Qabbani's preferred therapeutic regimen is particularly salient to this study, for it emphasizes one of the points at which premodern ("Islamic") and modern ("bourgeois") ideologies intersected, the general disapproval of sexual activity outside the context of legally defined and sanctioned relationships.[73]

But this prescription was not appropriate or feasible for all of the "addicts" seeking al-Qabbani's help, as many were too young or impoverished to marry. In such cases, the doctor recommended various forms of sublimation, as he did for those suffering from more generic sexual frustration. This treatment clarifies al-Qabbani's psychoanalytically informed conception of addiction as a pathology that is best treated by busying first the mind through cultural and intellectual pursuits, and then the body through vigorous physical exercise.[74]

All of the above is present in al-Qabbani's exchange with "Mr. M. H. from Qamishli," who sought a treatment that would help him "abstain from bad habits." As several elements of al-Qabbani's reply are of interest, it is reproduced in full:

> You are in need of a hobby that will distract you from thinking about sex, and thus help you abstain from worldly pleasures. In this way, you can strive to set a noble example, thereby serving your homeland, your nation, and your family. You need an athletic or musical hobby, or to devote yourself to stamp collecting and the like . . . and try to participate in clubs and organizations so that you do not spend time alone practicing your habit. And get out of bed as soon as you awaken.[75]

Today, al-Qabbani's suggestion that the rewards of stamp collecting consti-tuted an effective substitute for an adolescent's experience of "worldly plea-sures" reads like satire, but such an assertion was perfectly in keeping with prevailing medical thought in the 1950s.[76] More importantly, al-Qabbani's answer implied that the mere abstention from said worldly pleasures was in-sufficient to redeem "Mr. M. H." Instead, true redemption would be found in the nature of the activities that replaced "bad habits," that is, they must "set a noble example" to the homeland, the nation, and the family.

Occasionally, a case would present such extraordinary particulars that none of the doctor's previously mentioned treatments would avail. The "be-wildered A. M. from Damascus" provided the most jarring example. In a question that obviously had been severely edited, the petitioner complained of the "irregularity of her menstrual periods and the complete mastery of 'the habit' over her life." In a response that conceals as much as it reveals, al-Qabbani told "bewildered" that "the intensity of your sexual desire, and its awakening before you were five years of age, indicate an imbalance of your internal glands, specifically the secretions of the ovaries." After leaving this tantalizing morsel—abounding in Freudian promise—hanging in the air, the doctor assured his correspondent that there was "no relationship between the irregularity of the menstrual periods you are suffering and the habit that holds sway over you."[77]

Al-Qabbani's clinical diagnosis aside, this exchange is extraordinary. While women constituted a sizeable minority of al-Qabbani's interlocutors, I have encountered no other instance of a female reader discussing masturba-tion in the first person. As a coda to his diagnosis, al-Qabbani advised "A. M." to consult her family doctor "in order to regulate your periods and *reform your heart*." This and other elements of the exchange with "A. M." display a gender bias. First, al-Qabbani's tried-and-true prescriptions for male "prison-ers of the habit," marriage and various forms of sublimation, were apparently judged ineffective for females, whose condition required immediate medical intervention.[78]

The implications are obvious. Al-Qabbani assumed that males' "surren-der" to addiction, however shameful and deplorable, was driven by natural and otherwise "healthy" biological forces that could be channeled into pro-ductive and honorable activities. In contrast, when confronted with a single case of female addiction, al-Qabbani did not recommend a regimen of diet, exercise, and diversion. Nor did he assure his interlocutor that marriage would yield the satisfaction of her sexual desires. Instead, he immediately suspected an underlying physiological pathology.

FOLLOWING THE "UNNATURAL PATH":
SEXUAL DEVIANCE IN MODERN ARAB SOCIETY

In Sabri al-Qabbani's estimate, one form of sexual activity was considerably more transgressive of existing norms than the "excessive" practice of masturbation: the array of desires and practices currently encompassed by the term "homosexuality." Relying almost exclusively on Western medical literature, the doctor conceptualized same-sex desires and practices as both medical conditions and social problems, much as he had with addiction to "the secret habit."[79] His discussion of same-sex relations bears another striking resemblance to his treatment of masturbation: it is almost exclusively concerned with the phenomenon among males.[80]

In one respect, however, al-Qabbani's observations on this violation of sexual norms constituted a departure: his abiding interest in the topic was matched by its apparent sensitivity for his readers. Only two exchanges on same-sex relations appeared in al-Qabbani's columns. Despite his readers' apparent reluctance to enquire, al-Qabbani's interest was such that he dedicated a lengthy article—"al-Shudhudh al-Jinsi Mushkila Ijtima'iyya" (Sexual Deviance Is a Social Problem)—to the subject in *Your Doctor*'s debut issue, as well as several passages in his book *Our Sexual Life.*[81] Yet in order to understand al-Qabbani's observations on "sexual deviance" as a medical and social phenomenon, the topic requires contextualization.

A particular focus of recent scholarship has been the historicization of perceptions of male same-sex desires and practices in the Middle East. Scholars examining medical and legal treatises, biographical dictionaries, belles lettres, and more "popular" genres of literature have demonstrated that the concept of homosexuality was unknown in the premodern Arab-Islamic context. Instead, a very different epistemology governed the understanding of same-sex desires and practices, a system that employed its own particular vocabulary to express significant distinctions between (1) desires and actions, and (2) a given individual's role in the sexual act. This second distinction "was (and still is) imbued with symbolic significance: that between the penetrator and the penetrated."[82]

Prior to the nineteenth century, a male engaging in same-sex relations was assigned one of two defining roles, as either a *luti,* the "active," penetrating partner, or a *ma'bun,* the "passive," penetrated partner.[83] The *luti* was a juridical object, a "morally dissolute person" defined exclusively by his illegal and reprehensible behavior. However disreputable a figure, the *luti* was perceived as "masculine," and his desire to penetrate was deemed thoroughly explicable. Therefore, he was of no interest to physicians. Conversely, the *ma'bun* was perceived as effeminate in nature due to his role in the act of sodomy. The *ma'bun's* willingness, even desire, to be penetrated was perceived as an inherently feminine characteristic and a transgression of "culturally sanctioned gender roles."[84] As a result, the *ma'bun* was, much more than his counterpart, "dishonored and stigmatized." More significantly, his baffling proclivity to "subvert the natural order" and endure the resulting social opprobrium was attributed to an "an inner condition," that is, a physiological pathology, *ubna*.[85]

As with masturbation, elite and popular perceptions of same-sex desire and practice underwent a transformation in the modern period. The nineteenth-century *al-nahda,* or Arab intellectual renaissance, entailed an exponential increase in knowledge production, most of which was heavily influenced by prolonged exposure to European thought in the legal, medical, social, and pseudo-sciences.[86] The literature produced by the new medical specializations of psychology and psychiatry was of particular significance for it introduced Arab intellectuals to a previously unknown "distinct type of person," the homosexual, a new "species" that encompassed the old categories of the *luti,* the *ma'bun,* and all others who experienced same-sex desire.[87]

Exposure to the psychological literature also produced a new term to denote the desires, practices, and characteristics associated with this category of person, and to situate him in relationship to normative practice. The Arabic appellation *al-shudhudh al-jinsi* is a literal translation of "sexual deviance," the umbrella concept under which Western science located a catalog of "abnormal" desires.[88] *Al-shudhudh al-jinsi* became "the most common term used in monographs, the press, and polite company to refer to the Western concept of 'homosexuality.'"[89] Like the euphemism used for masturbation, this "polite" designation for same-sex desires and practices had become entrenched in Arabic's medical and journalistic lexicons by the time al-Qabbani launched his career.[90]

The evidence of al-Qabbani's engagement with the topic of "sexual deviance" is slim in his advice columns. The two rather terse exchanges in which the term appears deal exclusively with the phenomenon among males, are almost exclusively concerned with treatments, and include no attempt to define the condition. We must turn to the other sources mentioned above to delineate the doctor's general understanding of the phenomenon.

The term *al-shudhudh al-jinsi* "ignores the question of who does what to whom," thereby conflating and/or eliding a host of distinctions deemed significant in the premodern era.[91] Al-Qabbani's employment of the concept was in keeping with this trend in two ways. First, his only recorded effort to proffer a definition was suitably expansive: "The practice of sexual activity by means of fornication, sodomy, and lesbianism," all of which were, along with prostitution, characterized as "deviations from the path of reason."[92] In other words, virtually all forms of sexual activity outside the confines of lawful marriage constituted deviance from the norm. Second, he used the terms "deviance" and "sodomy" (*liwata*), as well as their corollaries *shadh* (deviant) and *luti* (sodomite), interchangeably.[93] In the process, he also conflated the "active" *luti* and the "passive" *ma'bun,* collapsing the latter into the former, which in turn became a synonym for "deviant."

Another feature of al-Qabbani's pronouncements on deviance is his apparent acceptance of the phenomenon's "naturalness" and its ubiquity across spatial, temporal, and other boundaries. According to the doctor, male deviance is prevalent in the animal kingdom (particularly among the primates) and in "primitive" societies, was visible and frequently a topic of discussion in ancient civilizations, and is, to varying degrees, present in all modern societies, where it can be detected "in any social class."[94]

Al-Qabbani's observations on the outward signs of deviance are also of interest. Here the modern change in popular and medical perceptions is most apparent. In response to his own rhetorical question about "the characteristics of *lutis,*" the doctor declared, "The very word evokes the image of a thin young man, weak of constitution, soft of voice, and of mostly feminine characteristics. But the truth is that most of them do not display these characteristics clearly."[95] Thus the previously visible and consistent distinction between the *luti* and the effeminate *ma'bun* no longer obtained. Finally, al-Qabbani noted that "due to their vile cravings," *lutis* "live the entirety of their lives as victims of internal torment," producing powerful feelings of self-loathing that are often visible to those around them, especially psychologists and other medical professionals.[96]

The *fuqaha',* or jurisprudents of Islamic law, long debated the origins and nature of *liwat* (sodomy). Some argued that it was "contrary to the natural order of things," while others concluded that it was "a common temptation to be kept in check by reason and religion."[97] A similar tension is present in modern "scientific" discourse, as physicians and secularly inclined social reformers have displayed considerable confusion and disagreement when discussing the causes of same-sex desire and practice.

This ambiguity is reflected in al-Qabbani's discussion of the topic. Al-Qabbani's empirical bent compelled him to acknowledge the near universality of same-sex desire as an easily observable historical phenomenon. Yet he *issue of homosexuality*

also acknowledged the role that social and environmental factors played in enabling the expression of such desires in human societies. Both perspectives are manifest in *Our Sexual Life,* in which al-Qabbani blandly observed, "Some people satisfy their sexual hunger by means of seeking pleasure among individuals of their [own] sex." More significantly, the doctor asserted that, historically, this "satisfaction" had most often been realized "among young females in boarding schools and in the harems of sultans," among "soldiers in barracks," and "especially" among "sailors forced to remain on vessels at sea throughout months-long voyages, far from the opposite sex."[98] Orientalist fantasies about the harem aside, al-Qabbani's "situational" explanation for same-sex practices, which apparently originated with Sigmund Freud, was common among nineteenth-century European and twentieth-century Arab intellectuals.[99]

Ultimately, al-Qabbani yielded to the homiletic, employing a variety of arguments to condemn the "perverted form of love."[100] First, by way of repudiating the "assumption" made by "a great number of sexual deviance's defenders" that "everything that is natural from the biological perspective is necessarily desirable and permissible," he declared that it was "not possible" to tolerate homicide merely because it is sometimes "an expression of a natural impulse."[101] This foray into the realm of moral philosophy, however objectionable to contemporary ears, at least tacitly acknowledged a biological foundation for same-sex desire. In a subsequent passage from the same article, al-Qabbani denied even that possibility, rejecting unattributed assertions that some people are born deviant. He assured the reader that this "false claim" was commonly held by deviants merely because it "absolves them of the sense of responsibility" for their actions.[102]

Sabri al-Qabbani's discussion of the treatment of sexual deviance was remarkably inconsistent, often displaying an even greater degree of confusion, frustration, and uncertainty than his analysis of the condition's causes. Most of these qualities are absent, however, from the two exchanges with readers referenced above. In the first example, al-Qabbani instructed "Mr. Sh. Y. from Syria," who was "afflicted with sexual deviance," to "use Testoviron, the guarantor of your return to the correct path."[103] The second exchange, while comparable in tone and gist, is longer, more detailed, and of greater interest:

QUESTION: Mr. Suhail al-Basha from Halab and Mr. Shukri N. from Hama both suffer from passive sexual deviance.

ANSWER: In view of the fact that you have decided to turn from this unnatural path and reclaim your manhood, you must first change your environment in order to escape from evil company. Then, take injections of 100 milligrams of Testoviron every ten days for a period of three months to be cured, and consult the book *Our Sexual Life*.[104]

This extended reply is notable for its particular designation of "passive sexual deviance," which signified the desire and willingness to be penetrated anally. Al-Qabbani routinely conformed to the modern, "scientific" idiom by conflating the "active" and "passive" partners under the terms *luti* or deviant. Here, however, he appears to have retained the premodern distinction, suggesting that loss of manhood was the inevitable outcome of practicing the "passive" form of deviance.[105] Furthermore, al-Qabbani's injunction to "escape from evil company" implicitly acknowledged the contingent nature of deviance. The doctor also prescribed Testoviron, a compound of testosterone and anabolic steroids, in the form of injections over a prolonged period.[106] This final instruction, and the assertion that this "guarantor" will effect a cure, was consistent with the doctor's customary praxis. It contradicted, however, many of his other observations on the topic. In a previously cited passage from the article "Sexual Deviance Is a Social Problem," al-Qabbani "refuted" claims that deviance was a congenital condition by asserting the impossibility of treating "the afflicted by means of treating the glands."[107] Thus, paradoxically, he appeared to deny the efficacy of hormone therapy and, by extension, all medical treatment targeting metabolic processes.

Elsewhere in the same article, the doctor appeared to abandon medical considerations entirely when discussing the "moral and legal justification for punishing *lutis*." While declaring such justifications "easy to find," he lamented the ineffectiveness and inappropriateness of imprisonment, because it merely "embitters" rather than "corrects" the incarcerated deviant "just as it contributes to the spread of *liwata* among men who would not have otherwise been exposed to it."[108] Here we see the dilemma for medical science: like other pathologies, sexual deviance displays identifiable symptoms and can be transmitted thorough intimate contact. Yet it refuses to disclose its secrets, i.e., its ultimate cause and appropriate remedy.

Unsurprisingly, this apparent intractability yielded frustration. Al-Qabbani cited the opinion of an unnamed "famous British psychologist" that deviants "don't see much hope of changing," and that the possibility of curing habitual practitioners of deviance was "almost nonexistent." The physician's only recourse was to treat the patient's symptoms without expecting a definitive cure. After summarizing the general failure of psychiatry and incarceration to solve the "social problem" of deviance in England, al-Qabbani concluded by presenting this fatalistic declaration of medical science's impotence: "Since there is no hope of a remedy to this problem, the most effective treatment possible is for all healthy [presumably, heterosexual] members of the population to act, in effect, as the doctors and prison guards of those afflicted with sexual deviance."[109]

Clearly, Sabri al-Qabbani considered it a moral imperative for all human beings to transcend their "elemental" desires. His appreciation that medical science alone could not always realize this goal is equally clear. This "anti-positivism" was uncharacteristic for al-Qabbani, and is perhaps the key to his designation of sexual deviance as primarily a social, rather than medical, problem. It also at least partially explains his Orwellian "solution," an informed (presumably via some form of "sex offender" registry) and vigilant citizenry mobilized to act as an army of "*luti* monitors." While this suggestion is horrifying to twenty-first-century ears, it was actually rather enlightened by the standards of the 1950s, when shock treatments (electroconvulsive therapy) and institutionalization were standard elements of American psychiatrists' therapeutic repertoire.

Throughout all of his medical discourse, al-Qabbani was almost silent about same-sex desires and practices among women. In *Our Sexual Life,* the word "lesbianism" is mentioned only in passing as one of several "deviations from the path of reason." In the oft-quoted article "Sexual Deviance Is a Social Problem," al-Qabbani's single reference to the phenomenon was the observation that female deviants were less numerous and less promiscuous than their male counterparts.[110] Finally, the topic was never raised in the doctor's advice columns. This relative silence on female same-sex desire was probably not due to the rarity of the phenomenon or the perceived sensitivity of the topic. As men were the default citizens/subjects of the developmental narrative, the "deviant" sexuality of women was simply less threatening to the "natural" order of things, and therefore of less interest.

Sabri al-Qabbani provided scientific information about sex and reproduction to Syria's citizens, not only to enhance their individual happiness and fulfillment (although this was integral to his mission) but also to channel potentially disruptive sexual desires into practices that enhanced, rather than undermined, the stability and progress of the state and nation. Given sexuality's sensitivity, as well as its productive and destructive capacities, al-Qabbani had to tread carefully when discussing the subject in a public forum. He had to maintain a family-friendly tone in *Your Doctor* in order to achieve the broadest circulation possible, to reach "every citizen," hence the reticence to discuss "openly in the pages of the magazine" issues "inappropriate for circulation among children and adolescents."[111] This need to "observe discretion in answers concerning sexual matters" clearly constrained al-Qabbani, requiring the use of polite but highly normative euphemisms and forestalling the frank discussion of certain topics.

Despite his best efforts to uphold the ideal of conjugal citizenship and to banish multiple forms of sexual deviance from Syrian life, al-Qabbani's exhortations implicitly acknowledged that his project could only achieve partial success. Even as he strove to present his advice in the context of medical science, al-Qabbani could not eschew the powerful cultural norm that demanded the moral condemnation of homosexuality. Such imperatives delimit scientific reason's capacity for social transformation. Furthermore, al-Qabbani was compelled to acknowledge that medical science was unable to explain or "treat" certain male same-sex desires and practices, "pathologies" that were manageable at best and then only with the support of various "civilizing" forces emerging from fields other than medicine. Women's sexuality was also effectively outside the mandate of his scientific-sexual project. Medical science appeared incapable of discussing the sexuality of Arab women as natural, empirically observable, and therefore explicable, as doctors did regarding the sexuality of men.

Despite these shortcomings of science, al-Qabbani achieved his immediate purpose of mounting a pedagogical project that described, defined, and upheld to the "citizens of the Arab East" his vision of a sexually normal, healthy society. The obstacles to fully translating this vision into reality serve as a reminder of the limits on any pedagogical project that seeks to mass-produce ideal citizens. The fallible mortals who are the objects of these efforts will almost always fall short of the modern expert's visions of reform.

Conclusion

Citizens on the Tenth Day

On the tenth day the trainer, the pupils, the tiger and the cage disappeared: the tiger became a citizen and the cage a city.

—ZAKARIYA TAMER, *Tigers on the Tenth Day*

THE QUOTATION ABOVE is taken from *Tigers on the Tenth Day,* an allegorical short story written by Zakariya Tamer, the Syrian master of that genre. In this story, a tiger, recently captured in the jungle and placed in a zoo cage, encounters an animal trainer who is pleased to demonstrate to his assistants the most effective means of breaking wild beasts. Over nine days of carefully calibrated manipulation, coercion, and humiliation, the proud, free tiger is rendered docile and conditioned to eager and unquestioning servitude.

On the morning of the tenth day, this broken creature becomes a "citizen" (*muwatin*). Tamer's use of this term to describe the tiger's new state reflects the outcome of one of the key processes unfolding throughout Syria's postcolonial history, the citizen's transformation from subject of "moral and material" development to object of authoritarian mobilization. In *Tigers on the Tenth Day,* originally published during the Islamist uprising (1976–1982) against the regime of Hafez al-Assad, Tamer knowingly used a pedagogical metaphor—the animal trainer's "education" of both the tiger and his assistants—to illustrate this process.

This Orwellian tale also expresses a concern informing much of the scholarly literature: why did Syria, a country with venerable traditions of international commerce, decentralized political authority, and religious and ethnic diversity, become a populist-authoritarian dictatorship of pronounced sectarian complexion, replete with oppressive security services; a bloated, corrupt, and incompetent bureaucracy; a stagnant command economy exploited by regime-crony oligarchs; and a stultifying official culture? One of my abiding research objectives is deflecting the normative and teleological aspects of this question while engaging with the serious historiographical concerns that underlie it. Thus this study has explored the role developmental visions for Syria's future played in the "practical politics" that produced this outcome.[1] It has also attempted to demonstrate that the undemocratic outcome was not inexplicable or antithetical to what preceded it. It was, instead, the product of a complex and contingent process that always contained authoritarian currents and tendencies.

This book has offered a cultural history of a critical episode in Syria's history, an abortive experiment with democratic governance in the context of postcolonial development. Although the specifics of this story are Syrian, the larger historical processes and trends were in operation throughout the region, the most significant of which was the increasing resort to authoritarian solutions. The editorial with which I opened this study—Najat Qassab Hasan's nostalgic recounting of the Syrian Army's ceremonial instantiation of its independence from foreign command—suggests the ease with which Qassab Hasan's civilian subject of "law and order" could be replaced by another representation of the model citizen, the professional soldier.[2]

Qassab Hasan's commemoration of 'Adnan al-Malki's role in the ceremony consecrating the army's new flag lauded that institution for its "spirit and its closeness to the people," and proclaimed the "abiding love" tying it to "the nation that offers its sons and the blood of its sons."[3] This assertion of the insoluble bond among people, army, and nation facilitates the slippage from the self-abnegation of domestic and bureaucratic service to self-sacrifice under arms. The militarization of citizenship flows from the unforgiving logic of developmentalism in the nationalist mode, which imbues such sacrificial acts with the character of a secular sacrament.[4]

THE NEXUS OF EXPERTISE AND MEDIA

The immediate purpose of the pedagogical discourses analyzed in this study was the construction of two subjects—the modern expert and the citizen— who formed a symbiotic relationship at the core of the developmental project. The experts—doctor, attorney, and professional soldier—described or exemplified complementary aspects, or "virtues," of civic-republican citizenship. These multiple forms of expertise were deployed to instruct citizens in the arts of governing the self, governing the family, and governing their fellow citizens, who were "always in the making" as part of an ongoing project that was an essential element of the French Mandate's "colonial legacy."[5] Imbued with the "doctrine of progress," this project framed the discursive landscape of the postwar Arab world.[6]

In the Syrian case, each form of expertise emphasized specific characteristics of the citizen. The doctor affirmed the citizen's rational engagement with—and triumph over—natural phenomena like disease and sexual desire. The lawyer upheld the civilizing influence of the citizen's service to socioeconomic institutions like the family, community, and state. The media campaign surrounding the soldier professed the redemptive power of the citizen's sacrifice on behalf of the nation. Collectively, medical, legal, and martial expertise worked to provide the scientific, moral, and ideological bases for a particular way of seeing and living in the world, and enumerated the consequences of failing to do so.

The discourse of developmental expertise in 1950s Syria, like its cognates throughout the developing world, was frequently presented as a "detached center of rationality" above politics while expressing cultural norms and contentious ideological commitments, and privileging certain modes of social and political thought and practice over others.[7] In the process, it presented a "normative construction" of citizenship that was unattainable in the volatile political environment of Syria's Democratic Years.[8] The pervasive presentation of this utopian ideal intensified developmental ambitions, contributing to an extant tendency to authoritarian measures.

This discourse of expertise emanated from a common political milieu and featured reformers who, while individually significant, also shared similar objectives and were well known to one another. Working in conjunction, these texts evoked countless individual acts of imagining a modern, strong, prosperous nation—an "imagined community" in the Andersonian sense. And, as in Benedict Anderson's compelling explanation for the persistence of nationalist sentiment, mass media had the most significant role in this process, supported by private capital, a cadre of professional bureaucrats, and (when necessary) the coercive power of the military and security establishments.[9]

Without access to mass media, however, the developmental aspirations analyzed in this study would have been little more than opinions shared at dinner tables, in cafés, or in professional gatherings. A stable platform from which to mount a sustained campaign of developmental suasion required considerable resources. While several wealthy members of Syria's political elite owned mass-media outlets, these were almost exclusively daily newspapers that served as mouthpieces for the narrow interests of their owners or the political parties with which they were affiliated. None of these men had the requisite vision, skills, or claims to developmental expertise to attempt such a campaign. Only those who enjoyed access to mass media *and* possessed credible expertise could exercise such authority effectively. As we have seen, these experts tended to emerge "from or below the median" of Syrian society.[10]

THE ELEMENTS OF VIRTUOUS CITIZENSHIP

why? this is a fascinating phenomenon

In postcolonial Syria, the virtuous citizen displayed several aspects: the rational citizen, the law-abiding citizen, the patriarchal citizen, the martial citizen, the hygienic citizen, the conjugal citizen, and others. As the project of constructing this citizen was an exercise in both inclusion and exclusion, the virtuous citizen also defined the subjects and forces that threatened it: the backward, ignorant peasant; the weak, foolish husband and father; the traitor to Arabism; and the sexual deviant. Together, this array of virtues and vices produced a developmentalist and teleological vision of modern citizenship.

Yet the civilizing of backward, ignorant, and dissolute members of the population was not an exclusively secular project. As other scholars have noted, Islamists and secular nationalists alike used state and private resources to pursue their dreams of the "moral transformation of entire populations."[11] Just as the modern state gradually absorbed many Islamic institutions (e.g., pious endowments and *shari'a* courts) and coopted prominent *'ulama'*, the progressive, modernist advocates of development adopted and assimilated Islamic concepts, vocabulary, modes of argumentation, and discursive genres. This untroubled synthesis raises a key epistemological question—"the relative authority of religious knowledge and scientific knowledge" during the twentieth century.[12]

This synthesis also indicates the durability and adaptability of Islamic discursive forms and undermines the stable, coherent binary of mutually exclusive categories—the Islamic and the secular—that have featured so frequently in Western scholarship on the Middle East. This purported dichotomy is absent from Syria's constitution, legal codes, predominant social and cultural practices, and public discussions of development and modernization in the 1950s, the putative apogee of secular thought and practice in the region.[13]

This absence demonstrates that the period 1967–1973, which was dominated by Israel's crushing defeat of so many ostensibly secular, leftist regimes and movements, did not, as many have asserted, constitute a watershed between two mutually exclusive eras, the first characterized by the predominance of secular-nationalist modes of thought, speech, and sociopolitical engagement, and the second just as clearly defined by the Islamist nature of these phenomena.[14] Islamic principles of whatever stripe were never absent from political discourse; even that of "men of science" like Sabri al-Qabbani, nominally irreligious nationalists like 'Adnan al-Malki, or avowed communists like Najat Qassab Hasan.

The concept of secularization cannot account for the modern period's defining historical processes or capture their complexity. The frequent conflation of secularism and democracy is equally unhelpful in explaining Syria's historical experience of the modern. In February 1954, a majority of Syria's political and military elites, intellectuals, and professionals collectively chose civilian, parliamentary government over the populist authoritarianism of military strongmen. It does not necessarily follow that the result would be anything Western observers would recognize as secular. In fact, the public discourse of the Democratic Years betrayed little evidence that opting for democratic governance demanded or even suggested a choice between the secular and the Islamic.

We lack sufficient evidence to assess how the majority of Syria's population responded to this pedagogical project. Nevertheless, the omnipresence of developmental discourse about citizenship and the volume of the public's correspondence with the doctor, the lawyer, and the soldier's hagiographers indicate that the literate segments of Syria's population engaged with—and largely accepted—many of the precepts underlying this construction of the citizen as the subject of development and progress. These precepts also informed the state's foundational documents, the ideology of virtually every political party, and the ethos of most state institutions.

Yet the perceived urgency of development—which inspired the fabrication of readers' questions—suggests the doubts its purveyors' harbored about the possibility of realizing its dreams. Anxieties about the people's capacity to bear the "normative burden" of citizenship are at the heart of this project.[15] The self-sacrificing devotion of the martial citizen can serve one ideology as easily as another, and can be turned against those whose aspirations engendered it. In other words, the martial citizen is inherently vulnerable to transformation from democratic subject into authoritarian object. Likewise, the variety and intensity of human sexual desire cannot be contained within (or tamed by) conjugality, and the law relies on people—even as it shapes them—to cultivate and practice virtue. It cannot efface self-indulgence, poor judgment, or foolishness from any human society. It can only seek to redress the damage caused by the free exercise of such character flaws.

Another less clearly articulated but nonetheless present threat to the project of modern citizenship was sectarianism. According to citizenship theory, a "structural and cultural precondition" underlying the phenomenon's "modernity" is "the erosion of particularistic commitments" like the assertion of sectarian over national identities.[16] The logic of the nation-state refuses such commitments and views their continuing salience as "an illegitimate and divisive force."[17] In post-independence Syria, nationalist narratives of various types shared certain interdependent assumptions about sectarianism. First, they assumed that sectarianism was an artificial phenomenon engendered and nourished by agents of foreign interests. Second, they perceived sectarianism as a developmental issue, that is, one of the chief indices of backwardness, and therefore a primary object of remediation. As a result, these narratives deemed those who displayed sectarian commitments to be agents of division who had, by definition, failed to embrace the default national identity of citizen.

But, as many scholars have noted, sectarianism (as minoritarian identity, majoritarian prejudice, and a host of other forms) is not a premodern, externally generated threat to Syria's modernity. It is a distinctly modern phenomenon produced by the same forces and processes that engendered the nation-state. In other words, modernity produces the nation-state, the citizenry, the sect, and the discourses surrounding and linking all three.[18] Knowing sectarianism's divisive power, the exemplars of modern citizenship featured in this study were reticent to raise this specter in public forums like mass media. It appeared instead in allusions to places and practices with which sectarian identities were associated in popular consciousness.

CITIZENS SINCE THE DEMOCRATIC YEARS

Syria's experiment with democratic governance ended when the country was merged with Egypt to form the United Arab Republic, a pan-Arabist experiment that ended in a military coup in September 1961. The UAR experience, while dispelling most Syrians' illusions about the benevolence of Gamal Abdel Nasser and his colleagues in Egypt's Revolutionary Command Council, convinced Syria's developmentally minded military officers that popular mobilization in the service of national development could not be achieved via "bourgeois democratic" means like parliamentary elections. The country soon returned to and surpassed its previous patterns of civil-military conflict and political instability: army officers of various political affiliations mounted a dizzying series of coups, counter-coups, and unsuccessful coup attempts; Syria's cities witnessed general strikes and riots suppressed with ferocious violence; fratricidal conflict within the armed forces spilled into the streets of Damascus and Aleppo; and Syria's post-1963 Ba'thist governments appeared to be little more than engines of exile, imprisonment, and execution. Relative stability was finally achieved after Hafez al-Asad's "correctionist movement" coup in November 1970.

Throughout this period of instability and much of the Asad era (1970–2000), the project of shaping citizens continued, dramatically expanded in scope and ambition, and pursued with increasingly coercive, totalitarian means. The grotesque outcome is analyzed in Lisa Wedeen's study of Asad's personality cult, which produced armies of docile "citizens" compelled to participate in the "politics of public dissimulation." Repeatedly acting "as if" they venerated Syria's late president, citizens had to behave "as if they were children and Asad were their father."[19] Zakariya Tamer's *Tigers on the Tenth Day* renders this outcome allegorically. On the eighth day of the tiger's instruction, his trainer orders him to applaud enthusiastically and sincerely in response to a speech. Addressing his fellow "citizens," *muwatinun*, the trainer delivers a brief declaration of eternal steadfastness in the face of "hostile forces" that is a sublime parody of the turgid speeches delivered countless times by the region's populist authoritarian rulers.[20]

This, the tiger's penultimate lesson, was preceded by commands to behave "as if" he were a member of other species, mewing like a kitten and braying like a donkey for his food. This trope—the totalitarian ambition to transform nature—appears so frequently in Tamer's stories that it prompted a contemporary, the late poet and literary critic Muhammad al-Maghut, to compare Tamer to Charles Darwin: the latter "showing how humans developed from monkeys," and the former "how humans could be manipulated into becoming monkeys."[21]

In the 1990s, it appeared to many observers that the Asad regime had accomplished a similarly transformative project, producing "malleable and loyal citizens" on a mass scale.[22] Yet critics of the Arab world's authoritarian politics have questioned this apparent redefinition of the term, arguing that "one cannot . . . speak of 'citizens' in countries where the ruling powers, republicans though they may be, see only subjects" (in the political rather than the philosophical sense).[23] Such regimes obviously cannot see citizens as autonomous possessors of agency. These rulers see, instead, "objects of governmentality."[24]

Beyond semantics, however, lies a more significant issue. In 2011, the residents of the Syrian city of Daraa displayed their agency and autonomy by taking to the streets to protest local police and security service personnel's arbitrary exercise of power, inspiring similar actions across Syria and demonstrating the incompleteness of the transformative project. The Asad regime's security services crushed this initially peaceful movement, sparking an armed uprising. This new "struggle for Syria" makes its predecessor seem positively restrained and genteel, and the character of Syrian politics has descended from the merely "pathological" to the apocalyptic.[25]

One wonders what constructions of citizenship the ongoing nightmare will produce. The history of the Democratic Years provides many lessons to Syrians who wish to reclaim what "might have been," for the experience of such failed experiments need not be relegated to the realm of nostalgic sentiment or to general despair over the "irreversibility" of history. Such experiences can also inspire "prospective nostalgia," and thereby inform pluralistic and democratic visions of Syria's future.[26]

Notes

INTRODUCTION

1. Najat Qassab Hasan, "Sahib al-Raya," *al-Jundi,* May 5, 1955, 21.

2. This genre of literature emerged in the seventeenth century, in the wake of the Ottomans' conquest of the Arab lands. For an overview of the relevant literature, see Sajdi, *The Barber of Damascus,* 224n.

3. This specification of "moral and material" uplifting appeared frequently in the discourse of the period. See, e.g., special magazine *Syria* published in English by the Directorate-General of Information in 1953 to promote the upcoming Damascus International Exposition, 41.

4. This phrase is taken from the preface to the column "al-Muwatin wa al-Qanun" (The Citizen and the Law) in the magazine *al-Idhaʻa al-Suriyya* (Syrian Broadcasting), which stated, "Today we publish a question addressed by a citizen to the attorney Najat Qassab Hasan, who has, as is his custom, included in his response answers that have a variety of legal, social, and moral directives to elucidate the features of the virtuous citizen." *Al-Idhaʻa al-Suriyya,* October 16, 1955, 10.

5. Lynn Hunt, "Introduction," in Hunt, ed., *The New Cultural History,* 17.

6. Ibid., 12.

7. Chatterjee, *The Politics of the Governed,* 37–38.

8. These phrases are borrowed from Omnia El Shakry, who argues, "It is the *particularity* of European history and civilization *masquerading as the universal,* that constitutes the fundamental plot of colonialism." El Shakry, *The Great Social Laboratory,* 4.

9. Scott, *Gender and the Politics of History,* 2.

10. "The Covenant of the League of Nations," Avalon Project, Yale Law School, http://avalon.law.yale.edu/20th_century/leagcov.asp.

11. My interest in this and many related subjects is thanks to Timothy Mitchell's *Rule of Experts.*

12. Prakash, *Another Reason;* Chatterjee, *The Nation and Its Fragments.*

13. Mustafa al-Hajj Ibrahim, "The Citizen and the Security Man," *Journal of the Police and Public Security,* April 1953, 24.

14. See, e.g., al-ʻAsh, "Who Is the Virtuous Citizen?" 6–7.

15. For a summary overview of "multilevel," "relational," and "transnational" forms of citizenship in recent theory, see Yarwood, *Citizenship,* 46, 174.

16. Ratib al-Husami, "The Citizen and the Radio," *al-Idhaʻa al-Suriyya,* April 1, 1954, 1.

17. The "ruralization" of the Syrian armed forces, as well as the civil service, began under al-Shishakli, accelerated during the Democratic Years, and was com-

pleted by the post-1963 regimes of the Ba'th Military Committee. Batatu, *Syria's Peasantry*, 156.

18. Abi-Mershed, *Apostles of Modernity*, 5.

19. Al-'Itri, *Hadith al-'Abqariyyat*, 210.

20. 'Isseh, a prominent leftist, would subsequently publish the daily newspaper *al-Ra'y al-'Amm* (Public Opinion), to which Qassab Hasan would contribute editorials under a pseudonym.

21. "Nashrat al-Akhbar," *al-Jami'a*, March 1, 1954, 32.

22. U.S. Department of State, DA Intelligence Report, August 10, 1956.

23. Surkis, *Sexing the Citizen*, 123.

24. Al-Malki's moniker is borrowed from Abu al-Hajjaj Hafiz's *Shahid al-'Uruba*.

25. Chatterjee, *The Politics of the Governed*, 139.

1. SYRIA DURING THE DEMOCRATIC YEARS

1. According to the prevailing periodization scheme, Syria's modern history is organized as follows: Colonialist Occupation (1920–1946), The Era of Nationalist Government (1946–1949), The Era of Military Coups (1949–1954), The Democratic Years (1954–1958), The United Arab Republic (1958–1961), The Secessionist Regime (1961–1963), The Ba'thist Revolution (1963–1966), The Era of the Neo-Ba'th (1966–1970), and The Era of the Correctionist Movement (1970–2000).

2. This is not to suggest that all share this view. A quite divergent reconstruction of Damascene history, one embraced by comparable numbers of "bourgeoisie" (including several relatives of Najat Qassab Hasan), is examined by Christa Salamandra in her "Consuming Damascus."

3. Syrian Republic, *al-Dustur al-Suri*. See also Khadduri, "Constitutional Development in Syria," and Manley, "Document." One significant exception concerned the peasants, whose "associational rights" were, unlike those of urban laborers, glaringly absent from the text. Heydemann, *Authoritarianism in Syria*, 65.

4. Petran, *Syria*, 107.

5. Kassir, *Being Arab*, 1–2.

6. Heydemann, *Authoritarianism in Syria*, 33, 53–54, 74–76.

7. Hallaq, *The Impossible State*, 96. The Ottoman Empire's initial legislation concerning nationality and citizenship appeared in 1869. Parolin, *Citizenship in the Arab World*, 73–74.

8. Thompson, *Colonial Citizens*.

9. Parolin, *Citizenship in the Arab World*, 88; Anderson, "The Syrian Law of Personal Status," 34, 35.

10. Ibid. For a brief overview of this process, see Sfeir, *Modernization of the Law*, 25, 26, 195–196. For the specifics of the Ottoman Family Code, the template for all future Syrian codes, see Tucker, "Revisiting Reform." For the various ways in which the "Islamic" component has been codified in Syria's post-independence constitutions and Codes of Personal Status, see Khadduri, "Constitutional Development in

Syria"; Winder, "The Establishment of Islam," 216–217; and Anderson, "The Syrian Law of Personal Status," 34–39.

11. Syrian Republic, *al-Dustur al-Suri,* 402–404.

12. Ibid., 402, 403, 411.

13. Heater, *A Brief History of Citizenship,* 4–5.

14. Such notions, which appear in Greek political discourse, medieval Islamic philosophy, and French Revolutionary discourse, were prevalent among Middle East intellectuals by the early twentieth century. See, e.g., Germani, *Jean-Paul Marat,* 166, and Schayegh, *Who Is Knowledgeable Is Strong,* 8–9.

15. Heater, *A Brief History of Citizenship,* 120.

16. This notion, of course, first gained currency with Patrick Seale's *The Struggle for Syria.*

17. See, e.g., ibid., and Malcolm H. Kerr's *The Arab Cold War,* which focuses more on Gamal Abdel Nasser and examines the continuation of the struggle after its (temporary) resolution in Syria.

18. For details of the defense pact, see Seale, *The Struggle for Syria,* and Heydemann, *Authoritarianism in Syria.*

19. Ibid., 80.

20. Yaqub, *Containing Arab Nationalism,* 49–50, 149. See also Thompson, *Justice Interrupted,* 229–230, and Ismael and Ismael, *The Communist Movement,* 49.

21. Yaqub, *Containing Arab Nationalism,* 155; Thompson, *Justice Interrupted,* 230.

22. Ismael and Ismael, *The Communist Movement,* 49.

23. Yaqub, *Containing Arab Nationalism,* 184; Ismael and Ismael, *The Communist Movement,* 49; Heydemann, *Authoritarianism in Syria,* 15.

24. Be'eri, *Army Officers,* 334.

25. Batatu, "Some Observations on the Social Roots," 341; Khoury, *Syria and the French Mandate,* 629; Halpern, "Middle Eastern Armies," 296–297.

26. Drysdale, "Ethnicity in the Syrian Officer Corps," 361.

27. Torrey, "The Role of the Military," 54.

28. For details of early development plans and objectives, see Petran, *Syria,* 88.

29. Heydemann, *Authoritarianism,* 10–11, 56, 61, 55, 14.

30. Ibid., 55–56, 32–33, 52–53, 47.

31. Sayigh, *The Economies of the Arab World,* 237. See also Makdisi, "Fixed Capital Formation in Syria."

32. Sayigh, *The Economies of the Arab World,* 229; Petran, *Syria,* 85.

33. Heydemann, *Authoritarianism in Syria,* 37, 42.

34. Hanan Qassab Hasan, interview, February 27, 2002.

35. Watenpaugh, "Bourgeois Modernity," xvii.

36. Sennett, *The Fall of Public Man,* 48.

37. See, e.g., Martin, "Presenting the 'True Face of Syria'."

38. While the total population of Syria increased by 29% between 1950 and 1960, Damascus experienced a 47.6% increase in population during the same period. Davis, *World Urbanization,* 74, 154, 201.

39. Ratib al-Husami, "The Citizen and the Radio," *al-Idha'a al-Suriyya*, April 1, 1954, 1.

40. International Bank for Reconstruction and Development, *The Economic Development of Syria*, 158–160.

41. El Shakry, *The Great Social Laboratory*, 91, 111, 114–115, 136–137.

42. The latter anxiety was clearly expressed in numerous pedagogical features about polite behavior in a modern environment. See, e.g., the "Studies in Etiquette" series in *Tabibak*, October 1957, 75–77; November 1957, 65–68; December 1957, 43–46; January 1958, 47–50; and February 1958, 25–28.

43. For details, see 'Uthman, *al-Sihafa al-Suriyya*, 241, 295, 310, 324–328; Khadur, *al-Sihafa al-Suriyya*, 373–421; Iliyas, *Tatawwur al-Sihafa al-Suriyya*, 2:89–94, 1:139–148; and McFadden, *Daily Journalism in the Arab States*, 44–56. To date, there has yet to appear a comprehensive study of Syria's press laws in the post–World War II period comparable to Shams al-Din Rifa'i's *Sharh Qawanin al-Sihafiyya*.

44. Founded in 1946, the Syrian Broadcasting Service was expanded greatly under the country's series of post–World War II military dictators. By the time Qassab Hasan's broadcasts began, all of Syria's five largest cities were receiving Arabic-language broadcasting for an average of thirteen hours daily. "Syrian Broadcasting Program," *al-Idha'a al-Suriyya*, October 16, 1955, 16–29; Boyd, *Broadcasting in the Arab World*, 84.

45. See, e.g., *al-Idha'a al-Suriyya*, May 16, 1954, 9; November 16, 1955, 2; January 1, 1956, 5; and January 16, 1956, 8.

46. For details of press legislation in the previous period, see 'Uthman, *al-Sihafa al-Suriyya*, 241, 295, 310, 324–328; Khadur, *al-Sihafa al-Suriyya*, 373–421; Iliyas, *Tatawwur al-Sihafa al-Suriyya*, 2:89–94, 1:139–148; and McFadden, *Daily Journalism in the Arab States*, 44–56. Additional legislative measures, like Law no. 169 of May 12, 1954, were passed to abrogate earlier ones (no. 53, October 8, 1949; no. 134, October 8, 1953) that had banned specific publications or categories of publication. Attempts to reinstate earlier controls were unsuccessful. For details of Law no. 169, see Khadur, *al-Sihafa al-Suriyya*, 410–413, and Iliyas, *Tatawwur al-Sihafa al-Suriyya*, 90. For details of Prime Minister Sabri al-'Asali's abortive attempt to ban newspapers through new licensing requirements, see Seale, *The Struggle for Syria*, 171. For details of how individual publishers operated under these conditions, see Babil, *Sihafa wa Siyasa*.

47. I identified more than 260 separate titles before I stopped counting.

48. The term "daily newspaper" is a self-description that appeared on both the periodical's masthead and its government license.

49. Thompson, *Colonial Citizens*, 210.

50. Anderson, *Imagined Communities*; Chartier, "Texts, Printings, Readings," 174–175.

51. The most notable of these examine an earlier period. See, e.g., Gelvin, *Divided Loyalties*; Thompson, *Colonial Citizens*; and Fahmy, *Ordinary Egyptians*.

52. McFadden, *Daily Journalism in the Arab States*, 9, 32–34.

53. For one such rare and humorous exception, see Martin, "Presenting the 'True Face of Syria'."

54. McFadden, *Daily Journalism in the Arab States,* 30–32, 74–80.

55. U.S. Department of State, DA Intelligence Report, August 10, 1956.

56. See Heydemann, *Authoritarianism in Syria.*

2. THE CITIZEN AND THE LAW

1. Najat Qassab Hasan is frequently mentioned in histories of the press and other media, and in the papers of the period's most prominent intellectual figures. See, e.g., al-Musuli, *al-Sihafa al-Suriyya wa Rijaluha,* 280, in which Qassab Hasan is afforded equal importance with Fu'ad al-Shayyib, Yahya al-Shihabi, Sa'id al-Jaza'iri, 'Abd al-Sallam al-'Ujayli, and Ahmad al-Jundi. See also 'Uthman, *al-Sihafa al-Suriyya,* 225–228; Iliyas, *Tatawwur al-Sihafa al-Suriyya,* 1:494–495; and al-Mashut, *Tarikh al-Sihafa al-Suriyya,* 319. The precise year of Qassab Hasan's birth is in dispute, with sources variously claiming 1919, 1920, or 1921.

2. When Qassab Hasan entered the Teachers' College, it represented the best education possible for a young man of limited means, as it offered free tuition and a monthly stipend. Hanan Qassab Hasan, interview, February 27, 2002.

3. The sources for this and all subsequent biographical information are Faris, ed., *Man Hum fi al-'Alam al-'Arabi,* 507–508; Moubayed, *Steel and Silk,* 565; and Hanan Qassab Hasan, interview, February 27, 2002.

4. The most famous example is perhaps Qassab Hasan's sister Najwa, who was, until September 2003, Syria's minister of culture. Qassab Hasan's younger brother, Burhan, was a politically active military officer, important figure in the petroleum industry, and author. See Faris, ed., *Man Hum fi al-'Alam al-'Arabi,* 507, and 'Ayyash, *Mu'jam al-Mu'allifin,* 419. Biographies of other relatives can be found in Farfur, *A'lam Dimashq fi al-Qarn,* 6, 43, 121.

5. The most important of Qassab Hasan's earliest journalistic endeavors was his role, along with Nash'at al-Tighilbi, Sabri al-Qabbani, and others, in the foundation of the satirical publication *'Asa al-Janna* (Heaven's Wand) in 1947. He subsequently contributed to Sidqi Isma'il's satirical samizdat publication *al-Kalb* (The Dog), and was solely or partially responsible for similar publications like *al-Qindil* (The Lantern), *Brazil al-Sham* (Brazil of Damascus), and *al-Gazetta* (The Gazette).

6. For the context, see Laqueur, *Communism and Nationalism,* 154–156; Ismael, *The Communist Movement,* 40–58; and Batatu, *Syria's Peasantry,* 120.

7. See Moubayed, *Steel and Silk,* 565. Qassab Hasan subsequently hosted numerous television programs. The one most comparable to *al-Muwatin wa al-Qanun* was *Wamadat* (Reflections), which dealt with the "basics of civil law as they concerned the citizen, i.e., the proper behavior of the citizen in society." Hanan Qassab Hasan, interview, February 27, 2002.

8. The popularity of *al-Muwatin wa al-Qanun* and Qassab Hasan's resultant fame are confirmed by the fact his biographical sketch was not included in George

Faris's *Man Huwa fi Suriya 1949* but did appear in the subsequent (1957) Faris, ed., *Man Hum fi al-'Alam al-'Arabi.*

9. As many of these program's transcripts are unavailable to researchers, I have occasionally drawn cases from Qassab Hasan's subsequently published *Qisas al-Nas.* I supplement this analysis by drawing on an interview with his daughter Hanan and on his editorials in other periodicals. These include the previously cited Qassab Hasan, *Qisas al-Nas,* as well as *Qanun al-Ahwal* and *Qanun wa Qada'.* The editorials appeared under the self-deprecating pseudonym Fasih (Eloquent) in a regular column, *Bi al-'Arabi al-Fasih* (Plain Speaking), which appeared in the former director of Syrian Broadcasting Ahmad 'Isseh's daily newspaper *al-Ra'y al-'Amm* (Public Opinion). I am grateful to Professor Hanan Qassab Hasan for making me aware of this column and her late father's role in writing it.

10. Qassab Hasan, *Qisas al-Nas,* 11–13.

11. Hanan Qassab Hasan, interview, February 27, 2002.

12. Turner, *Religion and Modern Society,* xv–xvi; Asad, *Formations of the Secular,* 253–254.

13. Qassab Hasan, *Qisas al-Nas,* 12.

14. Ibid.

15. See Deeb, *An Enchanted Modern,* and Stanton, *"This Is Jerusalem Calling,"* 139–148.

16. Muhammad Khalid Masud, Brinkley Messick, and David S. Powers, "Muftis, Fatwas, and Islamic Legal Interpretation," in Masud et al., eds., *Islamic Legal Interpretation,* 26–27.

17. Reid, *Lawyers and Politics,* 183, 224; Khoury, *Syria and the French Mandate,* 414.

18. Berkey, *Popular Preaching and Religious Authority,* 89–90. The most illuminating survey of such opinions appears in Masud et al., "Muftis, Fatwas, and Islamic Legal Interpretation," 8, 18, 27.

19. Berger, "The Sharia and Legal Pluralism," 116, 117.

20. The most succinct scholarly definition of the fatwa is a "formal statement of authoritative opinion on a point of Shari'a [Islamic law]." Holt et al., eds., *The Cambridge History of Islam,* 907.

21. The program first appeared in the schedule at 2:45 PM on Saturday, January 1, 1955. *Al-Idha'a al-Suriyya,* January 1, 1955, 25. The title of the program then changed to *al-Muwatin wa al-Qanun* as of Saturday, January 22, 1955. *Al-Idha'a al-Suriyya,* January 16, 1955, 24.

22. The classic interpretation of the "judgment/application" dichotomy is as follows: "The authority of a judgment is narrowly specific (*khass*), applying only to a particular case and its participants, while that of the fatwa is general (*'amm*), potentially extending beyond the circumstances of the given questioner to govern all equivalent cases." Masud et al., "Muftis, Fatwas, and Islamic Legal Interpretation," 19.

23. Ibid., 18, 22.

24. See, e.g., *al-Idha'a al-Suriyya,* October 16, 1955, 10–11.

25. Gaffney, *The Prophet's Pulpit*, 35.

26. These included Nash'at al-Tighilbi, 'Uthman Shahrur, Tal'at Tighalbi, Hasib Kayyali, Yahya Shihabi, George Shatila, Sabri al-Qabbani, and Nizar al-Qabbani, to name but a few.

27. Ahmad 'Isseh was one of al-Shishakli's closest and most trusted advisers. He, his private secretary Qadri al-Qal'aji, and Director of Information and Propaganda Nazih Hakim, were known collectively as "the three graces."

28. For biographical information on 'Isseh, see Moubayed, *Steel and Silk,* 505–506; Seale, *The Struggle for Syria*, 125; Faris, ed., *Man Huwa fi Suriya 1949,* 513; and Faris, ed., *Man Hum fi al-'Alam al-'Arabi,* 421–422.

29. This is a region-wide phenomenon that has been understudied. For an exception, see Stanton, *"This Is Jerusalem Calling."* See, e.g., *al-Idha'a al-Suriyya*, May 16, 1954, 9; November 16, 1955, 2; January 1, 1956, 5; and January 16, 1956, 8. See also the regular feature "al-'Alam Yataqaddam" (The World Advances). Other "professional" advice programs appeared on *al-Idha'a al-Suriyya*. Perhaps the most notable of these was "The Peasant Asks and the Radio Answers." See, e.g., *al-Idha'a al-Suriyya,* June 16, 1954, 31.

30. See, e.g., Ahmad 'Isseh's inaugural effort, which stressed the journal's low price and its calculated balance between "simplicity and elegance," between "specialist" and "comprehensive" content, and between the "light" and the "serious," all of which were designed to make it "the magazine for every member of the family." 'Isseh, "This Magazine," *al-Idha'a al-Suriyya*, September 1, 1953, 1.

31. Ratib al-Husami, "The Citizen and the Radio," *al-Idha'a al-Suriyya*, April 1, 1954, 1.

32. Qassab Hasan, *Qanun al-Ahwal,* 10.

33. Masud et al., "Muftis, Fatwas, and Islamic Legal Interpretation," 22.

34. Najat Qassab Hasan, "Introduction to al-Muwatin wa al-Qanun," *al-Idha'a al-Suriyya,* October 16, 1955, 10.

35. Hanan Qassab Hasan, interview, February 27, 2002. While convention prohibits muftis from exploring "purely hypothetical or imaginary" issues, Qassab Hasan's other invention, the names of his correspondents, is a classic convention of the traditional fatwa noted in chapter 1. See, e.g., Masud et al., "Muftis, Fatwas, and Islamic Legal Interpretation," 22–23.

36. Chatterjee, *The Politics of the Governed,* 30.

37. Hanan Qassab Hasan, interview, February 27, 2002.

38. Qassab Hasan, *Qisas al-Nas,* 11.

39. Both cities are routinely declared the oldest continuously inhabited settlements on earth.

40. When addressing the rancor of urban life, Qassab Hasan often declared, "How good it would be if every relationship were based on cordiality and friendship instead of being a cause for conflict or enmity." See, e.g., *al-Idha'a al-Suriyya,* November 1, 1955, 12.

41. *Al-Idha'a al-Suriyya,* January 16, 1955.

42. The Midan, far outside the walls of Old Damascus and long since absorbed by the city, was once divided into three sections, Lower Midan, Middle Midan, and Upper Midan. For more on the history of the Midan, see Rafeq, "The Social and Economic Structure of Bab al-Musalla."

43. *Al-Idha'a al-Suriyya*, January 16, 1955, 8.

44. Ibid.

45. *Al-Idha'a al-Suriyya*, January 16, 1956, 10.

46. Ibid. Such invocations were yet another common feature of the fatwa adopted by Qassab Hasan. Masud et al., "Muftis, Fatwas, and Islamic Legal Interpretation," 24.

47. This term is derived from the Arabic root that describes states of emptiness or vacancy and processes of voiding or evacuation. It denotes a practice by which a person who, by virtue of longstanding practice and/or a legally binding contract, possesses the right (usufruct for land or a lease for structures) to use a piece of property and sells said right for a sum of money upon which all parties to the transaction (the seller[s] and purchaser[s] of this right and the actual owner[s] of the property) agree. Qassab Hasan also uses the colloquial *khuluw* as a popular synonym for *furughiyya*. *Al-Idha'a al-Suriyya*, January 16, 1955, 8.

48. Qassab Hasan, *Qisas al-Nas*, 11.

49. *Al-Idha'a al-Suriyya*, January 16, 1955, 8.

50. He could, for example, have mentioned the principle of *majlis al-'aqd*, developed by Hanafi jurists and incorporated into the Syrian Civil Code, which required full disclosure of all potential costs and benefits of any business contract so as to prevent upsetting "the balance of benefits by allowing one party to acquire illicit profit at the expense of the other." Comair-Obeid, *The Law of Business Contracts*, 128.

51. Qassab Hasan, *Qisas al-Nas*, 11.

52. The material here and in the next three paragraphs comes from *al-Idha'a al-Suriyya*, November 1, 1955, 12.

53. *Al-Idha'a al-Suriyya*, January 16, 1955, 8, 9.

54. Ibid., 9.

55. Heydemann, *Authoritarianism in Syria*, 59–61.

56. *Al-Idha'a al-Suriyya*, January 16, 1955, 9.

57. *Al-Idha'a al-Suriyya*, January 16, 1955, 8.

58. Ibid.

59. *Al-Idha'a al-Suriyya*, January 16, 1956.

60. Qassab Hasan's relative lack of interest in criminal law is reflected in his *Qisas al-Nas*, only one chapter (chapter 2, "Criminal and Penal Issues") of which is dedicated to the topic.

61. *Al-Idha'a al-Suriyya*, January 16, 1956, 10.

62. Ibid.

63. Chatterjee, *The Politics of the Governed*, 141.

64. Qassab Hasan, *Qisas al-Nas*, 11.

65. Ibid.

66. *Al-Idha'a al-Suriyya*, January 16, 1956, 10 (emphasis added).

67. Ibid.

68. "So this citizen, bearing a fictional name chosen by me, was placed at the center of the public's interest and his case became a focus for the sympathy of millions." Passage from an unpublished manuscript. Hanan Qassab Hasan (daughter of Najat Qassab Hasan), in discussion with the author, February 27, 2002.

69. Qassab Hasan, *Qisas al-Nas,* 12, 11.

70. Ibid., 11.

3. SOCIAL JUSTICE AND THE PATRIARCHAL CITIZEN

1. While the term literally translates as "personal affairs," in the legal context it is always rendered "personal status." The provisions of this code comprise all issues of "consummation, birth, paternity, custody, age, support of the child, as well as marital relations—marriage, divorce, alimony, marital property and inheritance." Sfeir, *Modernization of the Law,* 25. For more, see El-Alami and Hinchcliffe, *Islamic Marriage and Divorce Laws.*

2. Ibid., xii. For more, see Sfeir, *Modernization of the Law.*

3. *Al-Idha'a al-Suriyya,* October 16, 1955, 10.

4. Hanan Qassab Hasan, interview, February 27, 2002.

5. Ibid.

6. Najat Qassab Hasan's most sustained legal reform efforts advocated a more general provision of divorce with cause (independent of individual marriage contracts) and access to daycare for divorced, working mothers. Ibid.

7. Qassab Hasan, *Qisas al-Nas,* 12.

8. Najmabadi, "The Morning After," 367.

9. The material here and over the next four paragraphs comes from *al-Idha'a al-Suriyya,* 57 (January 1, 1956), 9.

10. Ibid.

11. *Al-Idha'a al-Suriyya,* November 1, 1955, 12.

12. Qassab Hasan pointed out that by contracting the second marriage without first receiving a divorce, the woman had committed an act that was "not only incompatible with Islamic law" but also "subject to the harshest criminal penalties" under Article 471 of the Syrian Penal Code. Similar penalties, however, could be imposed on all who knowingly participated in such a fraudulent ceremony. Thus, if evidence emerged that the family perpetrated a similar fraud prior to that involving the petitioner, the authorities could argue that he was aware of the circumstances, leaving him vulnerable to criminal prosecution. Ibid.

13. Ibid.

14. Qassab Hasan, *Qisas al-Nas,* 11.

15. Syria has subsequently undergone several administrative reforms, modifying the boundaries and changing the names of several provinces.

16. Qassab Hasan, *Qisas al-Nas,* 12.

17. This and the next four paragraphs comes from *al-Idha'a al-Suriyya,* October 16, 1955, 10–11.

18. The quotations here and over the next five paragraphs comes from *al-Idhaʻa al-Suriyya,* January 1, 1956, 9.

19. A more literal translation of the proverb is "A body's ingrained habits are not changed until it meets the burial shroud."

20. The material for this and the next five paragraphs comes from *al-Idhaʻa al-Suriyya,* November 16, 1955, 14–15.

21. The material for this and the next six paragraphs comes from *al-Idhaʻa al-Suriyya,* October 16, 1955, 10.

22. The analogy with the nineteenth-century European experience is, once again, striking. See Surkis, *Sexing the Citizen,* 54–55.

4. PUNISHING THE ENEMIES OF ARABISM

1. Sharabi, *Governments and Politics,* 129.

2. *Al-Jundi,* July 7, 1955, 30–32.

3. See, e.g., *al-Anbaʼ,* September 9, 1955, 1, 4.

4. Anderson, *Imagined Communities,* 114.

5. Al-Malki's widely known habitual attendance at various Syrian soccer teams' matches facilitated the planning of his murder. An avid player in his youth, al-Malki also personally sponsored the al-Salhiyya neighborhood team. Al-Shamʻa, *Awraq Sahafi,* 34–35.

6. Hafiz, *Shahid al-ʻUruba,* 41.

7. Ibid., 48, 53, 85; al-Malki, *Rasaʼil min al-Sijn,* introduction.

8. *Al-Jundi,* July 14, 1955, 11.

9. The dedication of Damascus's Martyrs' Square quite accurately mirrored the city's geographical expansion to the north and west during the twentieth century. For the notables' exploitation of al-Hashimi's memory, see Wien, "The Long and Intricate Funeral."

10. Sipress, "Syria Creates Cult."

11. *Al-Jundi,* July 14, 1955, 11. The famous included prominent academics intellectuals, journalists, and political activists like Ahmad al-Samman, Ahmad al-Jundi, Nazir Fansa, and Yahya al-Shihabi.

12. Rosoux, "The Politics of Martyrdom," 86–87.

13. Cook, *Martyrdom in Islam,* 1–2.

14. Gay, *The Cultivation of Hatred,* 7. The reference to "illuminating treason" is taken from ʻAli Shariʼati, "Shahadat," in Taleqani et al., eds., *Jihad and Shahadat,* 209.

15. Derrida, *The Work of Mourning,* 51.

16. Gray, "Explaining Conspiracy Theories," 169.

17. Seale, *The Struggle for Syria,* 242–243.

18. Ibid.

19. During the investigation of al-Malki's assassination, ʻAbd al-Hamid al-Sarraj was shocked to discover that 55% of "noncommissioned officers belonged to the ʻAlawi sect." Batatu, *Syria's Peasantry,* 157.

20. Both of these entities had their origins under the regime of Colonel Adib al-Shishakli (1949–1954), whose government also boasted a Ministry of Propaganda and National Guidance.

21. Al-Malki, *Sirat al-Shahid*, 132–133.

22. For a summary overview in English, see U.S. Department of State, Confidential Department of State Incoming Telegram, April 26, 1955.

23. For details and differing perspectives, see Seale, *The Struggle for Syria*, 240; Rathmell, *Secret War in the Middle East*, 98–102; Haddad, *Revolutions and Military Rule*, 2:224; Maʻruf, *Ayyam ʻAshtuha*, 220; Torrey, *Syrian Politics and the Military*, 282; Beʼeri, *Army Officers*, 132; and Qubrusi, "Maqtal ʻAdnan al-Malki," 26. Subsequent accounts revealed that ʻAdnan's brother Riyad even accused Syrian Chief of Staff Shawkat Shuqayr immediately after the assassination. Jumʻa, *Awraq min Daftar*, 185; al-Shamʻa, *Awraq Sahafi*, 41–42.

24. *Al-Qabas*, April 28, 1955, 1; al-Malki, *Sirat al-Shahid*, 134.

25. Torrey, *Syrian Politics and the Military*, 282.

26. *Al-Qabas*, April 28, 1955, 4.

27. Examples of the screaming, large-font headlines characteristic of this campaign can be seen in *al-Anbaʼ*, July 6, 1955, 1, and *al-Anbaʼ*, July 10, 1955, 1.

28. For parallels with French revolutionary discourse, see Germani, *Jean-Paul Marat*, 40, 55, and Gay, *The Cultivation of Hatred*, 68.

29. "University Professors Condemn the Assassination of al-Malki: Intellectuals Demand Combating the Criminals and Their Supporters with the Harshest Measures," *al-Raʼy al-ʻAmm*, May 3, 1955, 2. The twenty-nine signatories included Sami al-Droubi, ʻAbdallah ʻAbd al-Dayim, Amjad Tarabulsi, Shafiq Jabri, Wajih al-Qudsi, Tawfiq al-Munjid, Nazim al-Mawsuli, ʻAbd al-Hakim Swaydani, Ibrahim al-Kilani, Nadir al-Nabulsi, ʻAbd al-Halim Mansur, Zayd Haydar, Musa al-Khuri, ʻAmir Furukh ʻIzz al-Din al-Tannukhi, and Ismaʻil ʻIzzat.

30. Al-Farʻ al-Thaqafi al-ʻAskari, *al-Malki*, 42–43.

31. *Al-Qabas*, May 8, 1955, 2; *al-Qabas*, May 9, 1955, 2; Torrey, *Syrian Politics and the Military*, 283–285; Rathmell, *Secret War in the Middle East*, 99–100. See also Seale, *The Struggle for Syria*, 241–242.

32. Torrey, *Syrian Politics and the Military*, 283–284; Sharabi, *Governments and Politics*, 130; "Delay in Publishing the Indictment: Progress in the Investigation of the Death of Colonel ʻAdnan al-Malki," *al-Anbaʼ*, May 21, 1955, 1.

33. U.S. Department of State, Foreign Service Despatch 529, June 29, 1955; *al-Sayyad*, June 16, 1955, 6. Tribunal records indicate that witnesses as young as fifteen were detained and questioned in Mezze. See, e.g., the deposition of Mutiʻa Baghdadi in Anonymous, "Malki Trial," file 3, Middle East Files, AUB, Jafet Library.

34. Qubrusi, "Maqtal ʻAdnan al-Malki," 16–17. See also Lesch, *Syria and the United States*, 68, and Rathmell, *Secret War in the Middle East*, 98.

35. These documents survive in the "Malki Trial" files held in the special collections of the Jafet Library at the American University of Beirut. Four files totaling more than four hundred pages including these documents, surveillance reports,

memoranda among government offices, and much else appear to be parts of an investigation dossier provided to Lebanese defense attorneys participating in the trials. The tribunal dossier is mentioned in *al-Jundi,* September 8, 1955, 6. For an example of "hints of coercion," see the interrogation of Yunis 'Abd al-Rahim's sister in Anonymous, "Malki Trial," file 2.

36. The depositions of more "elite" prisoners like Antun Sa'ada's widow, Juliette al-Mir, include explicit statements that they were obtained "without any pressure, beating, or torture." Anonymous, "Malki Trial," file 3.

37. Anonymous, "Malki Trial," file 2. During this session, Dabbusi denied even that he was a member of the SSNP.

38. Anonymous, "Malki Trial," file 2.

39. *Al-Anba',* June 30, 1955, 1; *al-Anba',* July 7, 1955, 1. For an overview, see Seale, *The Struggle for Syria,* 241. For further details, see Anonymous, "Malki Trial," file 1.

40. Torrey, *Syrian Politics and the Military,* 283.

41. *Al-Qabas,* April 29, 1955, 1.

42. U.S. Department of State, Foreign Service Despatch 520, June 23, 1955. See also Torrey, *Syrian Politics and the Military,* 285.

43. U.S. Department of State, Foreign Service Despatch 499, June 10, 1955.

44. For a summary of 'Ulush's professional resumé, see Faris, ed., *Man Huwa fi Suriya 1949,* 541, and Faris, ed., *Man Huma fi al-'Alam al-'Arabi,* 445–446.

45. *Al-Jundi,* September 8, 1955, 6.

46. Fischer-Lichte, *Theatre, Sacrifice, Ritual,* 121; Rathmell, *Secret War in the Middle East,* 99; Seale, *The Struggle for Syria,* 242.

47. *Al-Anba',* June 30, 1955, 1.

48. *Al-Anba',* September 2, 1955, 2.

49. U.S. Department of State, Foreign Service Despatch 499, June 10, 1955.

50. *Al-Anba',* September 1, 1955, 1.

51. Haddad, *Revolutions and Military Rule,* 2:225.

52. "Islamic criminal law requires the discerning judgment and freewill of the perpetrator as the basis for recognition of criminal responsibility," and explicitly "affirms that no individual can be responsible for the acts of others." Paradelle, "The Notion of 'Person' between Law and Practice," 236–237.

53. See, e.g., *al-Jami'a,* July 17, 1955, 9–10.

54. *Al-Jundi,* September 8, 1955, 7.

55. These included Ma'ruf al-Dawalibi, Bashir al-'Awf, Prime Minister Sabri al-'Asali, former President Hisham al-Atassi, and former cabinet ministers Fakhir al-Kayyali and Wajih al-Haffar. *Al-Anba',* October 2, 1955, 1, 4; *al-Anba',* October 3, 1955, 1, 4; *al-Anba',* October 8, 1955, 1, 4; *al-Jundi,* October 13, 1955, 6–7; *al-Jundi,* October 20, 1955, 8–10.

56. *Al-Anba',* September 18, 1955, 1, 4; *al-Jundi,* October 20, 1955, 8–10.

57. *Al-Jundi,* September 22, 1955, 46.

58. *Al-Anba',* September 1, 1955, 1, 5; *al-Qabas,* August 31, 1955, 1, 4; *al-Qabas,* September 1, 1955, 2, 3; *al-Anba',* September 21, 1955, 1, 4.

59. U.S. Department of State, Foreign Service Despatch 93, September 23, 1955. See also Rathmell, *Secret War in the Middle East,* 99, and Torrey, *Syrian Politics and the Military,* 296.

60. *Al-Jundi,* September 22, 1955, 46.

61. *Al-Anba',* September 1, 1955, 1, 4. See also U.S. Department of State, Foreign Service Despatch 93, September 23, 1955.

62. *Al-Anba',* July 14, 1955, 2; *al-Anba',* September 16, 1955, 2; *al-Anba',* November 21, 1955, 4.

63. *Al-Anba',* September 18, 1955, 1, 4.

64. *Al-Anba',* September 20, 1955, 1. The incongruity of these noble and sincere sentiments and the kangaroo court with which his name had been associated apparently became too much for 'Ulush, who resigned without explanation in January 1956, shortly after the court rendered its sentences of death. He was quickly persuaded to return, only to quit for good in February. *Al-Qabas,* January 20, 1956, 1, 4; *al-Qabas,* February 13, 1956, 1, 4.

65. *Al-Anba',* December 15, 1955, 1, 3. See also *al-Qabas,* December 15, 1955, 2, and Torrey, *Syrian Politics and the Military,* 308. The prosecutor general had requested death sentences against thirty-one of the defendants. *Al-Qabas,* November 6, 1955, 2.

66. U.S. Department of State, Incoming Telegram, January 12, 1956. See also Yamak, *The Syrian Social Nationalist Party,* 70, and Torrey, *Syrian Politics and the Military,* 308–309.

67. Ibid., 309. For details, see *al-Qabas,* April 29, 1956, 1, 4.

68. All three—Fu'ad Jadid, 'Abd al-Mun'im Dabbusi, and Badi' Makhlouf—were Army NCOs and 'Alawis. Four of those sentenced to death and listed above had escaped the court's jurisdiction. In February 1957, one of these, Fu'ad's elder brother Colonel Ghassan Jadid, was assassinated in Beirut, presumably by agents of Syrian Military Intelligence.

69. Torrey, *Syrian Politics and the Military,* 311; Haddad, *Revolutions and Military Rule,* 2:225; U.S. Department of State, Confidential Department of State Incoming Telegram, August 4, 1956.

70. Torrey, *Syrian Politics and the Military,* 311–312.

71. "Yawm al-Mansura," *al-Jundi,* September 13, 1956, 7.

72. Ibid.

73. "The Echo of Bullets," *al-Jundi,* September 27, 1956, 17. The author's chosen pen name invites speculation about its intended meaning. The name is associated with the Muslim conqueror of the Persian Sasanid Army in 636, and with the Muthanna Club, an Iraqi pan-Arab society that manifested fascist tendencies in the 1930s and 1940s.

74. Lesch, *Syria and the United States,* 69; *al-Qabas,* July 3, 1955, 1; U.S. Department of State, Foreign Service Despatch 25, June 14, 1955.

75. *Al-Qabas,* April 28, 1955, 4; U.S. Department of State, Incoming Telegram, April 27, 1955. See also *al-Anba',* July 6, 1955, 1.

76. Torrey, *Syrian Politics and the Military,* 285; *al-Anba',* October 26, 1955, 1; *al-Qabas,* January 27, 1956, 1, 4; *al-Qabas,* April 11, 1956, 4. See also *al-Sayyad,* June 16, 1955, 6, and U.S. Department of State, Foreign Service Despatch 529, June 29, 1955.

77. U.S. Department of State, Foreign Service Despatch 93, September 23, 1955.

78. See, e.g., *al-Anba',* June 26, 1955, 1, 4; June 27, 1955, 1, 4; September 1, 1955, 1, 4; September 7, 1955, 1, 4; *al-Ra'y al-'Amm,* September 8, 1955, 3, 4; *al-Jundi,* October 6, 1955, 5; *al-Raqib,* September 29, 1955, 3; "The Interrogation of 180 of the Accused," *al-Anba',* June 15, 1955, 1, 4. Isam al-Mahayri and his cousin Fahmi were the proprietors of the company, which at one time owned and operated the Damascus dailies *al-Sham* (Damascus), *al-Hadara* (Civilization), *Dimashq al-Masa'* (Damascus Evening), and variously named pro-ssnp publications.

79. U.S. Department of State, Confidential Department of the Army Staff Communications Office Message, May 14, 1955.

80. Al-Sham'a, *Awraq Sahafi,* 44–49.

81. *Al-Anba',* September 28, 1955, 1, 4.

82. Kaylani, "The Rise of the Syrian Ba'th," 17; Yamak, *The Syrian Social Nationalist Party,* 70; al-Sham'a, *Awraq Sahafi,* 41. Al-Sham'a's account of these events implies a conspiracy, as they occurred before "people knew anything, even the name of the killer." See also *al-Anba',* September 9, 1955, 1, 7; U.S. Department of State, Secret Department of the Army Staff Communications Office Message, July 8, 1955; and U.S. Department of State, Foreign Service Despatch 529, June 29, 1955.

83. *Al-Qabas,* July 21, 1955, 2; July 27, 1955, 2; August 5, 1955, 1; May 29, 1956, 1; *al-Anba',* September 21, 1955, 2.

84. Anonymous, *Man Qatala Yunis,* 3–4; *al-Qabas,* May 29, 1956, 1. See also U.S. Department of State, Foreign Service Despatch 529, June 29, 1955.

85. *Al-Anba',* September 20, 1955, 1; *al-Jundi,* September 29, 1955, 40; *al-Qabas,* May 9, 1956, 1; Torrey, *Syrian Politics and the Military,* 296. See also U.S. Department of State, Foreign Service Despatch 93, September 23, 1955, and *al-Qabas,* May 9, 1956, 1.

86. Seale, *Asad of Syria,* 23.

87. The most detailed version asserts that a search of Yunis's corpse uncovered the "following written statement . . . : 'I am going to kill Adnan Malki to defend my personal honor.'" U.S. Department of State, Incoming Telegram, May 17, 1955.

88. Chief of Staff Shuqayr was aware of such rumors. See, e.g., U.S. Department of State, Secret Memorandum of Conversation, June 24, 1955.

89. For details of the officer corps' demography during this period, see Drysdale, "The Syrian Armed Forces," 57–61.

90. Occasionally, witnesses referenced their own sectarian identities in open court. The press simply repeated these statements without comment. See, e.g., the testimony of Yunis 'Abd al-Rahim's brother Yasin. *Al-Jundi,* October 20, 1955, 8–10.

91. *Al-Anba',* July 2, 1955, 1, 4.

92. See, e.g., "Abu Yu'arrib," "In Memory of 'Adnan al-Malki," *al-Hadara,* April 25, 1956, 2. I found just one published editorial that explicitly addressed the issue of sectarianism in both its headline and text: "Acts of Sabotage That Are Inspired by

Blind Factionalism: The Syrian Social Nationalist Party Promotes Sectarianism, Collaborates with Zionism, and Works for the Partition of the Arab Homeland," *al-Jundi,* May 5, 1955, 30–32.

93. The Orthodox Patriarch's secondary school in Damascus's Christian neighborhood of Bab Sharqi was most frequently mentioned in this regard. Anonymous, "Malki Trial," files 1, 4.

94. Anonymous, "Malki Trial," file 2.

95. Shuqayr also asserted that Syria's Communist Party appealed almost exclusively to the country's ethnic minorities, "particularly the Kurds." All of this is rendered more interesting by the fact that Shuqayr was a member of the Druze minority and was born in Lebanon. U.S. Department of State, Secret Memorandum of Conversation, June 24, 1955.

96. Seale, *Asad of Syria,* 50.

97. Silverstein and Makdisi, "Introduction," 7.

98. Gay, *The Cultivation of Hatred,* 35–36.

99. *Al-Jundi,* September 27, 1956, 17; Sharabi, *Governments and Politics,* 130.

100. Yamak, *The Syrian Social Nationalist Party,* 70.

101. Seale, *Asad of Syria,* 241.

102. For a highly partisan account of this process, see Zakariyya, *al-Sultan al-Ahmar.*

103. U.S. Department of State, Confidential Memorandum of Conversation, June 4, 1955; Torrey, *Syrian Politics and the Military,* 283, 381.

104. *Al-Anba',* December 15, 1955, 1, 3.

105. *Al-Jundi,* September 8, 1955, 6.

106. Haddad, *Revolutions and Military Rule,* 2:224.

107. The army staged a similar spectacle in 1956, trying dozens of civilians who were accused of participating in a U.S.-sponsored coup attempt. Yaqub, *Containing Arab Nationalism,* 149. Soon thereafter in Iraq, Fadil 'Abbas al-Mahdawi presided over "People's Court" tribunals on behalf of the Qasim regime (1958–1962).

5. MAKING THE MARTIAL CITIZEN

1. Zerubavel, "Patriotic Sacrifice and the Burden of Memory," 73; Strenski, *Contesting Sacrifice,* 9.

2. Fields, "The Psychology and Sociology of Martyrdom," 25; Gillis, "Memory and Identity," 11; Rosoux, "The Politics of Martyrdom," 88; Mosse, *Fallen Soldiers,* 90.

3. Germani, *Jean-Paul Marat,* 1; Cook, *Martyrdom in Islam,* 2.

4. Party founder and chief ideologue Michel 'Aflaq famously argued that nationalism, like all other forms of "love," was inextricably "linked to sacrifice," the "high price" required to realize his movement's "great goal" of Arab spiritual rebirth and political unity. 'Aflaq, "Nationalism Is Love before Everything Else," 242–243.

5. Bodnar, *Remaking America,* 28.

6. Germani, *Jean-Paul Marat,* 1; Cook, *Understanding Jihad,* 155.

7. Marnham, *Resistance and Betrayal,* 8. The quote refers to Jean Moulin.

8. I have borrowed the concept of inverse transubstantiation from Anne Norton's *Bloodrites of the Post-Structuralists.* The original concept, "And the Word became flesh, and dwelt among us," is taken from John 1:14.

9. Seale, *The Struggle for Syria*, 223, 239, 243; Moubayed, *Damascus between Dictatorship and Democracy*, 136; Commins, *Historical Dictionary of Syria*, 150; Fansa, *al-Nakabat wa al-Mughamarat*, 361; al-Shamat, "Syria under Civilian Rule," 95–96, 99, 136; Moubayed, *Steel and Silk*, 70.

10. Kamrava, "Military Professionalization," 69–70, 76. See also Be'eri, "The Waning of the Military Coup," 73; Rubin, "The Military in Contemporary Middle East Politics"; and Perlmutter, "The Praetorian State," 383.

11. This concept dates back, as do so many others, to the French Revolution. See Bertaud, "The Revolutionary Role of the Army," 37.

12. Rubin, "The Military in Contemporary Middle East Politics," 1.

13. Cook, *Martyrdom in Islam*, 3.

14. Ibid.

15. Schilcher, *Families in Politics*, 55n102; al-Malki, *Sirat al-Shahid*, 13; al-Baytar, *Hilyat al-Bashar*, 243–244.

16. Khoury, *Urban Notables*, 34–35, 114n60; Schilcher, *Families in Politics*, 55n102.

17. Khoury, *Urban Notables*, 34–35. The most detailed list of al-Malki *a'yan* (notables) in Damascus appears in al-Husni, *Kitab Muntakhabat al-Tawarikh li-Dimashq*, 873–874.

18. See, e.g., Faris, ed., *Man Huwa fi Suriya 1949*, 679–685.

19. Ibid., 681. According to 'Adnan's brother Riyad, Shams al-Din "frequently repeated the story of this disaster to his sons in order to witness its effects in their eyes." See al-Malki, *Sirat al-Shahid*, 18.

20. 'Adnan was the notional ancestor of the Arabic speakers in the northern and western parts of the peninsula, while Qahtan was assigned the same role in the south and east. Muhammad Shams al-Din would have been aware of the Qahtan Society, a late Ottoman secret society that "stressed the idea of Arabism in reaction to the unveiling of Unionist 'Turkification' policy." Khoury, *Urban Notables*, 64.

21. For a detailed retrospective on 'Adnan's childhood in the shadow of anti-imperialist struggle, see al-Malki, *Sirat al-Shahid*, 14–23, 18 (quotation).

22. Hafiz, *Shahid al-'Uruba*, 25. A shorter and less detailed version of Hafiz's martyrology, featuring many of the same childhood anecdotes and family photographs, appeared in the press just two weeks after al-Malki's assassination. *Al-Jundi*, May 5, 1955, 24–25.

23. Al-Shamat, "Syria under Civilian Rule," 99; Be'eri, *Army Officers*, 132.

24. Hamdani, *Shahid 'ala Ahdath*, 140.

25. See, e.g., al-Sham'a, *Awraq Sahafi*, 34–35; Zakariyya, *al-Sultan al-Ahmar*, 15; and Seale, *The Struggle for Syria*, 239.

26. Ibid. See also Ma'ruf, *Ayyam 'Ashtuha*, 86; al-Malki, *Sirat al-Shahid*, 133; Zakariyya, *al-Sultan al-Ahmar*, 15; and al-Sham'a, *Awraq Sahafi*, 34–35. See also *al-Qabas*, September 26, 1955, 1, 4.

27. One prominent scholar who interviewed most of al-Malki's contemporaries concluded that he was "not a particularly remarkable young man." Seale, *The Struggle for Syria*, 243.

28. See, e.g., *Sawt Suriya*, August 1954, 32–33; and *al-Jundi*, June 1, 1954, 5; July 16, 1954, 4; August 5, 1954, 4, 10, 35; September 16, 1954, 9; September 30, 1954, 8; October 7, 1954, 8.

29. Faris, ed., *Man Huwa fi Suriya 1949*.

30. Moubayed, *Damascus between Dictatorship and Democracy*, 70, 136; Lentz, *Assassinations and Executions*, 114–115; Commins, *Historical Dictionary of Syria*, 150. U.S. government documents also attest to al-Malki's perceived influence. See, e.g., U.S. Department of State, Foreign Service Despatch 281, January 22, 1955. See also U.S. Department of State, Foreign Service Despatch 331, February 15, 1955.

31. Be'eri, *Army Officers*, 132; al-Malki, *Sirat al-Shahid*, 43–50, 115; Hafiz, *Shahid al-'Uruba*, 17, 20. The posthumous narrative made much of al-Malki's service in Palestine, when it was actually common for his generational cohort.

32. Be'eri, *Army Officers*, 132; al-Malki, *Sirat al-Shahid*, 98–107; Fansa, *al-Nakabat wa al-Mughamarat*, 361; Seale, *The Struggle for Syria*, 126–127; Commins, *Historical Dictionary of Syria*, 150; Kaylani, "The Rise of the Syrian Ba'th," 13; Moubayed, *Damascus between Dictatorship and Democracy*, 91; Moubayed, *Steel and Silk*, 70.

33. Moubayed, *Damascus between Dictatorship and Democracy*, 136; Seale, *The Struggle for Syria*, 239; U.S. Department of State, Confidential Memorandum from J. S. Moose, Jr., June 12, 1954. See also U.S. Department of State, Confidential Office Memorandum, April 15, 1954.

34. Seale, *The Struggle for Syria*, 239–240. After the assassination, Shuqayr confided to U.S. officials that he had long considered al-Malki a "loudmouthed" troublemaker. U.S. Department of State, Secret Memorandum of Conversation between U.S. Ambassador James S. Moose, Jr., U.S. Embassy Counselor Robert C. Strong, Nazir Fansa, and Brigadier General Shawkat Shuqayr, June 24, 1955.

35. The quotation in the heading is from Tlas, *Mir'at Hiyati*, 1:465.

36. al-Malki, *Rasa'il min al-Sijn*, foreword.

37. Rosoux, "The Politics of Martyrdom," 87.

38. The citizen-martyr's immortality is also a venerable component of the republican tradition, appearing as early as the Peloponnesian War and becoming particular visible during the French Revolution. See ibid., 84, and Schama, *Citizens*, 744.

39. Rosoux, "The Politics of Martyrdom," 92; Cook, *Martyrdom in Islam*, 2.

40. The earliest of such book-length treatments appeared in August 1956: al-Far' al-Thaqafi al-'Askari, *al-Malki*. Subsequent efforts, particularly Hafiz's *Shahid al-'Uruba*, merely expanded the scope and fulsomeness of the hagiographic project.

41. Cook, *Martyrdom in Islam*, 11, 119; Shari'ati, "On Martyrdom," 363; Fields, "The Psychology and Sociology of Martyrdom," 27; Murtada Mutahhari, "Shahid," in Taleqani et al., eds., *Jihad and Shahadat*, 128. This notion, that foreknowledge of his murder is one of the defining characteristics of the martyr, is actually much older than nationalism, Islam, or Christianity. See, e.g., Woolf, *Et Tu, Brute*.

42. See, e.g., al-Far' al-Thaqafi al-'Askari, *al-Malki*, 210; "al-Faqid Kana 'ala 'Ilm bi al-Mu'amara" (The Deceased Had Knowledge of the Conspiracy), *al-Jundi*, September 29, 1955, 13–15; Saunders, *The United States and Arab Nationalism*, 42; U.S. Department of State, Foreign Service Despatch 136, November 1, 1955; U.S. Department of State, Incoming Telegram, September 24, 1955; al-Madani, *'Adnan al-Malki*, 118; and Hamdani, *Shahid 'ala Ahdath*, 139.

43. See, e.g., "Mawkib al-Shuhada'" (The Procession of Martyrs), *al-Anba'*, December 15, 1955, 2. For the martyrs of Jamal Pasha, see "Fi Dhikra al-Shuhada': Umma Lan Tamut" (In Memory of the Martyrs: The Nation Will Not Die), *al-Jundi*, May 9, 1957, 5–9. For Yusuf al-'Azma, see "In the Neighborhood of the Hero of Maysalun," quoted in al-Malki, *Sirat al-Shahid*, 16.

44. The most prominent early example was the naval officer Jules Jammal, who was credited with crashing an explosives-laden vessel into a French ship during the Suez War of 1956. *Al-'Idha'a al-Suriyya*, December 10, 1956, 36–37; January 1, 1957, 30–33; *al-Sanabil*, December 8, 1956, front cover.

45. See, e.g., Wien, "The Long and Intricate Funeral."

46. Ben-Amos, *Funerals, Politics, and Memory*, 3, 5.

47. Wien, "The Long and Intricate Funeral," 276, 279. See also Volk, *Memorials and Martyrs*, 24.

48. Ibid., 25.

49. Moubayed, *Damascus between Dictatorship and Democracy*, 137. On at least two occasions, parliamentary deputies, many of whom had hated or feared al-Malki, felt compelled to observe a minute of silence in honor of his memory and to report these observances to the press. "In the Chamber of Deputies," *al-Anba'*, December 15, 1955, 4; U.S. Department of State, Incoming Telegram, April 27, 1955; Torrey, *Syrian Politics and the Military*, 282–283.

50. Al-Madani, *'Adnan al-Malki*, 60; al-Malki, *Sirat al-Shahid*, 134–135; U.S. Department of State, Incoming Telegram, April 23, 1955; U.S. Department of State, Foreign Service Despatch 446, April 27, 1955.

51. Fischer-Lichte, *Theatre, Sacrifice, Ritual*, 109.

52. *Al-Anba'*, June 20, 1955, 2.

53. *Al-Jundi*, July 7, 1955, 5.

54. "Al-Malki's Memorial Service Causes Tears to Flow: The Speeches of al-Qasimi, Shuqayr, al-Hajjar, 'Arila, al-'Alayli, and Abu Risha about the Glorious Deeds of the Deceased and the Immortality of Arab Principles," *al-Anba'*, July 2, 1955, 1. See also *al-Jundi*, July 7, 1955, 4–6, which features photos of the "tearful eyes all around."

55. For biographical information on Abu Risha, see Faris, ed., *Man Huwa fi Suriya 1949*, 16–17; Faris, ed., *Man Huma fi al-'Alam al-'Arabi*, 14–15; and Moubayed, *Steel and Silk*, 512–513.

56. *Al-Qabas*, July 1, 1955, 1; July 3, 1955, 3; *al-Anba'*, July 2, 1955, 1, 4; *al-Jundi*, July 7, 1955, 7–9, 11–13, 16–18; *al-Anba'*, July 2, 1955, 1, 4; U.S. Department of State, Secret Department of the Army Staff Communications Office Message, July 2, 1955.

57. Zafir al-Qasimi was the scion of an old Damascene family of *'ulama'* and suq merchants who were prominent in Islamic modernist, i.e., salafist, circles. 'Abdallah al-'Alayli was a Sunni cleric from Lebanon who was closely associated with the politics of Kamal Jumblatt's Progressive Socialist Party.

58. *Al-Anba'*, July 2, 1955, 1.

59. For 1956, see *al-Qabas*, April 20, 1956, 4; April 29, 1956, 2; and U.S. Department of State, Incoming Telegram, May 1, 1956.

60. "April 22nd . . . 'Adnan Day," "'Adnan in the Procession of Martyrs," and "He Served His Nation in Life and Death," *al-Jundi*, April 25, 1957, 5–10, 46–47. The opening remarks were presented by Lieutenant Colonel Hisham al-'Azm.

61. For example, a small number of such poems were composed in tribute to the Iraqi soldier and politician Yasin al-Hashimi. Wien, "The Long and Intricate Funeral," 287.

62. A (very) small sampling of such essays: Corporal Namiq Kamal Ziyada, "He Will Return . . . ," *al-Jundi*, September 8, 1955, 41; First Sergeant Najib Rahmun Najjar, "This I Promise, Oh Martyr Hero," and Staff Sergeant Iskander Mu'ammar, "Departure of a Soul," *al-Jundi*, July 14, 1955, 32; Sergeant Major Muhammad al-Yamani, "The Eternal Image," *al-Jundi*, September 22, 1955, 37; 'Izzat 'Abd al-Razzaq of Qamishli, "Why We Loved 'Adnan al-Malki," *al-Jundi*, September 1, 1955, 37; First Sergeant Badr al-Din al-Suqi, "Rest in Peace," *al-Jundi*, September 22, 1955, 37; "The Name of 'Adnan al-Malki Has Fallen" and "Tears over 'Adnan," *al-Jundi*, July 7, 1955, 27–29.

63. For speeches, see, e.g., Staff Sergeant Sa'id Jawish, "To the Spirit of the Martyr," *al-Jundi*, July 14, 1955, 32.

64. See, e.g., "Officer Candidate Muwwaffaq Ja'fari" and "The Procession of Heroes," *al-Jundi*, July 14, 1955, 18; and First Sergeant Sahtun Qasim, "The Logic of Colonialism," *al-Jundi*, September 1, 1955, 38.

65. For soldiers' poems and letters that ascribe this condition to al-Malki, see, e.g., Sergeant Subhi Majwaz, "The Immortal Martyr of the Arab Nation," and First Sergeant Matanyus As'ad, "The Living Martyr," *al-Jundi*, September 1, 1955, 38.

66. "The Cause of the Hero," *al-Jundi*, September 8, 1955, 19–21.

67. "In Memory," *al-Jundi*, July 7, 1955, 19–20. For biographical information, see Moubayed, *Steel and Silk*, 555–556.

68. "Alas for 'Adnan," *al-Jundi*, July 7, 1955, 21. For biographical information, see Faris, ed., *Man Huwa fi Suriya 1949*, 135.

69. "Crowned," *al-Jundi*, July 25, 1957, 11; "Private Papers," *al-Jundi*, May 1, 1958, 38. For biographical information and a sample of his work in translation, see Jayyusi, ed., *Modern Arabic Fiction*, 225.

70. *Al-Jundi*, May 1, 1958, 35–36. For biographical information, see Faris, ed., *Man Huwa fi Suriya 1949*, 458, and Moubayed, *Steel and Silk*, 462–463.

71. "He Was Disgusted by Weakness and the Weak," *al-Jundi*, July 7, 1955, 27. Al-Shihabi was a contributor to or editor of numerous state and private publications and the former director of the department of broadcasting at the Syrian broadcasting

authority. Faris, ed., *Man Huwa fi Suriya 1949*, 423; Faris, ed., *Man Huma fi al-'Alam al-'Arabi*, 352.

72. Al-'Isa subsequently functioned as a sort of court poet for the neo-Ba'th and Hafiz al-Asad regimes. For biographical information, see Moubayed, *Steel and Silk*, 541–542.

73. *Al-Jundi*, July 7, 1955, 27.

74. Ibid., 22–23.

75. These missives numbered in the thousands. For just a few examples, see Staff Sergeant 'Abd al-Kafi 'Abbas, "Catastrophe," *al-Jundi*, June 30, 1955, 37; First Sergeant Isma'il 'Amud, "Oh Martyr of the Fatherland," *al-Jundi*, July 14, 1955, 32; Private Baha' al-Din Hafiz, "Beloved Martyr of the Fatherland," *al-Jundi*, September 8, 1955, 41; Corporal Sulayman al-Fa'ur, "To the Dearly Departed Colonel of the General Staff 'Adnan al-Malki," and Sergeant Raghib Wahba, "The Hero Martyr," *al-Jundi*, September 15, 1955, 34, 42; and NCO Cadet Saqar Tali', "And the Procession Departed," *al-Jundi*, October 6, 1955, 40. Space constraints have prevented the inclusion of letters appearing in *al-Jundi*'s regular feature "The Student's Page." They also numbered in the hundreds. For examples, see Muti' Farhan al-Masalah from Dar'a, "'Adnan . . . Ruh," *al-Jundi*, September 8, 1955, 42, and Hani Hamwi, "To the Martyr 'Adnan," *al-Jundi*, October 20, 1955, 44.

76. *Al-Jundi*, July 7, 1955, 36–37.

77. Ibid.

78. Ibid., 37.

79. Flight Officer Khalil Hamdi al-Dabbagh, "'Adnan al-Malki Did Not Die," and "Words from Readers," *al-Jundi*, September 15, 1955, 13.

80. Sergeant Muhammad al-Yamani, "With the Hero-Martyr," *al-Jundi*, September 29, 1955, 33; Sergeant Muhammad al-Yamani, "With the Hero Martyr: Magnificent Heroism," *al-Jundi*, October 13, 1955, 42.

81. Sergeant Muhammad al-Yamani, "With the Hero-Martyr in Palestine," *al-Jundi*, June 30, 1955, 37; Sergeant Muhammad al-Yamani, "With the Hero-Martyr," *al-Jundi*, September 29, 1955, 33; Sergeant Muhammad al-Yamani, "With the Hero Martyr," *al-Jundi*, October 6, 1955, 40; Sergeant Muhammad al-Yamani, "With the Hero Martyr: Magnificent Heroism," *al-Jundi*, October 13, 1955, 42.

82. The most famous examples concern Cato the Younger, who is said to have survived "not in his own words, but as a character described by others." Woolf, *Et Tu, Brute*, 141.

83. Cook, *Martyrdom in Islam*, 116; Rosoux, "The Politics of Martyrdom," 83; Germani, *Jean-Paul Marat*, 58.

84. Cook, *Martyrdom in Islam*, 129; Germani, *Jean-Paul Marat*, 58.

85. Schama, *Citizens*, 744.

86. The army, as an institution, also engaged in this practice. See, e.g., al-Far' al-Thaqafi al-'Askari, *al-Malki*, 2, where al-Malki is quoted as saying, "We don't want military pacts, we don't want to join one of the military camps, we don't want the death of our people."

87. *Al-Jundi*, July 7, 1955, 20.

88. These excerpts were almost certainly provided by 'Adnan's brother and Ba'th Party activist Riyad, who subsequently published an annotated collection of these "prison letters"; see al-Malki, *Rasa'il min al-Sijn*.

89. *Al-Jundi*, July 7, 1955, 6. Al-Malki also asserted that he and his cellmates had written a "shining page in the modern history of Syria." Ibid., 9.

90. Thucydides, *History of the Peloponnesian War*, 145; Cook, *Understanding Jihad*, 2, 26.

91. *Al-Jundi*, July 7, 1955, 6, 34, 49, 9, 18.

92. Ibid., 9, 18, 49.

93. *Al-Tali'a*, April 27, 1956, 1–2; Germani, *Jean-Paul Marat*, 58; Mosse, *Fallen Soldiers*, 100–101.

94. "Decisions of the Cabinet of Ministers: The Military Legion of Honor Is Awarded to the Martyr al-Malki," *al-Anba'*, June 27, 1955, 4; *al-Jundi*, April 25, 1957, inside front cover.

95. Seale, *The Struggle for Syria*, 243. See also "I Was at the Military Academy," which purports to present a "complete picture of life in the factory of heroes." *Al-Jundi*, September 26, 1957, 21–22.

96. Cook, *Martyrdom in Islam*, 131; Mutahhari, "Shahid," 127.

97. Shakespeare, *Julius Caesar*, Act 3, scene 2, lines 165–195.

98. "The Naming of a Street after Colonel al-Malki," *al-Anba'*, June 22, 1955, 4. The parallel with the young French Republic is striking. Shortly after the assassination of Jean-Paul Marat, the Jacobin regime changed the name of the rue des Cordeliers to rue Marat, and the Place de l'Observance was renamed Place de l'Ami du Peuple, a reference to Marat's most influential publication. Germani, *Jean-Paul Marat*, 58.

99. Haddad, *Revolutions and Military Rule*, 2:225; Seale, *The Struggle for Syria*, 243.

100. "'Adnan's Service Comrades Escort Him to His Final Resting Place," *al-Jundi*, July 18, 1957, 5–7. Such photographic depictions of officers saluting or otherwise displaying the respect and/or grief were quite common, even many predating al-Malki's reinterment. See, e.g., *al-Jundi*, July 7, 1955, 48.

101. *Al-Jundi*, July 18, 1957, 4, 15–16.

102. "Independence Day" is actually known as "Evacuation Day" in Syria, for it commemorates the day on which French armed forces were compelled to evacuate Syrian territory in 1946, some three years after Syria was granted nominal independence. As noted above, Martyrs' Day commemorates those hanged by Ottoman governor Jamal Pasha in 1916. Army Day commemorates the founding of the Syrian Army in 1946.

103. Khalili, *Heroes and Martyrs of Palestine*, 132. For Independence Day, see "'Adnan in the Celebration of Independence," *al-Jundi*, April 18, 1957, 15.

104. See, e.g., "Remembrance of 'Adnan al-Malki," *al-'Idha'a al-Suriyya*, April 27, 1956, 5; *al-Jundi*, July 7, 1955, 44–48; "Day of the Martyr," *al-Jundi*, April 25, 1957,

4; *al-Qabas,* April 23, 1956, 1, 4; U.S. Department of State, Incoming Telegram, April 23, 1955; U.S. Department of State, Foreign Service Despatch 446, April 27, 1955.

105. Editorial by the publishers of *al-Jundi,* "The Cultural Section of the Armed Forces," *al-Jundi,* May 1, 1958, 3. This name is, of course, very reminiscent of the "festivals of Marat" staged by militants during the French Revolution. Germani, *Jean-Paul Marat,* 166–167.

106. Anderson, *Imagined Communities,* 10.

107. Hunt, "Foreword," xi.

108. *Al-Qabas,* April 28, 1955, 1.

109. The relevant passage states, "Dying for one's country . . . assumes a moral grandeur which dying for the Labour Party, the American Medical Association, or perhaps even Amnesty International can not rival." Anderson, *Imagined Communities,* 144.

110. Morrison, "Acts of Commemoration," 289.

111. Rosoux, "The Politics of Martyrdom," 87.

112. Moubayed, *Steel and Silk,* 71.

113. See, e.g., al-Sham'a, *Awraq Sahafi,* 23–49. This rhetorical tactic, emphasizing or exaggerating one's proximity to dramatic historical events, is common among journalists. See, e.g., Zelizer, *Covering the Body,* 2, 3, 36, 42.

114. One line of inquiry that I have not pursued is the influence that the al-Malki narrative may have exerted on the discourse of Algerian and Palestinian resistance movements, whose martyrologies also displayed complex syntheses of Christian, Islamic, and secular nationalist vocabulary, symbols, and tropes. Khalili, *Heroes and Martyrs of Palestine,* 140; Rosoux, "The Politics of Martyrdom," 99.

115. Schama, *Citizens,* 741; Germani, *Jean-Paul Marat,* 2. In this, I clearly disagree with Lisa Wedeen, who has argued in her otherwise excellent book that "in Syria, there was no state-sponsored cult prior to that of Asad." Wedeen, *Ambiguities of Domination,* 28. The letter from Flight Officer Khalil Hamdi al-Dabbagh quoted above suggests that al-Malki photographs and memorabilia were being merchandized, which would constitute another precursor to the Hafez/Basil/Bashar al-Asad cults.

116. Rosoux, "The Politics of Martyrdom," 83.

117. Moubayed, *Damascus between Dictatorship and Democracy,* 140.

6. THE MAGIC OF MODERN PHARMACEUTICALS

1. *Tabibak,* September 1956, 3.

2. The most obvious example of this tendency is found in the writings of Ba'th Party founder Michel 'Aflaq. See, e.g., the excerpt from his *Fi Sabil al-Ba'th,* "Nationalism Is Love before Everything Else."

3. These images usually appeared in the form of a multicolor cover illustration purporting to depict aspects of medical theory or praxis in, for example, Ancient Babylon or Ancient Egypt. *Tabibak,* September, October 1956.

4. *Tabibak,* November 1956, back cover. The illustration was the work of the Russian artist Vsevold Nicouline, a long-term resident of Italy who is best known for illustrating the 1944 edition of Carlo Collodi's *Pinnochio.* The scene, one of a "staid dignified session," was not a historically accurate depiction of Arab-Islamic medical education, yet such anachronisms were common features of Orientalist imagery. See Conrad, "Arab-Islamic Medicine," 711. Al-Qabbani's use of and comments on the image are doubly ironic in this context, as the clothes and facial features of the students depicted suggest a Persian or Central Asian setting rather than an "Arab" one.

5. For a classic example of al-Qabbani's overriding faith in progress, see his response to "Mr. 'Abd al-Hafiz Ibrahim from Beirut," *Tabibak,* June 1957, 89, in which al-Qabbani asserts the constant evolution of medical science and the accompanying improvement in clinical practice.

6. Kleinman, "What Is Specific to Western Medicine?" 1:20.

7. Turner, *The Politics of Expertise,* 6, 42.

8. Articles displaying such attitudes appeared in almost every issue of *Your Doctor.* A classic example is "Murakkab al-Naqs: Na'm, lahu Diwa'" (Inferiority Complex: Yes, There Is a Remedy for That), *Tabibak,* August 1957, 12–14.

9. The most unusual example is "Junun taht al-Talab" (Madness upon Request), which described Albert Hoffman's synthesis of lysergic acid diethylamide (LSD) and the ongoing efforts to identify that drug's possible psychotherapeutic applications. *Tabibak,* January 1957, 27–33.

10. The biographical information is culled, in part, from the standard sources, i.e., Faris, ed., *Man Huwa fi Suriya 1949,* 596, and *Man Hum fi al-'Alam al-'Arabi,* 496. Yet I have drawn most heavily on al-'Itri's *Hadith al-'Abqariyyat,* 202–213.

11. *Al-Jami'a* was a "variety" magazine featuring sports and entertainment news, pulp fiction, and "girlie" pictures.

12. See, e.g., *al-Jami'a,* March 1, 1954, 11, and October 9, 1954, 25.

13. Billed as an "illustrated, weekly magazine," *al-Dunya* was very similar to *al-Jami'a* in appearance, structure, and content, and was clearly competing for the same audience.

14. The tradition of medically oriented publications in Syria dates at least to 1928 and the first appearance of the Damascene journal *al-Tibb al-Hadith* (Modern Medicine). Al-Mashut, *Tarikh al-Sihafa al-Suriyya,* 176. Yet al-Qabbani's "advice to readers" columns were unprecedented in the history of Syrian medical journalism.

15. The formulaic description in Arabic is *majalla sihhiyya 'ilmiyya ijtima'iyya,* literally, "a social, scientific, healthful magazine." Syria's press laws required that such descriptions appear on the mastheads of all licensed publications.

16. He also published a second magazine, *al-Riyada wa al-Jamal* (Sports and Beauty), that failed after a very brief period. Al-'Itri, *Hadith al-'Abqariyyat,* 204. For a complete list of his published works, consult the bibliography at the end of this study.

17. The *History of Medicine* appeared in the first eleven issues of *Tabibak*, then intermittently thereafter. The articles were abridged or amended excerpts from Victor Robinson's *The Story of Medicine* in Arabic translation. Robinson, perhaps the first to combine successfully the roles of physician and medical journalist, was the publisher of the journal *Medical Life*, and thus one of al-Qabbani's heroes. The "backwardness and inventiveness" slant was particularly evident in "al-Tibb fi al-'Asr al-Jabri" (Medicine during the Stone Age), *Tabibak*, September 1956, 71–76, and "al-Tibb fi Masr al-Qadima" (Medicine in Ancient Egypt), *Tabibak*, October 1956, 69–73.

18. Surkis, *Sexing the Citizen*, 197.

19. Occasionally, al-Qabbani declined to make such long-distance diagnoses, but this was the exception rather than the rule. See, e.g., the response to the question from "Mr. Khalid al-Mahayni" about "weak nerves," in *al-Dunya*, March 9, 1956, 24.

20. *Al-Dunya*, January 22, 1954, 24.

21. *Tabibak*, June 1957, 85; November 1956, 85; *al-Dunya*, March 2, 1956, 30; *Tabibak*, July 1957, 92; June 1957, 88; January 1958, 87; February 1957, 93; February 1958, 97; October 1957, 95.

22. *Tabibak*, October 1956, 64–68.

23. *Tabibak*, November 1956, 91. Such descriptions of folk practices were often provided, as in this case, in conjunction with the prescription of powerful medications. Less common was the recommendation of herbal compounds that required no prescription. For the latter, see *al-Dunya*, January 22, 1954, 24, and *Tabibak*, November 1956, 87.

24. See, e.g., *Tabibak*, June 1957, 90; March 1957, 91; April 1957, 92; May 1957, 87; December 1957, 96.

25. For Ovomaltine, see, e.g., *Tabibak*, May 1957, 39; for Eno Fruit Salts, see, e.g., *Tabibak*, June 1957, 66; for Evian, see, e.g., *Tabibak*, March 1957, 26; for Johnson and Johnson's Baby Powder, see, e.g., *Tabibak*, December 1956, 82. Al-Qabbani's special relationship with these companies transcended conventional advertising, including items like the "most beautiful baby" photo contest cosponsored by Johnson and Johnson's Baby Powder. *Tabibak*, January 1958, 98–99; February 1958, 86–87.

26. Other than *Your Doctor*, the only exceptions to this general rule were the covers of some monthly entertainment magazines and special issues of more general-interest periodicals associated with specific events like the opening of the Damascus International Exposition or celebrations associated with national or religious holidays. For the former, see *al-Dunya, al-Raqib, al-Jami'a*, or the cartoons on the cover of *al-Mudhik al-Mabki* (The Tragi-Comic). For the latter, see *al-Mukhtar* (The Select), September 2, 1954.

27. The rare exceptions included advertisements for Syrian Airlines (*Tabibak*, September 1957, 88; October 1957, 84; November 1957, 99), for Crème Nivea (*Tabibak*, January 1958, 82), and for the Lottery of the Damascus International Exposition (*Tabibak*, August 1957, 42), which were ubiquitous in other publications.

28. One indication is the fact that *Your Doctor* was priced lower per page than the overwhelming majority of its "popular" contemporaries. Precise comparisons are difficult because *Tabibak* was a monthly magazine, like most professional journals, whereas virtually all other mass circulation magazines were weeklies. The average length of *Tabibak* was 100 pages. Its price was 50 qurush (there were 100 qurush to the Syrian lira) per monthly issue, and 7, 15, or 25 lira (depending on income) for a yearly subscription. The oft-mentioned weekly *al-Dunya* averaged 37 pages in length and was priced at 25 qurush per issue and 20 lira for a yearly subscription in Syria or Lebanon.

29. See, e.g., *Tabibak*, March 1957, 22, and January 1957, 26.

30. See, e.g., *Tabibak*, February 1957, 61.

31. See, e.g., *Tabibak*, July 1957, 97.

32. The active pharmaceutical ingredient in Armonil was diazepam, the generic name for Valium. The ad appears in *Tabibak*, February 1957, 90, and January 1957, 79.

33. The causal relationship between this location, on the one hand, and the abiding interest of al-Qabbani's readers in the topic of bodybuilding on the other, is impossible to document. The sole exception to this observation is a letter seeking specific instructions for "the way to use the fortifying drink Armonil." *Tabibak*, February 1957, 95–96. Advertisements for other products claiming to support muscle growth also appeared in *Your Doctor*. See, e.g., the advertisement for Rinocilline, manufactured by the Swiss Company Vifor, *Tabibak*, March 1957, 45.

34. *Tabibak*, October 1956, 45–50.

35. Other examples include ads for Urodonal, which claimed to prevent and treat "urinary stones," and Apragon, the cold medicine manufactured by Schering. See, e.g., *Tabibak*, June 1957, 67, and February 1957, 72.

36. Appearing in *Tabibak*, October 1957, inserted between pages 52 and 53, and in *Tabibak*, September 1957, inserted between pages 100 and 101.

37. *Tabibak*, November 1956, 57–59.

38. Surkis, *Sexing the Citizen*, 213–214.

39. Advertisements for Camoquin, a Parke-Davis product used to treat malaria and giardia, were among those frequently appearing on the same pages as "Your Doctor Is at Your Service." See, e.g., *Tabibak*, September 1957, 119, and December 1957, 83.

40. See, e.g., *al-Dunya*, March 2, 1956, 30; March 9, 1956, 24; and *Tabibak*, February 1958, 92.

41. *Tabibak*, June 1957, 86.

42. *Al-Dunya*, March 25, 1955, 20.

43. Ibid.

44. *Al-Dunya*, March 9, 1956, 24.

45. See, for example, the previously referenced exchanges with "Miss Samira M. from Suwayda'" (a town almost entirely inhabited at this time by Druze of rural origins), who feared she may have contracted rabies, in *al-Dunya*, March 25, 1955, 20, and with "Mr. Fathi M. from Syria" ("from Syria" was a standard formulation

employed by al-Qabbani when the town or village was too obscure for his readers to recognize), who had contracted some unidentified type of intestinal worms, in *al-Dunya*, March 9, 1956, 24.

46. *Al-Jami'a*, February 22, 1954, 13–14.

47. *Tabibak*, October 1957, 93–94.

48. Further clarification of al-Qabbani's position on this issue is found in his response to a question from "Mr. M. 'Ayn, the Iraqi residing in Damascus" about the "benefits and harm of beer" in *Tabibak*, September 1957, 130–131. Al-Qabbani addressed other religious taboos from a clinical perspective. See, e.g., his response to "Mr. Bassam Sa'i," which addresses "the medical harm of [eating] pork." *Tabibak*, December 1957, 80–81. Al-Qabbani also discussed the Ramadan fast from this perspective. See, e.g., the exchange with "Mr. Zuhayr Burka from Tripoli [Lebanon]," *Tabibak*, October 1956, 92.

49. Further evidence supporting this conclusion is al-Qabbani's occasional practice of invoking God's name or quoting the Qur'an to introduce, contextualize, and validate his medical advice. For the former, see *Tabibak*, February 1957, 95, and December 1957, 93. A classic example of the latter appears in *Tabibak*, January 1958, 85, in which al-Qabbani quoted verse 30 of Sura 21 ("The Prophets")—"We made from water every living thing"—to encourage the petitioner to maintain a healthy level of hydration. The Qur'anic translation is from Ali, *The Holy Qur'an*, 828. *Your Doctor* also featured the occasional quote from prominent figures in Islamic history. See, e.g., the quotation from "the Imam 'Ali," in *Tabibak*, December 1956, 31. The ruling, which concludes that wine's "harm is greater than its benefit," conveys the principle that any practice not expressly forbidden or enjoined by doctrine should be evaluated in terms of its relative potential harm and benefit to the individual and/or the community. "Response to Mr. Ahmad 'Ayn from Hama," *al-Dunya*, January 22, 1954, 24. Such formulations are "characteristic of virtually all fatwas." Muhammad Khalid Masud, Brinkley Messick, and David S. Powers, "Muftis, Fatwas, and Islamic Legal Interpretation," in Masud et al., eds., *Islamic Legal Interpretation*, 24; "Response to Mr. M. Z. from Dayr al-Zawr," *Tabibak*, October 1956, 88. One frequent postscript—"and for every event there is an explanation"—employs a commonly used aphorism to make a positivist assertion of scientific certainty, and thereby inverts the mufti's standard recapitulation of human fallibility in the face of divine omniscience. See, e.g., *Tabibak*, December 1957, 91, and January 1958, 94.

50. Among the most interesting of these were questions about the potential harm of drinking too many Pepsi colas and about the possibility of "exchanging a diseased heart for a healthy one," some ten years before the first such surgery was attempted. See *Tabibak*, October 1957, 97, and January 1957, 93.

51. For headaches, see *Tabibak*, October 1956, 91, and June 1957, 88. For hemorrhoids, see *al-Dunya*, March 2, 1956, 30, and *Tabibak*, February 1958, 93. For allergies, see *Tabibak*, June 1957), 85, and October 1957, 94. For arteriosclerosis, see *Tabibak*, January 1957, 93. For cancer, see *Tabibak*, January 1957, 91. For irregular heartbeats, see *Tabibak*, June 1957, 91; October 1956, 90; and November 1956, 89. For epilepsy, see

Tabibak, January 1957, 88. For digestive/intestinal ailments, see *Tabibak,* September 1956, 91; October 1956, 90, 92, 93; June 1957, 88, 90; and October 1957, 94.

52. Al-Qabbani's interest in such matters was also manifested in feature articles. See, e.g., Dr. Hisham Sabah al-Husni, "Hypersensitivity: A Medical and Social Problem," *Tabibak,* September 1957, 56–59.

53. For stuttering, see *al-Dunya,* March 25, 1955, 20, and *Tabibak,* October 1956, 93–94. For insomnia, see *Tabibak,* September 1956, 91, and October 1957, 96.

54. See, e.g., *Tabibak,* October 1956, 91, and November 1956, 89.

55. For talking in one's sleep, see *Tabibak,* June 1957, 87. For nervous disorders, see *Tabibak,* December 1956, 87; June 1957, 91; and November 1956, 90. For dream interpretation, see *al-Dunya,* March 14, 1954, 24. For the movie-induced stomach cramps, see *Tabibak,* January 1958, 93. The issue of "police stories" is raised in *Tabibak,* October 1956, 91.

56. The most common of such queries came from students desiring medications that enhanced memory. See, e.g., *Tabibak,* November 1956, 92, and March 1957, 84.

57. See, e.g., *Tabibak,* November 1956, 88.

58. For sunbathing, see *Tabibak,* November 1956, 89–90; June 1957, 87, 91; and September 1957, 118. For the "pleasing voice" issue, see *al-Dunya,* January 22, 1954, 24. For acne, see *Tabibak,* November 1956, 86, and June 1957, 90.

59. *Tabibak,* February 1957, 84–85.

60. For augmentation, see *Tabibak,* November 1956, 91, and February 1957, 96. For reduction, see *Tabibak,* October 1956, 92, and January 1958, 87.

61. For the wavy hair issue, see *Tabibak,* November 1956, 87. For gray hair, see *Tabibak,* November 1956, 86. For hair loss/baldness, see *al-Dunya,* March 9, 1956, 24; *Tabibak,* November 1956, 86, 89; and *Tabibak,* October 1957, 94. For unwanted hair, see *al-Dunya,* March 25, 1955, 20, and *Tabibak,* June 1957, 85, 86.

62. For bodybuilding, etc., see *Tabibak,* November 1956, 89, and October 1957, 94. For height issues, see *Tabibak,* November 1956, 89; June 1957, 87; and February 1957, 96. One letter contained a complaint of excessive height. *Tabibak,* January 1957, 86.

63. *Al-Dunya,* March 25, 1955, 20. Before the development of recombinant DNA research, the only source of these compounds, precursors to synthesized human growth hormone (somatotropin, or HGH), was the pituitary glands of cadavers.

64. *Tabibak,* June 1957, 90.

65. *Al-Dunya,* March 25, 1955, 20.

66. *Tabibak,* October 1956, 89.

67. The identical initials are pure coincidence.

68. Conrad, "Arab-Islamic Medicine," 712.

69. For a treatment of transplant surgery in Islamic societies, see Hamdy, *Our Bodies Belong to God.*

70. Examples abound. See, e.g., the letters from "L 'Ayn F." and "Miss M. W. Z. from Aleppo" in *al-Dunya,* March 25, 1955, 20, and more than twenty examples in *Tabibak,* June 1957, 85–95.

71. Again, the practice was frequent and ubiquitous. See, e.g., the letters from "A rebellious young man from Homs" in *Tabibak*, October 1956, 91; "Ibn al-Rafidain ['a son of Mesopotamia'] from Iraq" in *Tabibak*, November 1956, 86; "Mistreated from Dayr al-Zawr" in *Tabibak*, December 1956, 87; and "Seaside Girl from Latakiya" in *Tabibak*, June 1957, 91.

72. See, e.g., letters from "the 'Perplexed' 'Ayn M. 'Ayn from Abla" in *Tabibak*, November 1956, 86, and "Miss W. 'Euphrates River' from Iraq" in *Tabibak*, June 1957, 85.

73. Masud et al., "Muftis, Fatwas," 22–23.

74. *Tabibak*, September 1956, 1. This exact format and language was maintained until the December 1957 issue, when the changes described below were instituted.

75. See, e.g., the query from "a reader in Iraq" who was coughing up blood after his x-rays showed no sign of tuberculosis. *Tabibak*, June 1957, 88.

76. The policy statement and justification appears in *Tabibak*, March 1957, 92. The example of its enforcement, addressed to nineteen named individuals, appears in *Tabibak*, December 1957, 91.

77. In the case of the traditional mufti, this has been described as a manifestation of the "restricted control of the essential cultural capital that sharia knowledge represents." Masud et al., "Muftis, Fatwas," 21.

78. Al-'Itri, *Hadith al-'Abqariyyat*, 212.

79. A quick comparison of his responses to questions in the September through December 1956 issues with those for November 1957 through February 1958 reveals the dramatic difference.

80. See, e.g., "al-Sharika allati Tumaris A'zam Daman Tibbi" (The Company That Provides the Very Best Medical Insurance), *Tabibak*, May 1957, 71–75, which lauds the work of "the illustrious" Dr. Iman al-Kuzbary in his capacity as supervisor of medical care at the Khumasiyya Company, the largest Syrian industrial conglomerate of the day.

81. "For Doctors Only" first appeared in *Tabibak*, September 1957, then in issues for October 1957 through April 1958, August 1958 through January 1959, and intermittently thereafter.

82. *Tabibak* also featured advertisements addressed exclusively to physicians. See, e.g., the advertisement for the East German state chemical manufacturer that is addressed to "le corps Medical Syrien," *Tabibak*, October 1957, 4.

83. Ruhi al-Khayyat, a "specialist in internal medicine and diseases of the chest," was the product of an old family that was, in this period, very prominent in medicine and science. 'Abd al-Latif al-Sadat, a "specialist in urology and general practitioner," was also at this time director of the Department of Health in the Syrian Army. Nashat al-Kahhal, a "specialist in gynecology and obstetrics," and Zuhdi al-Munjid, a "specialist in psychiatry and nervous disorders," were scions of families that produced some of the most prominent physicians in Syria during this period. Faris, ed., *Man Huwa fi Suriya 1949*, 275, 346, 529, 633; Faris, ed., *Man Hum*

fi al-'Alam al-'Arabi, 331–332, 292, 730, 600–601. Reflecting the additional expertise provided by these specialists, the name of al-Qabbani's advice column was briefly changed to "Your Doctor's Hospital." See *Tabibak,* September–December 1958.

84. *Tabibak,* January 1958, 93, 100.

85. This practice of using specialists became a permanent feature, continuing at least until the issue for August 1971.

86. Al-Qabbani's rhetorical invocation of medical doctors' collective expertise resembles another common feature of the fatwa, the citation of external authority in support of the judgment rendered. By evoking an external authority, al-Qabbani situated the medical profession's practitioners as the collective guardians and transmitters of an authoritative intellectual tradition, effectively making them the secular counterparts of Islam's jurisprudents, the *fuqaha'* (sing. *faqih*). During the Ottoman period, the citation of previous precedent-setting judgments by reputed scholars was common for Syria's "provincial muftis" like Hamid al-'Imadi and Khayr al-Din al-Ramli. Masud et al., "Muftis, Fatwas," 12, 25.

87. See, for example, the responses to "Ahmad Ayyub from Kafr Takharim" and "Sergeant Farid Kamil" in *al-Dunya,* March 25, 1955, 20, and March 2, 1956, 30.

88. Turner, *The Politics of Expertise,* 4.

89. Masud et al., "Muftis, Fatwas," 16–20. On this issue, the authors rely heavily on the medieval scholar Yahya Ibn Sharif al-Nawawi.

90. This is what T. J. Jackson Lears calls the "dream of metamorphosis." See Lears, *Fables of Abundance,* 42–46.

7. SEX AND THE CONJUGAL CITIZEN

1. The identical statement in the epigraph also appears in *Tabibak,* June 1957, 84. Similar statements appeared in October 1956, 89; November 1956, 87; February 1957, 83; March 1957, 93; April 1957, 86; May 1957, 81; June 1957, 84; and September 1957, 121. Al-Qabbani published numerous books devoted exclusively to educating the public about sexuality and reproduction including *Atfal taht al-Talab, Hayatuna al-Jinsiyya, Mi'at Su'al,* and *Alif Ba' al-Jins.*

2. For a detailed analysis of this phenomenon in France's Third Republic, see Surkis, *Sexing the Citizen.*

3. Sexuality had, of course, been the subject of Arab-Islamic medical treatises for centuries. One of the earliest examples was Qusta Ibn Luqa's (d. 300/912) *Fi al-Bah* (On Sexuality). Yet, for a variety of reasons, chief among them low literacy rates, the prohibitive expense of books, and propriety, such canonical works were circulated among a very small number of the male, educated elite. Conrad, "Arab-Islamic Medicine," 698, 703.

4. For other examples of this phenomenon, see Turner, *The Politics of Expertise,* 18.

5. Surkis, *Sexing the Citizen,* 1, 5, 13, 16, 21, 43, 58, 136, 158–160, 243, 240.

6. I have borrowed and adapted Jean-François Lyotard's concept of the "libidinal economy." Lyotard, *Libidinal Economy.*

7. See, e.g., *al-Dunya*, January 22, 1954, 24; *Tabibak*, October 1956, 92, 93; February 1957, 91–92; June 1957, 86; July 1957, 90; September 1957, 119.

8. *Tabibak*, September 1957, 121. This "sexual vices and their consequences are Western imports" narrative continued throughout the twentieth century. See, e.g., the comments of Muhammad 'Ali al-Barr, quoted in Massad, *Desiring Arabs*, 214.

9. Exchange with "Mr. 'Ayn S. from Dayr al-Zawr," *Tabibak*, October 1956, 91; al-Qabbani, *Hayatuna al-Jinsiyya*, 78–79.

10. "Circumcision," *Tabibak*, June 1957, 19–23.

11. Gollaher, "From Ritual to Science."

12. Exchange with "Mr. Muhammad Rashid Salim," *Tabibak*, October 1956, 92.

13. See, e.g., *al-Dunya*, March 25, 1955, 20; *Tabibak*, October 1956, 92; November 1956, 86, 87; December 1956, 28–31, 89; January 1957, 89; February 1957, 93; March 1957, 88; April 1957, 20–23; May 1957, 40–41; June 1957, 85–86, 90; August 1957, 16–18; September 1957, 117; October 1957, 97; December 1957, 86; and January 1958, 88.

14. The complaint was so common that al-Qabbani dedicated an entire chapter of his sex primer to it. "Are You a Stallion or the Opposite?" in *Hayatuna al-Jinsiyya*, 55–58.

15. See, e.g., the response to "'Imad 'Ali Muhammad from Lebanon," who the doctor advised to first get tested for diabetes. *Tabibak*, February 1958, 91.

16. See, e.g., the exchanges with "Mr. Ramsis al-Laythi from Damascus" in *Tabibak*, November 1956, 90–91, and with "Mr. S. 'Ilm al-Din from al-Manbah in Lebanon," who was told he "must receive an intramuscular injection of 25 milligrams of testosterone every two days." *Tabibak*, June 1957, 91.

17. *Tabibak*, February 1957, 94; December 1957, 93.

18. *Tabibak*, October 1956, 89. See also the response to the question from "Mr. 'Ali K.," which attributes "the spread of 'sexual weakness' in our country" to "the secret habit, sexual repression with the presence of numerous agitating factors, and the perception of psychological inferiority." *Tabibak*, January 1957, 94.

19. The phrase routinely employed, *sur'at al-inzal*, translates literally as "rapidity of ejaculation." See, e.g., the response to "Mr. Iskandar Bey from Damascus, Mr. Hassun Sa'id Sa'di from Baghdad, and Mr. 'Adil Mahmud from Baghdad," *Tabibak*, March 1957, 84.

20. A classic example is the response to "Mr. Zaidun from Damascus, Mr. Fu'ad from Koura, and Mr. D. A. M. from Riyadh," who, in addition to being told that "marriage is guaranteed to cure this malady," were also ordered ("you must") to take "half a tablet of Largactil after every meal." A powerful sedative and antipsychotic, Largactil (chlorpromazine) was marketed and prescribed in the United States as Thorazine. *Tabibak*, February 1957, 94.

21. This interpretation is supported by the fact that al-Qabbani modified the above prescription on subsequent occasions, omitting the injunction to marry and replacing it with the provision of more varied and comprehensive measures to delay ejaculation. See, e.g., the exchange with "Mr. J. B. D. from Damascus," *Tabibak*, January 1958, 89.

22. The chapter of *Our Sexual Life* dedicated to the male orgasm, "The Happy Moment That Men Await," deals exclusively with the mechanics of ejaculation. Qabbani, *Hayatuna al-Jinsiyya*, 80–83.

23. Examples appear in the above discussion of fertility, contraception, and reproduction.

24. See, e.g., the exchanges with "A. M. from Damascus," *Tabibak*, February 1958, 96, and "Mr. Muhammad Hashim," *Tabibak*, January 1957, 88.

25. See, e.g., the exchange with "Mr. M. F. from Damascus," *Tabibak*, September 1957, 119.

26. For the sole exception, see the exchange with "Mr. Muhammad Darwish from Kuwait and Mr. M. S. from Damascus," *Tabibak*, February 1957, 85.

27. Responses to "Mr. M. 'Ayn. A. from Hama," who was told, "you are not in need of hormones," in *Tabibak*, October 1957, 93, and to "Mr. A. B. S. from Dayr al-Zawr," *Tabibak*, February 1957, 94.

28. *Tabibak*, March 1957, 83–84.

29. See, e.g., Surkis, *Sexing the Citizen*, 51.

30. See, for example, Tucker, *In the House of the Law*, 151–156, and Surkis, *Sexing the Citizen*, 248.

31. This view is expressed in all of al-Qabbani's discourses on sexuality and is particularly prevalent in his advice to male readers. See, e.g., *al-Dunya*, March 9, 1956, 24, in which al-Qabbani advises his worried young correspondent that the "sexual physical exercises" afforded by marriage will "guarantee the onset of his virility" and "lead him onto the path of happiness and success." See also *Tabibak*, December 1956, 87, and June 1957, 88. It also is in keeping with the main currents of Islamic and Christian thought. Wasil, *Mushkilat al-Shabab*, 5.

32. *Al-Dunya*, March 2, 1956, 29.

33. *Tabibak*, January 1958, 88.

34. *Tabibak*, November 1956, 87–88.

35. This was certainly the view expressed by Abdelwahab Boudhiba, summarized in Ze'evi, *Producing Desire*, 4.

36. In closing, al-Qabbani could not resist offering another customary bit of counsel, urging the petitioner to take "Basiflourine" until the situation was resolved. *Tabibak*, March 1957, 95 (emphasis added).

37. *Tabibak*, September 1956, 29–31.

38. *Tabibak*, February 1957, 93.

39. See, e.g., his article "Masculinity . . . a Suicidal Doctrine," *Tabibak*, June 1957, 25–28.

40. *Hayatuna al-Jinsiyya*, 111–118, 111 (quotation).

41. In its absence, other features, e.g., "20 Questions about Your Beauty, My Lady," "Your Beauty, My Young Lady," and "Yes, My Lady, You Are Beautiful," appeared. See *Tabibak*, April 1957, 74–79; May 1957, 53–60; and June 1957, 68–73.

42. See, e.g., the responses to "the suffering girl in Latakiyya," *al-Dunya*, March 2, 1956, 29; to "Miss 'Afaf K., Mrs. Mimi Khatib from Damascus, and

Miss Haifa' from Aleppo," *Tabibak*, November 1970, 94; and to "Mrs. F. 'Ayn," *Tabibak*, February 1958, 89.

43. *Tabibak*, January 1957, 91.

44. *Tabibak*, March 1957, 86.

45. *Tabibak*, November 1956, 88.

46. Response to "Salwa Marjani [from] Idlib," *Tabibak*, January 1957, 85.

47. For the quotation in the heading, see the exchange with a reader in *Tabibak*, February 1957, 94. For examples of questions related to reproduction, see *al-Dunya*, March 25, 1955, 20; *Tabibak*, November 1956, 85; and *Tabibak*, June 1957, 88, 90.

48. See, e.g., exchange with "Mrs. B. B. from Damascus," *Tabibak*, February 1957, 96.

49. *Tabibak*, November 1956, 91. This was actually the first of two exchanges with "Mrs. B. B.," who, after reading the book, wrote again to inquire about the efficacy of monthly injections of a medication called Diyujinun, presumably a brand name for progestogen. *Tabibak*, February 1957, 96.

50. The first installment in *Your Doctor*, which emphasized the potential medical and social dangers of unplanned pregnancies, appeared in the journal's debut issue. "Atfal Bidun Talab" (Unplanned Children), *Tabibak*, September 1956, 19–20.

51. The evidence indicates that the book was available to all but the poorest strata of Syrian society, for I acquired a copy of its thirty-first printing in 2001 at a Ministry of Culture book fair for the equivalent of U.S. $2.00.

52. Ze'evi, *Producing Desire*, 9. Whenever possible, al-Qabbani rhetorically solidified this connection with Islamic tradition. See, e.g., the chapter of *Our Sexual Life* entitled "Human Beings Were Created from a Clot of Blood!" *Hayatuna al-Jinsiyya*, 88–95.

53. For the most concise treatment of this issue, see Farah, *Marriage and Sexuality in Islam*, 35–36.

54. See, e.g., *al-Dunya*, January 22, 1954, 24; *Tabibak*, November 1956, 85, 87; *Tabibak*, January 1957, 86, 89, 91, 93; "Mr. H. K.," *Tabibak*, February 1957, 84, 93, 94; *Tabibak*, June 1957, 87; and *Tabibak*, February 1958, 99. See also al-Qabbani, "The Secret of Human Existence Lies in the Testicles," *Hayatuna al-Jinsiyya*, 42–49.

55. *Tabibak*, October 1956, 93, 89.

56. There is a dearth of empirical studies of masturbation. The few exceptions have been severely criticized. See Melikian and Prothro, "Sexual Behavior of University Students," and Klausner, "Inferential Visibility and Sex Norms."

57. I was unable to examine every issue of *al-Dunya* and *al-Idha'a al-Suriyya*. The total number is almost certainly higher, as is evidenced by al-Qabbani's frequent referral of petitioners to the discussion of masturbation in previous issues. See, e.g., his response to "N. W. K. from Damascus," *Tabibak*, March 1957, 90.

58. Al-Qabbani, "al-Istimna'" (Masturbation), *Hayatuna al-Jinsiyya*, 178–184. Masturbation and other "secret habits" also feature prominently in another chapter of *Our Sexual Life*, "The Scientist's Efforts to Explain the Issue of Sex," 219–225.

59. Ze'evi, *Producing Desire*, 32, 34. See also Farah, *Marriage and Sexuality in Islam*, 36–37. For a more unorthodox minority position, see Boudhiba, *Sexuality in Islam*, 31. Boudhiba locates "auto-eroticism" adjacent to "female homosexuality, bestiality or necrophilia" in the hierarchy of "sexual perversions."

60. *Al-Dunya*, January 22, 1954, 24. Al-Qabbani's recommended treatments for these conditions were "regulating the digestive system," consuming more "meats and fats," and abstaining from "excessive vital secretions," respectively.

61. See, e.g., Massad, *Desiring Arabs*, 307–308.

62. The only two exceptions I have located appear in the title of the chapter of *Our Sexual Life* referenced above and in al-Qabbani's response to "Mr. H. Q. from Beirut," in which he used both a colloquial phrase (*jald 'umayra*) and the more literal term *al-istimna'*. *Tabibak*, January 1958, 88.

63. Laqueur, *Solitary Sex*, 17. Laqueur's book is the most comprehensive and theoretically sophisticated study of the subject of "onania," which refers to an eighteenth-century pseudo-medical publication and to the hysteria it fostered.

64. Massad, *Desiring Arabs*, 307. According to Massad, the term's first documented use in Arabic appears in the memoirs of Lebanese author and journalist Jurji Zaydan (1861–1914), and was popularized by the prolific Egyptian author, journalist, and activist Salama Musa (1887–1958). Ibid., 130.

65. The psychological implications loomed so large that al-Qabbani eventually began to assign some questions about masturbation to one of his new colleagues, "specialist in psychiatry and nervous disorders" Dr. Zuhdi al-Munjid. See, e.g., his response to "Lost," *Tabibak*, February 1958, 89–90.

66. See, e.g., the response to "Mr. Muhammad Hashim," which attributes the curvature of Mr. Hashim's penis to "a bad habit established in youth." *Tabibak*, January 1957, 88. The "weakness of the nerves and poverty of the blood" mantra appeared much more frequently. See, e.g., the response to "the helpless, tormented student, Mr. R. F. from Damascus, and Mr. B. S. J. from Aleppo," *Tabibak*, December 1957, 94; the response to "the young 'Ayn D. from Damascus," *Tabibak*, February 1958, 99; and the response to "'Ayn S. from Latakiyya," *Tabibak*, January 1957, 85. For the expression of similar concerns in premodern treatises, see Ze'evi, *Producing Desire*, 34.

67. *Tabibak*, December 1957, 79. Al-Qabbani closes with "read the book *Our Sexual Life* by Dr. Sabri al-Qabbani in which is found a detailed discussion of this subject."

68. See, e.g., *Tabibak*, January 1957, 85; December 1957, 94; and February 1958, 99. These tropes are also ubiquitous in the writings of the aforementioned Egyptian journalist Salama Musa. Musa, *al-Shakhsiyya al-Naji'a*, 174–75.

69. Al-Qabbani appears to have defined excess as practicing the secret habit more than "once or twice a week." *Tabibak*, October 1957, 94; November 1957, 98–100. Here again, Salama Musa seems to have established the standard. Musa, *Ahadith ila al-Shabab*, 122. See also Surkis, *Sexing the Citizen*, 107.

70. See, e.g., the responses to "Mr. 'M. H.' from Qamishli," *Tabibak*, December 1956, 87, and to "Mr. Abu Firas from Iraq," *Tabibak*, November 1957, 94.

71. This exchange also included discussion of a hernia, which al-Qabbani dismissed as unrelated to "the habit." *Tabibak,* November 1957, 98–100. See also the response to "Mr. H. Q. from Beirut," *Tabibak,* January 1958, 88.

72. Response to "Mr. Dh. S. from Aleppo," *Tabibak,* November 1956, 88–89.

73. Al-Qabbani's certainty notwithstanding, marriage did not yield the desired result in every instance, as is evidenced by the letter from "Desperate from Aleppo," who suffered "addiction to the secret habit despite being married." *Al-Dunya,* January 22, 1954, 24.

74. See, e.g., the response to "the helpless, tormented student, Mr. R. F. from Damascus, and Mr. B. S. J. from Aleppo," *Tabibak,* December 1957, 94; the response to "Mr. Abu Firas from Iraq," *Tabibak,* November 1957, 94; the response to "H. M. from Basra," *Tabibak,* September 1957, 117. This prescription, once again, echoes that of Salama Musa, quoted in Massad, *Desiring Arabs,* 130–131.

75. *Tabibak,* December 1956, 87. A similar response was proffered to "'Ayn S. from Latakiyya," *Tabibak,* January 1957, 85.

76. Perhaps this an example of al-Qabbani's "celebrated wit." Al-'Itri, *Hadith al-'Abqariyyat,* 203–204.

77. In support of this diagnosis, al-Qabbani's complete answer also includes the sentence "and there is no better proof of this than the irregular periods that afflict you." *Tabibak,* November 1956, 91.

78. Ibid. (emphasis added).

79. Al-Qabbani repeatedly cited British and American studies, particularly the publications of Alfred Kinsey, in support of his conclusion that "it is impossible to deny the enormity of the social problems caused by sexual deviance." *Tabibak,* September 1956, 48–49. Al-Qabbani's use of Kinsey's research displays a fundamental misunderstanding of its intent. In this, he was far from alone. To cite just one example, the late leader of the Egyptian Muslim Brotherhood, Sayyid Qutb, cited Kinsey as evidence of the depravity and moral bankruptcy of Western society. Qutb, *Fi Zilal al-Qur'an,* 126.

80. For comparisons with nineteenth-century thought on this issue, see Surkis, *Sexing the Citizen,* 10–19.

81. *Tabibak,* September 1956, 45–50; al-Qabbani, *Hayatuna al-Jinsiyya,* 219–225. In the article's preface, al-Qabbani characteristically boasted that it presented "the most recent science with regard to the causes of sexual deviance and its methods of treatment in addition to a number of important recommendations regarding legal and social opinions surrounding this problem." *Tabibak,* September 1956, 45.

82. El-Rouayheb, *Before Homosexuality,* 15–16.

83. A literal translation of *luti* is "sodomite," as both terms are derived from the Biblical/Qur'anic story of Lot and the destruction of Sodom and Gomorrah.

84. El-Rouayheb, *Before Homosexuality,* 136, 19, 21, 22–23. This perception is also prevalent in the extant popular literature. Ibid., 9–10.

85. Ibid., 153, 20, 19.

86. See Massad, *Desiring Arabs,* 51–98, for a comprehensive overview of this process.

87. The quotes are from Foucault, *The History of Sexuality,* 1:43. See also El-Rouayheb, *Before Homosexuality,* 44–45.

88. The precise chain of transmission has yet to be established beyond doubt. Some scholars locate the source exclusively in medical/scientific literature, while others note its contemporaneous use in the popular discourse of the Victorian period. For the former, see Massad, *Desiring Arabs,* and Ze'evi, *Producing Desire.* For the latter, see El-Rouayheb, *Before Homosexuality.*

89. Massad, *Desiring Arabs,* 172. Massad notes that the current and more politically correct term *mithliyya* also emerged from the translation of Western psychological texts, in this case Freud.

90. El-Rouayheb, *Before Homosexuality,* 158–159; Massad, *Desiring Arabs,* 99. Initially, variant translations of sexual deviance were in circulation. Massad attributes the term's popularization to the tireless Salama Musa. Ibid., 134, 138, 129–130.

91. El-Rouayheb, *Before Homosexuality,* 161.

92. Al-Qabbani, *Hayatuna al-Jinsiyya,* 224–225. This observation appears in a chapter entitled "The Scientist's Efforts to Resolve the Problem of Sex."

93. See, e.g., his discussion of "sexual deviance in ancient Greece." *Tabibak,* September 1956, 45. For good measure, al-Qabbani occasionally employed an appositive structure to create a new concept, "sodomy sexual deviance." See, e.g., ibid., 48.

94. Ibid., 45, 50.

95. Ibid., 49. In passing, al-Qabbani mentioned the *mutakhannithin,* a variant form of the plural "effeminates," noting that they are "a minority who attract undue attention to themselves." The more common form, *mukhannath,* was sometimes used as a synonym for *ma'bun* in the premodern period. See El-Rouayheb, *Before Homosexuality,* 16–19.

96. *Tabibak,* September 1956, 50.

97. El-Rouayheb, *Before Homosexuality,* 128.

98. Al-Qabbani, *Hayatuna al-Jinsiyya,* 224. Elsewhere, al-Qabbani noted the prevalence of sexual deviance at "the colleges of the ancient English universities," where there was "segregation of the sexes." *Tabibak,* September 1956, 49.

99. In the twentieth century, several prominent Arab social reformers adopted Freud's concept of "contingent homosexuality" to argue that the social segregation of the sexes, particularly in youth, inevitably resulted in the practice of "emergency homosexuality." For numerous examples, see Massad, *Desiring Arabs,* 134–144, 176–177. See also Surkis, *Sexing the Citizen,* 48, 83–84.

100. *Tabibak,* September 1956, 45.

101. Ibid., 47. One is, of course, tempted to ask where al-Qabbani located and surveyed the opinions of so many "defenders of sexual deviance" in the 1950s Arab world.

102. Ibid., 50.

103. *Tabibak,* February 1957, 95.

104. *Tabibak,* October 1957, 85.

105. This conceptual difference remained salient in popular discourse throughout the modern period. El-Rouayheb, *Before Homosexuality,* 161.

106. The intramuscular injection of such compounds was a common experimental therapy for homosexuality in the 1940s.

107. *Tabibak,* September 1956, 50.

108. Ibid. It is not clear if al-Qabbani drew the obvious inference regarding his discussion of "contingency"—that the prison is, by definition, a site of institutionalized gender segregation and a natural breeding ground for deviance.

109. Ibid., 49.

110. Ibid., 48. Once again, al-Qabbani's source for this assertion was the research of Albert Kinsey.

111. Specific examples of the policy in operation are numerous. See, e.g., *Tabibak,* September 1956, 91; November 1956, 86–87; January 1957, 89, 94; June 1957, 90; November 1957, 95, 96; and December 1957, 80.

CONCLUSION

1. Shotter, "Psychology and Citizenship," 115. See also Parolin, *Citizenship in the Arab World,* 17.

2. Hallaq, *The Impossible State,* 180.

3. Qassab Hasan, "Sahib al-Raya," *al-Jundi,* May 5, 1955, 21.

4. Hallaq, *The Impossible State,* 28, 91–92, 180.

5. Chatterjee, *The Politics of the Governed,* 7; El Shakry, *The Great Social Laboratory,* 5.

6. Hallaq, *The Impossible State,* 16.

7. Mitchell, *Rule of Experts,* 242. See also Turner, *The Politics of Expertise,* 20–21.

8. Surkis, *Sexing the Citizen,* 12, 244.

9. Anderson, *Imagined Communities.*

10. Hanan Qassab Hasan, interview, February 27, 2002.

11. Asad, *Formations of the Secular,* 198.

12. Dallal, *Islam, Science, and the Challenge of History,* 3.

13. For comparable arguments, see Asad, *Formations of the Secular,* 25, and Hurd, *The Politics of Secularism,* 137. Benedict Anderson takes a more ecumenical position regarding the secular and the religious. Anderson, *Imagined Communities,* 12.

14. This presumption reflected general perceptions of Arab intellectuals. For overviews, see Abu-Rabi', *Contemporary Arab Thought,* and Kassab, *Contemporary Arab Thought.* For an overview of the ongoing revision among Arab intellectuals, see Abu-Rabi', *Contemporary Arab Thought,* 1–62.

15. Chatterjee, *The Politics of the Governed,* 34.

16. Turner, "Preface," vi.

17. Makdisi, *The Culture of Sectarianism,* 166. See also Weiss, *In the Shadow of Sectarianism,* 5–6.

18. See, e.g., White, *The Emergence of Minorities,* 3, and Makdisi, *The Culture of Sectarianism,* 2–3, 7, 166.

19. Wedeen, *Ambiguities of Domination,* 6, 65.

20. Tamer, *Tigers on the Tenth Day,* 16.

21. Ibid., 7–8.

22. Rabo, "Gender, State and Civil Society," 168.

23. Kassir, *Being Arab,* 26.

24. Chatterjee, *The Politics of the Governed,* 35–36.

25. Sharabi, *Governments and Politics.*

26. Boym, *The Future of Nostalgia,* xvi.

Bibliography

ARCHIVAL COLLECTIONS AND OTHER UNPUBLISHED SOURCES

American University of Beirut (AUB), Jafet Library
Anonymous. "Malki Trial." Files 1–4, Middle East Files

National Archives, College Park, MD
U.S. Department of State. Confidential Department of State Incoming Telegram, April 26, 1955. General Records of the Department of State, 1955–1959. Folder 783.0000/1–555; Central Decimal File Box 3745; Record Group 59.

———. Confidential Department of the Army Staff Communications Office Message, May 14, 1955. General Records of the Department of State, 1955–1959. Folder 783.00(W)/1–755; Central Decimal File Box 3747; Record Group 59.

———. Confidential Incoming Telegram, August 4, 1956. General Records of the Department of State, 1955–1959. Folder 783.00/7–656; Central Decimal File Box 3745; Record Group 59.

———. Confidential Memorandum from J. S. Moose, Jr., June 12, 1954. Foreign Service Records of the Department of State, 1954–1956. Folder "Damascus, Secret, 1955"; Syria; Damascus Embassy; Record Group 84.

———. Confidential Memorandum of Conversation, June 4, 1955. Foreign Service Records of the Department of State, 1954–1956. Folder "Damascus, Secret, 1955"; Syria; Damascus Embassy; Record Group 84.

———. Confidential Office Memorandum, April 15, 1954. Classified General Records of the Foreign Service Posts of the Department of State, 1946–1963. Folder 350 "Syrian Coup d'État," February, March 1954; Syria; U.S. Embassy, Legations and Consulates; Damascus; 1950–1954, Record Group 84.

———. DA Intelligence Report, August 10, 1956. Records of the Foreign Service Posts of the Department of State, Syria. Folder A1–6 "Activities of Other Governments"; Box 1 UD 3253; U.S. Information Service, Damascus; Record Group 84.

———. Foreign Service Despatch 25, June 14, 1955. Records of the Foreign Service Posts of the Department of State, Syria. Folder A; Box 1 UD 3253; U.S. Information Service, Damascus; Record Group 84.

———. Foreign Service Despatch 93, September 23, 1955. General Records of the Department of State, 1955–1959. Folder 783.00/6–255; Central Decimal File Box 3745; Record Group 59.

———. Foreign Service Despatch 136, November 1, 1955. General Records of the Department of State, 1955–1959. Folder 783.00/6–255; Central Decimal File Box 3745; Record Group 59.

———. Foreign Service Despatch 281, January 22, 1955. General Records of the Department of State, 1955–1959. Folder 783.0000/1–555; Central Decimal File Box 3745; Record Group 59.

———. Foreign Service Despatch 331, February 15, 1955. General Records of the Department of State, 1955–1959. Folder 783.0000/1–555; Central Decimal File Box 3745; Record Group 59.

———. Foreign Service Despatch 446, April 27, 1955. General Records of the Department of State, 1955–1959. Folder 783.0000/1–555; Central Decimal File Box 3745; Record Group 59.

———. Foreign Service Despatch 499, June 10, 1955. General Records of the Department of State, 1955–1959. Folder 783.00/6–255; Central Decimal File Box 3745; Record Group 59.

———. Foreign Service Despatch 520, June 23, 1955. General Records of the Department of State, 1955–1959. Folder 783.00/6–255; Central Decimal File Box 3745; Record Group 59.

———. Foreign Service Despatch 529, June 29, 1955. General Records of the Department of State, 1955–1959. Folder 783.00/6–255; Central Decimal File Box 3745; Record Group 59.

———. Incoming Telegram, April 23, 1955. General Records of the Department of State, 1955–1959. Folder 783.0000/1–555; Central Decimal File Box 3745; Record Group 59.

———. Incoming Telegram, April 27, 1955. General Records of the Department of State, 1955–1959. Folder 783.0000/1–555; Central Decimal File Box 3745; Record Group 59.

———. Incoming Telegram, May 17, 1955. General Records of the Department of State, 1955–1959. Folder 783.0000/1–555; Central Decimal File Box 3745; Record Group 59.

———. Incoming Telegram, September 24, 1955. General Records of the Department of State, 1955–1959. Folder 783.00/6–255; Central Decimal File Box 3745; Record Group 59.

———. Incoming Telegram, January 12, 1956. General Records of the Department of State, 1955–1959. Folder 783.00/1–456; Central Decimal File Box 3745; Record Group 59.

———. Incoming Telegram, May 1, 1956. General Records of the Department of State, 1955–1959. Folder 783.00/1–456; Central Decimal File Box 3745; Record Group 59.

———. Secret Department of the Army Staff Communications Office Message, July 2, 1955. General Records of the Department of State, 1955–1959. Folder 783.00(W)/1–755; Central Decimal File Box 3747; Record Group 59.

———. Secret Department of the Army Staff Communications Office Message, July 8, 1955. General Records of the Department of State, 1955–1959. Folder 783.00(W)/1–755; Central Decimal File Box 3747; Record Group 59.

———. Secret Memorandum of Conversation, June 24, 1955. Foreign Service Records of the Department of State, 1954–1956. Folder "Damascus, Secret, 1954, 57F121"; Syria; Damascus Embassy; Record Group 84.

———. Secret Memorandum of Conversation between U.S. Ambassador James S. Moose, Jr., U.S. Embassy Counselor Robert C. Strong, Nazir Fansa, and Brigadier General Shawkat Shuqayr, June 24, 1955. Foreign Service Records of the Department of State, 1954–1956. Folder "Damascus, Secret, 1955"; Syria; Damascus Embassy; Record Group 84.

Personal Interviews

Qassab Hasan, Hanan. February 27, 2002
Anonymous, March 3, 2001
Anonymous, October 9, 2001

ARABIC-LANGUAGE PUBLISHED SOURCES

Syrian Newspapers

Alif Ba' (The ABCs)
Al-Anba' (The News)
Al-Bina' (The Structure)
Brazil al-Sham (Brazil of Damascus)
Dimashq al-Masa' (Damascus Evening)
Al-Gazetta (The Gazette)
Al-Hadara (Civilization)
Al-Kalb (The Dog)
Al-Mudhik al-Mabki (The Tragi-Comic)
Al-Mukhtar (The Select)
Al-Nas (The People)
Al-Qabas (The Firebrand)
Al-Qindil (The Lantern)
Al-Ra'y al-'Amm (Public Opinion)
Al-Sham (Damascus)
Al-Tali'a (The Vanguard)

Syrian Magazines

Al-Dunya (The World)
Al-Idha'a al-Suriyya (Syrian Broadcasting)
Al-Jami'a (The Community)
Al-Jundi (The Soldier)
Al-Majalla al-'Askariyya (The Military Gazette)
Majallat al-Shurta wa al-Amm al-'Amm (The Journal of the Police and Public Security)
Majallat Kulliyat al-Tarbiyya (The Journal of the College of Education)

Majallat Niqabat al-Muhandisin (The Journal of the Engineers' Union)
Al-Raqib (The Observer)
Al-Sanabil (The Spike)
Sawt Suriya (The Voice of Syria)
Al-Sayyad (The Hunter)
Tabibak (Your Doctor)

Other Published Works

'Aflaq, Michel. *Fi Sabil al-Ba'th al-'Arabi* (For the Sake of Arab Revival). 3rd ed. Beirut: Dar al-Tali'a, 1963.

Anonymous. *Man Qatal Yunis 'Abd al-Rahim?* (Who Killed Yunis 'Abd al-Rahim?). N.p.: N.p., 1955.

al-'Ash, Yusuf. "Man Huwa al-Muwatin al-Salih?" ("Who Is the Virtuous Citizen?"). *Journal of the Police and Public Security,* November 1953, 6–7.

'Ayyash, 'Abd al-Qadir. *M'jam al-Mu'allifin al-Suriyyin fi al-Qarn al-'Ashrin* (A Biographical Dictionary of Syrian Writers in the Twentieth Century). Damascus: Dar al-Fikr, 1985.

al-'Azm, Khalid. *Mudhakkirat Khalid al-'Azm* (The Memoirs of Khalid al-'Azm). 3 vols. Beirut: Dar al-Muttahida lil-Nasr, 1972.

Babil, Nasuh. *Sihafa wa Siyasa: Suriyya fi al-Qarn al-'Ashrin* (Journalism and Politics: Syria in the Twentieth Century). London: Riad El-Rayyes, 1987.

al-Baytar, 'Abd al-Razzaq Razzaq. *Hilyat al-Bashar fi Ta'rikh al-Qarn al-Thalith 'Ashar* (The Life of Human Beings in the 23th Century). Vol. 1. Damascus: Majma' al-Lugha al-'Arabiyya, 1961.

Fansa, Bashir. *Al-Nakabat wa al-Mughamarat: Tarikh ma Ahmalihi al-Tarikh min Asrar al-Inqilabat al-'Askariyya al-Suriyya, 1949–1958* (Disasters and Reckless Adventures: The Secrets of Syrian Military Coups d'État That History Has Ignored, 1949–1958). Damascus: Dar Ya'rib, 1996.

al-Far' al-Thaqafi al-'Askari (The Military Cultural Branch). *Al-Malki: Rajul wa Qadiya* (al-Malki: Man and Affair). Damascus: Manshurat al-Far' al-Thaqafi al-'Askari, 1956.

Farfur, Muhammad 'Abd al-Latif Salih. *A'lam Dimashq fi al-Qarn al-Rabi' 'Ashar al-Hijri* (Eminent Personalities in Damascus in the Fourteenth Century—Hijra). Damascus: Dar al-Malla li al-Tiba'a wa al-Nashr wa Dar Hassan li al-Tiba'a wa al-Nashr, 1987.

Faris, George, ed. *Man Hum fi al-'Alam al-'Arabi. Al-Juz' al-Awwal: Suriya* (Who's Who in the Arab World, volume 1, Syria). Damascus: Maktab al-Dirasat al-Suriyya wa al-'Arabiyya, 1957.

———. *Man Huwa fi Suriya 1949* (Who's Who in Syria 1949). Damascus: Matba't al-'Ulum wa al-Adab Hashimi Ikhwan, 1951.

Hafiz, Abu al-Hajjaj. *Shahid al-'Uruba 'Adnan al-Malki, 1919–1955* (Martyr of Arabism 'Adnan al-Malki, 1919–1955). Damascus: Matba'at Ahmad Mukhayyam, 1961.

al-Hakim, Husayn. *La'na al-Inqilabat min 1946 ila 1966* (The Curse of Military Coups from 1946 to 1966). Damascus: Matba'at al-Dawadi, 1999.

Hamdani, Mustafa Ram. *Shahid 'ala Ahdath Suriya wa 'Arabiya wa Asrar al-Infisal: Mudhakkirat* (Witness to Syrian and Arab Events and the Secrets of the Secession: Memoirs). Damascus: Dar Tlas, 1999.

Hilan, Rizq Allah. *Suriya bayna al-Takhalluf wa al-Tanmiya* (Syria between Backwardness and Development). Damascus: N.p., 1973.

———. *Al-Thaqafa wa al-Tanmiya fi Suriya wa al-Buldan al-Mukhallifa* (Culture and Development in Syria and Backward Countries). Damascus: Matb'at Dar al-'Ilm, 1980.

al-Husni, Muhammad Adib Taqi al-Din. *Kitab Muntakhabat al-Tawarikh li-Dimashq* (The Book of Selected Damascus Genealogies). Beirut: Dar al-Afaq al-Jadida, 1979.

Iliyas, Juzif. *Tatawwur al-Sihafa al-Suriyya fi Mi'at 'Am—1865–1965* (The Development of Syrian Journalism over 100 Years—1865–1965). 2 vols. Beirut: Dar al-Nidal li al-Taba'a wa al-Nashar wa al-Tawzi', 1982–1983.

Isma'il, Sidqi. *Jaridat al-Kalb* (The Newspaper "The Dog"). Damascus: Matabi' al-Idara al-Siyasiya, 1983.

al-'Itri, 'Abd al-Ghani. *'Abqariyyat* (Geniuses). Damascus: Dar al-Basha'ir, 1997.

———. *'Abqariyyat Shamiyya* (Damascene Geniuses). Damascus: N.p., 1982.

———. *'Abqariyyat wa A'lam* (Geniuses and Eminent Personalities). Damascus: Dar al-Basha'ir, 1996.

———. *Hadith al-'Abqariyyat* (The Story of Geniuses). Damascus: Dar al-Basha'ir, 2000.

Jum'a, Sami. *Awraq min Daftar al-Watan, 1946–1961* (Pages from the Notebook of the Homeland, 1946–1961). Damascus: Dar Tlas, 2000.

Khadur, Adib. *Al-Sihafa al-Suriyya: Nasha'tuha, Tatawwuruha, Waqi'ha al-Rahin* (The Syrian Press: Its Origins, Development, and Factual Circumstances). Damascus: Dar al-Ba'th li al-Sihafa wa al-Nashr wa al-Tawzi', 1972.

al-Khalidi, Ghassan. *Al-Hizb al-Qawmi wa Qissat al-Malki: Haqiqa Am Ittiham?* (The Nationalist Party and the Malki Case: Truth or Accusation?). 2 vols. Beirut: Dar wa Maktabat al-Turath al-Adabi, 2000.

al-Madani, Muhammad Nimr. *'Adnan al-Malki: Thalath Rasasat fi al-Mal'ab al-Baladi* ('Adnan al-Malki: Three Bullets in the National Stadium). Damascus: al-Dar al-Hadith, 1996.

al-Malki, 'Adnan. *Rasa'il min al-Sijn* (Letters from Prison). Damascus: Dar al-Thaqafa fi Dimashq, 1960.

al-Malki, Riyad. *Sirat al-Shahid 'Adnan al-Malki, 1919–1955: Bi Munasabat 50 'Am 'ala Istishhadihi* (The Biography of the Martyr 'Adnan al-Malki, 1919–1955: On the Occasion of the Fiftieth Anniversary of His Assassination). Damascus: Dar Tlass, 2005.

Ma'ruf, Muhammad. *Ayyam 'Ashtuha, 1949–1969: al-Inqilabat al-'Askariyya wa Asraruha fi Suriya* (The Days I Lived, 1949–1969: The Military Coups and Their Secrets in Syria). Beirut: Riad al-Rayyes, 2003.

Marwa, Adib. *Al-Sihafa al-'Arabiyya: Nasha'tuha wa Tatawwuruha* (The Arab Press: Its Origins and Its Development). Beirut: Matabi' Fudul, 1961.

al-Mashut, Muhammad 'Ulyan. *Tarikh al-Sihafa al-Suriyya wa al-'Arabiyya* (The History of the Syrian and Arab Press). Damascus: Matba'at Dar al-Kitab, 1988.

Musa, Salama. *Ahadith ila al-Shabab* (Conversations of the Youth). Cairo: Salama Musa lil-Nashr wa al-Tawzi', n.d.

———. *Al-Shakhsiyya al-Naji'a* (The Efficient Personality). Cairo: Salamah Musa lil-Nashr wa al-Tawzi', 1943.

al-Musuli, Mundhir. *Al-Sihafa al-Suriyya wa Rijaluha: I'lam wa A'lam* (The Syrian Press and Its Leading Personalities: Information and Luminaries). Damascus: Dar al-Mukhtar, 1997.

al-Qabbani, Sabri. *Alif Ba' al-Jins* (The ABCs of Sex). N.p.: N.p., n.d.

———. *Atfal taht al-Talab wa Man' al-Haml* (Children upon Demand and the Prevention of Pregnancy). 28th ed. Beirut: Dar al-'Ilm li al-Milayin, 2001.

———. *Hayatuna al-Jinsiyya* (Our Sexual Life). 31st ed. Beirut: Dar al-'Ilm li al-Milayin, 1994.

———. *Mi'at Su'al wa Su'al Hawla al-Jins* (A Hundred and One Questions about Sex). 22nd ed. Beirut: Dar al-'Ilm li al-Milayin, 1979.

Qassab Hasan, Najat. *Qanun al-Ahwal al-Shakhsiyya ma'a Sharh Qanuni wa Insani Kamil* (Personal Status Law with a Complete Legal and Personal Elucidation). Damascus: s.n., 1985.

———. *Qanun wa Qada' 'ala Mustawa al-Mustaqbal* (Law and Issues with Regard to the Future). Damascus: Niqabat al-Mahamiin fi al-Jumhuriyya al-'Arabiyya al-Suriyya, n.d.

———. *Qisas al-Nas: Mi'tan wa Tisa'un Qadia Insania waradat fi Rukn al-Mawatin wa al Qanun* (Stories of the People: Two Hundred and Ninety Civil Cases That Appeared in the Column "The Citizen and the Law"). Damascus: Dar Tlas, 1989.

Qubrusi, Abdallah. "Maqtal 'Adnan al-Malki" (The Murder of 'Adnan al-Malki). In Ghassan al-Khalidi, *al-Hizb al-Qawmi wa Qadiyat al-Malki: Haqiqa am Ittiham?* (The National Party and the Malki Affair: Truth or Accusation?), 1:13–20. Beirut: Dar wa Maktabat al-Turath al-Adabi, 1999.

Qutb, Sayyid. *Fi Zilal al-Qur'an* (In the Shadow of the Qur'an). Cairo: Dar Shoroq, 1979.

Rafeq, Abdul-Karim. *Tarikh al-Jami'a al-Suriyya: al-Bidaya wa al-Numu, 1901–1946. Awwal Jami'a Hukumiyya fi al-Watan al-'Arabi. Bi Munasibat al-'Id al-Mi'awi li Kuliyyat al-Tib wa al-'Id al-Tis'ini li Kuliyyat al-Huquq* (The History of the Syrian University: The Beginning and the Growth, 1901–1946. The First State University in the Arab World. On the Occasion of the Centenary on the Faculty of Medicine and the Ninetieth Anniversary of the Faculty of Law). Damascus: Librairie Nobel, 2004.

Rifa'i, Shams al-Din. *Sharh al-Qawanin al-Sihafiyya al-Suriyya wa al-Riqaba 'alayha taht al-Hukm al-'Uthmani wa al-Intidab al-Faransi, 1800–1946* (Elucidation of the Syrian Press Laws and Censorship under Ottoman Rule and the

French Mandate, 1800–1946). Damascus: al-Matbuʿat al-Jamʿiyya al-Taʿawuniyya li al-Tibaʿa, 1979.

———. *Tarikh al-Sihafa al-Suriya* (The History of Syrian Journalism). 2 vols. Cairo: Dar al-Maʿrif bi Misr, 1969.

———. *Tarikh al-Tibaʿa fi al-Sharq al-ʿArabi* (The History of Printing in the Arab East). Cairo: Dar al-Maʿrif, 1958.

al-Shamʿa, Hani. *Awraq Sahafi: Mudhakirat wa Ahdath, 1955–1975* (A Journalist's Papers: Reminiscences and Events, 1955–1975). Damascus: N.p., n.d.

Syrian Republic. *Al-Dustur al-Suri* (The Syrian Constitution). Damascus: Press of the Syrian Republic, September 5, 1950.

Tamer, Zakariya. *Al-Numur fi al-Yawm al-ʿAshir* (Tigers on the Tenth Day). 5th ed. London: Riad El-Rayyis, 2002.

Tlas, Mustafa. *Mira'at Hayati* (The Mirror of My Life). 2 vols. Damascus: Tlasdar, 1991.

al-ʿUjayli, ʿAbd al-Salam. *Dhikrayat 'Ayyam al-Siyasa: al-Juz' al-Awwal min Kitab Sadara Juz'uhu al-Thani* (Memories of My Political Days: The First Volume of a Book Whose Second Volume Has Already Been Published). Beirut: Riad al-Rayyes, 2002.

ʿUthman, Hashim. *Al-Sihafa al-Suriyya: Madiha wa Hadiriha* (The Syrian Press: Its Past and Its Present). Damascus: Matabiʿ Wizarat al-Thaqafa, 1997.

Wasil, ʿAbd al-Rahman. *Mushkilat al-Shabab al-Jinsiyya wa al-ʿAtifiyya taht Adwa' al-Shariʿa al-Islamiyya* (The Sexual and Romantic Problems of Young People under the Gaze of Islamic Shariʿa). Cairo: Maktabat Wahbab, 1984.

Zakariyya, Ghassan. *Al-Sultan al-Ahmar* (The Red Sultan). London: Arados, 1991.

ENGLISH-LANGUAGE PUBLISHED SOURCES

Abi-Mershed, Osama W. *Apostles of Modernity: Saint-Simonians and the Civilizing Mission in Algeria.* Stanford, CA: Stanford University Press, 2010.

Abu-Rabiʿ, Ibrahim M. *Contemporary Arab Thought: Studies in Post-1967 Arab Intellectual History.* London: Pluto Press, 2004.

ʿAflaq, Michel. "Nationalism Is Love before Everything Else." In *Arab Nationalism: An Anthology,* edited by Sylvia Haim, 242–249. Berkeley: University of California Press, 1976.

Ali, A. Yusuf. *The Holy Qur'an: Text, Translation, and Commentary.* St. Brentwood, MD: Amana, 1983.

Anderson, Benedict. *Imagined Communities: Reflections on the Origin and Spread of Nationalism.* New ed. London: Verso, 2006.

Anderson, J. N. D. "The Syrian Law of Personal Status." *Bulletin of the School of Oriental and African Studies* 17:1 (1955): 34–49.

Armbrust, Walter, ed. *Mass Mediations: New Approaches to Popular Culture in the Middle East and Beyond.* Berkeley: University of California Press, 2000.

Asad, Talal. *Formations of the Secular: Christianity, Islam, Modernity.* Stanford, CA: Stanford University Press, 2003.

Asfour, Edmund Y. *Syria: Development and Monetary Policy.* Cambridge, MA: Harvard University Press, 1959.

Atiyeh, George N., and Ibrahim M. Oweiss, eds. *Arab Civilization: Challenges and Responses: Studies in Honor of Constantine K. Zurayq.* Albany: State University of New York Press, 1988.

Ayalon, Ami. *The Press in the Arab Middle East: A History.* New York: Oxford University Press, 1995.

Bakhtin, Mikhail Mikhailovich. *The Dialogic Imagination.* Edited by Michael Holquist. Translated by Carl Emerson and Michael Holquist. Austin: University of Texas Press, 1981.

Batatu, Hanna. "Some Observations on the Social Roots of Syria's Ruling, Military Group and the Causes for Its Dominance." *Middle East Journal* 35.3 (Summer 1981): 331–334.

———. *Syria's Peasantry, the Descendants of Its Lesser Rural Notables, and Their Politics.* Princeton, NJ: Princeton University Press, 1999.

Be'eri, Eliezer. *Army Officers in Arab Politics and Society.* New York: Praeger, 1970.

———. "The Waning of the Military Coup in Arab Politics." *Middle Eastern Studies* 18.1 (January 1982): 69–81.

Ben-Amos, Avner. *Funerals, Politics, and Memory in Modern France, 1789–1996.* New York: Oxford University Press, 2000.

Berger, Maurits S. "The Sharia and Legal Pluralism: The Example of Syria." In *Legal Pluralism and the Arab World,* edited by Baoudouin Dupret, Maurits Berger, and Laila al-Zwaini, 113–124. Cambridge, MA: Kluwer Law International, 1999.

Berkey, Jonathan P. *Popular Preaching and Religious Authority in the Medieval Islamic Near East.* Seattle: University of Washington Press, 2001.

Bertaud, Jean-Paul. "The Revolutionary Role of the Army: To Regenerate Man, to Form a Model Citizen, a Model for Civil Society?" In *Culture and Revolution: Cultural Ramifications of the French Revolution,* edited by George Levitine, 18–39. College Park: Department of Art History, University of Maryland at College Park, 1989.

Black, Cyril. *The Dynamics of Modernization: A Study in Comparative History.* New York: Harper and Row, 1966.

Blecher, Robert Ian. "The Medicalization of Sovereignty: Medicine, Public Health, and Political Authority in Syria, 1861–1936." Ph.D. dissertation, Stanford University, 2002.

Bodnar, John. *Remaking America: Public Memory, Commemoration, and Patriotism in the Twentieth Century.* Princeton, NJ: Princeton University Press, 1992.

Boudhiba, Abdelwahab. *Sexuality in Islam.* Translated by Alan Sheridan. London: Saqi Books, 1985.

Boyd, Douglas A. *Broadcasting in the Arab World: A Survey of the Electronic Media in the Middle East.* 3rd ed. Ames: Iowa State University Press, 1999.

Boym, Svetlana. *The Future of Nostalgia*. New York: Basic Books, 2001.

Bynum, W. F., and Roy Porter, eds. *Companion Encyclopedia of the History of Medicine*. Vol. 1. New York: Routledge, 1993.

Chartier, Roger. "Texts, Printings, Readings." In *The New Cultural History*, edited by Lynn Hunt, 154–175. Berkeley: University of California Press, 1989.

Chatterjee, Partha. *The Nation and Its Fragments: Colonial and Postcolonial Histories*. Princeton, NJ: Princeton University Press, 1993.

———. *The Politics of the Governed: Reflections on Popular Politics in Most of the World*. New York: Columbia University Press, 2004.

Comair-Obeid, Nayla. *The Law of Business Contracts in the Arab Middle East: A Theoretical and Practical Comparative Analysis (with Particular Reference to Modern Legislation)*. The Hague: Kluwer, 1996.

Commins, David Dean. *Historical Dictionary of Syria*. Lanham, MD: Scarecrow Press, 1996.

———. *Islamic Reform: Politics and Social Change in Late Ottoman Syria*. New York: Oxford University Press, 1990.

Connolly, William E. *Political Theory and Modernity*. Ithaca, NY: Cornell University Press, 1993.

Conrad, Lawrence I. "Arab-Islamic Medicine." In *Companion Encyclopedia of the History of Medicine*, edited by W. F. Bynum and Roy Porter, 1:676–708. London: Taylor and Francis, 1997.

Cook, David. *Martyrdom in Islam*. New York: Cambridge University Press, 2007.

———. *Understanding Jihad*. Berkeley: University of California Press, 2005.

Dallal, Ahmad. *Islam, Science, and the Challenge of History*. New Haven, CT: Yale University Press, 2010.

Darnton, Robert. *The Great Cat Massacre and Other Episodes in French Cultural History*. New York: Basic Books, 1984.

Davis, Kingsley. *World Urbanization 1950–1970*, volume 1, *Basic Data for Cities, Countries, and Regions*. Berkeley: University of California Press, 1969.

Deeb, Lara. *An Enchanted Modern: Gender and Public Piety in Shiʻi Lebanon*. Princeton, NJ: Princeton University Press, 2006.

Derrida, Jacques. *The Work of Mourning*. Chicago: University of Chicago Press, 2001.

Drysdale, Alisdair. "Ethnicity in the Syrian Officer Corps: A Conceptualization." *Civilisations* 29.3–4 (1982): 359–374.

———. "The Syrian Armed Forces: The Role of the Geographic and Ethnic Periphery." In *Soldiers, Peasants and Bureaucrats: Civil-Military Relations in Communist and Modernizing Societies*, edited by Roman Kolkowicz and Andrzej Korbonski, 52–76. London: George Allen and Unwin, 1982.

Economic Research Institute, American University of Beirut. *Middle East Economic Papers*. Beirut: Dar al-Kitab, 1954–1963.

El-Alami, Dawoud Sudqi, and Doreen Hinchcliffe. *Islamic Marriage and Divorce Laws of the Arab World*. Cambridge, MA: Kluwer, 1996.

El-Rouayheb, Khaled. *Before Homosexuality in the Arab-Islamic World, 1500–1800.* Chicago: University of Chicago Press, 2005.

Elshakry, Marwa. "Darwin's Legacy in the Arab East: Science, Religion and Politics, 1870–1914." Ph.D. dissertation, Princeton University, 2003.

El Shakry, Omnia. *The Great Social Laboratory: Subjects of Knowledge in Colonial and Postcolonial Egypt.* Stanford, CA: Stanford University Press, 2007.

Fahmy, Ziad. *Ordinary Egyptians.* Stanford, CA: Stanford University Press, 2011.

Farah, Madelain. *Marriage and Sexuality in Islam: A Translation of al-Ghazali's Book on the Etiquette of Marriage from the Ihya.* Salt Lake City: University of Utah Press, 1984.

Fields, Rona M. "The Psychology and Sociology of Martyrdom." In *Martyrdom: The Psychology, Theology, and Politics of Self-Sacrifice,* edited by Rona M. Fields, 23–82. Westport, CT: Praeger, 2004.

Fischer-Lichte, Erika. *Theatre, Sacrifice, Ritual: Exploring Forms of Political Theatre.* New York: Routledge, 2005.

Foucault, Michel. *The History of Sexuality,* volume 1, *An Introduction.* New York: Vintage, 1990.

Gaffney, Patrick D. *The Prophet's Pulpit: Islamic Preaching in Contemporary Egypt.* Berkeley: University of California Press, 1994.

Gay, Peter. *The Cultivation of Hatred: The Bourgeois Experience from Victoria to Freud.* Vol. 3. New York: Norton, 1993.

———. *Education of the Senses: The Bourgeois Experience from Victoria to Freud.* Vol. 1. New York: Oxford University Press, 1984.

Geertz, Clifford. *The Interpretation of Cultures.* New York: Basic Books, 1973.

Gelvin, James L. *Divided Loyalties: Nationalism and Mass Politics in Syria at the Close of Empire.* Berkeley: University of California Press, 1998.

———. *The Modern Middle East: A History.* 3rd ed. New York: Oxford University Press, 2011.

Germani, Ian. *Jean-Paul Marat: Hero and Anti-Hero of the French Revolution.* Lewiston, NY: Edwin Mellen Press, 1992.

Gillis, John R. "Memory and Identity: The History of a Relationship." In *Commemorations: The Politics of National Identity,* edited by John R. Gillis, 3–24. Princeton, NJ: Princeton University Press, 1994.

Gollaher, David L. "From Ritual to Science: The Medical Transformation of Circumcision in America." *Journal of Social History* 28.1 (Fall 1994): 5–36.

Gray, Matthew. "Explaining Conspiracy Theories in Modern Arab Middle Eastern Political Discourse: Some Problems and Limitations of the Literature." *Critique: Critical Middle Eastern Studies* 17.2 (Summer 2008): 155–174.

Haddad, George M. *Revolutions and Military Rule in the Middle East.* 3 vols. New York: R. Speller, 1965–1973.

Haim, Sylvia G., ed. *Arab Nationalism: An Anthology.* Berkeley: University of California Press, 1976.

al-Hajj Ibrahim, Mustafa. "The Citizen and the Security Man." *Journal of the Police and Public Security,* April 1953, 24.

Hallaq, Wael B. *The Impossible State: Islam, Politics, and Modernity's Moral Predicament.* New York: Columbia University Press, 2012.

Halpern, Manfred. "Middle Eastern Armies and the New Middle Class." In *The Role of the Military in Underdeveloped Countries,* edited by John J. Johnson, 277–315. Princeton, NJ: Princeton University Press, 1962.

Hamdy, Sherine. *Our Bodies Belong to God: Organ Transplants, Islam, and the Struggle for Human Dignity in Egypt.* Berkeley: University of California Press, 2012.

Heater, Derek. *A Brief History of Citizenship.* New York: New York University Press, 2004.

Henriques, John L., ed. *Syria: Issues and Historical Background.* New York: Nova Science, 2003.

Heydemann, Steven. *Authoritarianism in Syria: Institutions and Social Conflict, 1946–1970.* Ithaca, NY: Cornell University Press, 1999.

Hobsbawm, Eric. *Age of Extremes: The Short Twentieth Century 1914–1991.* London: Abacus, 1995.

Holt, P. M., Ann K. S. Lambton, and Bernard Lewis, eds. *The Cambridge History of Islam.* Vol. 2B. London: Cambridge University Press, 1977.

Hunt, Lynn. "Foreword." In Mona Ozouf, *Festivals and the French Revolution,* translated by Alan Sheridan, ix–xiii. Cambridge, MA: Harvard University Press, 1988.

———, ed. *The New Cultural History.* Berkeley: University of California Press, 1989.

Hurd, Elizabeth Shakman. *The Politics of Secularism in International Relations.* Princeton, NJ: Princeton University Press, 2008.

International Bank for Reconstruction and Development. *The Economic Development of Syria.* Baltimore: Johns Hopkins University Press, 1955.

Ismael, Tareq Y. *The Communist Movement in the Arab World.* New York: Routledge Curzon, 2005.

Ismael, Tareq Y., and Jacqueline S. Ismael. *The Communist Movement in Syria and Lebanon.* Gainesville, FL: University Press of Florida, 1998.

Jayyusi, Salma Khadra, ed. *Modern Arabic Fiction: An Anthology.* New York: Columbia University Press, 2005.

Johnson, John J., ed. *The Role of the Military in Underdeveloped Countries.* Princeton, NJ: Princeton University Press, 1962.

Kamrava, Mehran. "Military Professionalization and Civil-Military Relations in the Middle East." *Political Science Quarterly* 115.1 (Spring 2000): 67–92.

Kassab, Elizabeth Suzanne. *Contemporary Arab Thought: Cultural Critique in Comparative Perspective.* New York: Columbia University Press, 2010.

Kassir, Samir. *Being Arab.* Translated by Will Hobson. London: Verso, 2006.

Kaylani, N. M. "The Rise of the Syrian Ba'th 1940–1958: Political Success, Party Failure." *International Journal of Middle Eastern Studies* 3.1 (January 1972): 3–23.

Kerr, Malcolm H. *The Arab Cold War, 1958–1964: A Study of Ideology in Politics.* New York: Oxford University Press, 1965.

Khadduri, Majid. "Constitutional Development in Syria: With Emphasis on the Constitution of 1950." *Middle East Journal* 5.2 (Spring 1951): 137–160.

Khalili, Laleh. *Heroes and Martyrs of Palestine: The Politics of National Commemoration.* New York: Cambridge University Press, 2007.

Khoury, Philip. *Syria and the French Mandate: The Politics of Arab Nationalism, 1920–1945.* Princeton, NJ: Princeton University Press, 1987.

———. *Urban Notables and Arab Nationalism: The Politics of Damascus, 1860–1922.* Cambridge: Cambridge University Press, 1983.

Klausner, Samuel Z. "Inferential Visibility and Sex Norms in the Middle East." *Journal of Sex Research* 1.3 (November 1965): 201–220.

Kleinman, Arthur. "What Is Specific to Western Medicine?" In *Companion Encyclopedia of the History of Medicine,* edited by W. F. Bynum and Roy Porter, 1:15–23. New York: Routledge, 1993.

Laqueur, Thomas W. *Solitary Sex: A Cultural History of Masturbation.* New York: Zone Books, 2003.

Laqueur, Walter Z. *Communism and Nationalism in the Middle East.* London: Routledge and Kegan Paul, 1956.

Lears, T. J. Jackson. *Fables of Abundance: A Cultural History of Advertising in America.* New York: Basic Books, 1994.

Lentz, Harris M., III. *Assassinations and Executions: An Encyclopedia of Political Violence, 1900 through 2000.* Rev. ed. Jefferson, NC: McFarland, 2002.

Lesch, David W. *Syria and the United States: Eisenhower's Cold War in the Middle East.* Boulder, CO: Westview Press, 1992.

Lyotard, Jean-François. *Libidinal Economy.* Translated by Iain Hamilton Grant. Bloomington: Indiana University Press, 1993.

Makdisi, Samir A. "Fixed Capital Formation in Syria, 1936–1957." In *Middle East Economic Papers,* edited by Economic Research Institute, American University of Beirut, 95–112. Beirut: Dar al-Kitab, 1958.

Makdisi, Ussama. *The Culture of Sectarianism: Community, History, and Violence in Nineteenth-Century Ottoman Lebanon.* Berkeley: University of California Press, 2000.

Manley, Mary Louise. "Document: The Syrian Constitution of 1953." *The Middle East Journal* 7 (1953): 520–530.

Marnham, Patrick. *Resistance and Betrayal: The Death and Life of the Greatest Hero of the French Resistance.* New York: Random House, 2000.

Martin, Kevin W. "'Peasants into Syrians?' Quick Studies, As You See It." *International Journal of Middle East Studies* 41.1 (2009): 4–6.

———. "Presenting the 'True Face of Syria' to the World: Urban Disorder and Civilizational Anxieties at the First Damascus International Exposition." *International Journal of Middle East Studies* 42.3 (2010): 391–411.

Massad, Joseph. *Desiring Arabs.* Chicago: University of Chicago Press, 2007.

Masud, Muhammad Khalid, Brinkley Messick, and David S. Powers, eds. *Islamic Legal Interpretation: Muftis and Their Fatwas.* Cambridge, MA: Harvard University Press, 1996.

McFadden, Tom Johnston. *Daily Journalism in the Arab States.* Columbus: Ohio State University Press, 1953.

Melikian, Levon, and E. Terry Prothro. "Sexual Behavior of University Students in the Arab Near East." *Journal of Abnormal and Social Psychology* 49.1 (January 1954): 59–64.

Mitchell, Timothy. *Rule of Experts: Egypt, Techno-Politics, Modernity.* Berkeley: University of California Press, 2002.

Morrison, Ian. "Acts of Commemoration." In *Acts of Citizenship,* edited by Engin F. Isin and Greg M. Nielsen, 289–291. London: Zed Books, 2008.

Mosse, George L. *Fallen Soldiers: Reshaping the Memory of the World Wars.* New York: Oxford University Press, 1990.

Moubayed, Sami M. *Damascus between Dictatorship and Democracy.* Lanham, MD: University Press of America, 2000.

———. *Steel and Silk: Women and Men Who Shaped Syria 1900–2000.* Seattle: Cune Press, 2004.

Najmabadi, Afsaneh. "The Morning After: Travail of Sexuality and Love in Modern Iran." *International Journal for Middle East Studies* 36 (2004): 367–385.

Norton, Anne. *Bloodrites of the Post-Structuralists: Word, Flesh and Revolution.* New York: Routledge, 2002.

Paradelle, Murielle. "The Notion of 'Person' between Law and Practice: A Study of the Principles of Personal Responsibility and of the Personal Nature of Punishment in Egyptian Criminal Law." In *Standing Trial: Law and the Person in the Modern Middle East,* edited by Baudoin Dupret, 233–263. London: I. B. Tauris, 2004.

Parolin, Gianluca K. *Citizenship in the Arab World: Kin, Religion, and Nation-State.* Amsterdam: Amsterdam University Press, 2009.

Perlmutter, Amos. "The Praetorian State and the Praetorian Army: Toward a Taxonomy of Civil-Military Relations in Developing Polities." *Comparative Politics* 1.3 (April 1969): 382–404.

Petran, Tabitha. *Syria.* New York: Praeger, 1972.

Prakash, Gyan. *Another Reason: Science and the Imagination of Modern Idea.* Princeton, NJ: Princeton University Press, 1999.

Rabo, Annika. "Gender, State and Civil Society in Jordan and Syria." In *Civil Society: Challenging Western Models,* edited by Elizabeth Dunn and Chris Hann, 155–167. London: Routledge, 1996.

Rafeq, Abdul-Karim. "The Social and Economic Structure of Bab al-Musalla (al-Midan), Damascus, 1825–1875." In *Arab Civilization: Challenges and Responses: Studies in Honor of Constantine K. Zurayq,* edited by George N. Atiyeh and Ibrahim M. Oweiss, 272–311. Albany: State University of New York Press, 1988.

Rathmell, Andrew. *Secret War in the Middle East: The Covert Struggle for Syria, 1949–1961.* New York: St. Martin's Press, 1995.

Reid, Donald. *Lawyers and Politics in the Arab World, 1880–1960.* Chicago: Biblioteca Islamica, 1981.

Robinson, Victor. *The Story of Medicine.* New York: Tudor, 1931.

Rosoux, Valérie. "The Politics of Martyrdom." In *Martyrdom: The Psychology, Theology, and Politics of Self-Sacrifice,* edited by Rona M. Fields, 83–116. Westport, CT: Praeger, 2004.

Rubin, Barry. "The Military in Contemporary Middle East Politics." In *Armed Forces in the Middle East: Politics and Strategy,* edited by Barry Rubin and Thomas A. Kearney, 1–22. Portland, OR: Frank Cass, 2002.

Rubin, Barry, and Thomas A. Kearney, eds. *Armed Forces in the Middle East: Politics and Strategy.* Portland, OR: Frank Cass, 2002.

Sajdi, Dana. *The Barber of Damascus: Nouveau Literacy in the Eighteenth-Century Ottoman Levant.* Stanford, CA: Stanford University Press, 2013.

Salamandra, Christa. "Consuming Damascus: Public Culture and the Construction of Social Identity." In *Mass Mediations: New Approaches to Popular Culture in the Middle East and Beyond,* edited by Walter Armbrust, 182–202. Berkeley: University of California Press, 2000.

Saunders, Bonnie. *The United States and Arab Nationalism: The Syrian Case, 1953–1960.* Westport, CT: Praeger, 1996.

Sayigh, Yusif A. *The Economies of the Arab World: Development since 1945.* New York: St. Martin's Press, 1978.

Schama, Simon. *Citizens: A Chronicle of the French Revolution.* New York: Knopf, 1989.

Schayegh, Cyrus. *Who Is Knowledgeable Is Strong: Science, Class, and the Formation of Modern Iranian Society, 1900–1950.* Berkeley: University of California Press, 2009.

Schilcher, Linda Schatowski. *Families in Politics: Damascene Factions and Estates of the 18th and 19th Centuries.* Stuttgart: Franz Steiner, 1985.

Scott, Joan Wallach. *Gender and the Politics of History.* New York: Columbia University Press, 1988.

Seale, Patrick. *Asad of Syria: The Struggle for the Middle East.* Berkeley: University of California Press, 1989.

———. *The Struggle for Syria: A Study of Post-War Arab Politics, 1945–1958.* London: I. B. Tauris, 1986.

Sennett, Richard. *The Fall of Public Man.* New York: Norton, 1974.

Sfeir, George N. *Modernization of the Law in Arab States: An Investigation into Current Civil, Criminal and Constitutional Law in the Arab World.* San Francisco: Austin and Winfield, 1998.

al-Shamat, Hania Mounir Abou. "Syria under Civilian Rule: An Improbable Democracy, 1954–1958." M.A. thesis, American University of Beirut, 1999.

Sharabi, Hisham. *Governments and Politics of the Middle East in the Twentieth Century.* Princeton, NJ: Van Norstrand, 1962.

Shari'ati, 'Ali. "On Martyrdom." In *Islam in Transition: Muslim Perspectives,* edited by John J. Donohue and John L. Esposito, 361–365. New York: Oxford University Press, 2007.

Shotter, John. "Psychology and Citizenship: Identity and Belonging." In *Citizenship and Social Theory,* edited by Bryan S. Turner, 115–138. London: Sage, 1993.

Silverstein, Paul A., and Ussama Makdisi. "Introduction." In *Memory and Violence in the Middle East and North Africa,* edited by Paul A. Silverstein and Ussama Makdisi, 1–24. Bloomington: Indiana University Press, 2006.

Sipress, Alan. "Syria Creates Cult around Its President's Dead Son." *Philadelphia Inquirer,* November 8, 1996. http://articles.philly.com/1996-11-08/news/25647185 _1_syrians-basil-assad-president-hafez.

Stanton, Andrea L. *"This Is Jerusalem Calling": State Radio in Mandate Palestine.* Austin: University of Texas Press, 2013.

Strenski, Ivan. *Contesting Sacrifice: Religion, Nationalism, and Social Thought in France.* Chicago: University of Chicago Press, 2002.

Surkis, Judith. *Sexing the Citizen: Morality and Masculinity in France, 1870–1920.* Ithaca, NY: Cornell University Press, 2006.

Syria magazine (single issue). Damascus: Directorate-General of Information, 1953.

Taleqani, Mahmud, et al., eds. *Jihad and Shahadat: Struggle and Martyrdom in Islam.* Houston: Institute for Research and Islamic Studies, 1986.

Tamer, Zakariya. *Tigers on the Tenth Day and Other Stories.* Translated by Denys Johnson-Davies. London: Quartet Books, 1985.

Thompson, Elizabeth. *Colonial Citizens: Republican Rights, Paternal Privilege, and Gender in French Syria and Lebanon.* New York: Columbia University Press, 2000.

———. *Justice Interrupted: The Struggle for Constitutional Government in the Middle East.* Cambridge, MA: Harvard University Press, 2013.

Thucydides. *History of the Peloponnesian War.* Translated by Rex Warner. New York: Penguin Classics, 1972.

Torrey, Gordon H. "The Role of the Military in Society and Government in Syria and the Formation of the UAR." In *The Military in the Middle East: Problems in Society and Government,* edited by Sydney Nettleton Fisher, 53–70. Columbus: The Ohio State University Press, 1963.

———. *Syrian Politics and the Military, 1945–1958.* Columbus: The Ohio State University Press, 1964.

Tucker, Judith E. *In the House of the Law: Gender and Islamic Law in Ottoman Syria and Palestine.* Berkeley: University of California Press, 1997.

———. "Revisiting Reform: Women and the Ottoman Law of Family Rights, 1917." *Arab Studies Journal* 4.2 (Fall 1996): 4–17.

Turner, Bryan S. "Preface." In *Citizenship and Social Theory,* edited by Bryan S. Turner, vii–xii. London: Sage, 1993.

———. *Religion and Modern Society: Citizenship, Secularization and the State.* New York: Cambridge University Press, 2011.

Turner, Stephen P. *The Politics of Expertise.* New York: Routledge, 2014.

Volk, Lucia. *Memorials and Martyrs in Modern Lebanon.* Bloomington: Indiana University Press, 2010.

Watenpaugh, Keith David. "Bourgeois Modernity, Historical Memory, and Imperialism: The Emergence of an Urban Middle Class in the Late Ottoman and Interwar Middle East Aleppo, 1908–1939." Ph.D. dissertation, University of California at Los Angeles, 1999.

Wedeen, Lisa. *Ambiguities of Domination: Politics, Rhetoric and Symbols in Contemporary Syria*. Chicago: University of Chicago Press, 1999.

Weiss, Max. *In the Shadow of Sectarianism: Law, Shi'ism, and the Making of Modern Lebanon*. Cambridge, MA: Harvard University Press, 2010.

White, Benjamin Thomas. *The Emergence of Minorities in the Middle East*. Edinburgh: Edinburgh University Press, 2011.

Wien, Peter. "The Long and Intricate Funeral of Yasin al-Hashimi: Pan-Arabism, Civil Religion, and Popular Nationalism in Damascus, 1937." *International Journal of Middle East Studies* 43.2 (May 2011): 271–292.

Williams, Raymond. *The Country and the City*. London: Chatto and Windus, 1973.

Winder, R. Bayly. "The Establishment of Islam as the State Religion of Syria." *The Muslim World* 44.3 (July–October 1954): 215–226.

Winter, Jay. *Sites of Memory, Sites of Mourning*. Cambridge: Cambridge University Press, 1995.

Woolf, Greg. *Et Tu, Brute: A Short History of Political Murder*. London: Profile Books, 2006.

World Bank. *The Economic Development of Syria*. Baltimore: Johns Hopkins University Press, 1955.

Yamak, Labib Zuwaiyya. *The Syrian Social Nationalist Party: An Ideological Analysis*. Cambridge, MA: Center for Middle East Studies, Harvard University, 1969.

Yaqub, Salim. *Containing Arab Nationalism: The Eisenhower Doctrine and the Middle East*. Chapel Hill: University of North Carolina Press, 2004.

Yarwood, Richard. *Citizenship*. London: Routledge, 2014.

Ze'evi, Dror. *Producing Desire: Changing Sexual Discourse in the Ottoman Middle East*. Berkeley: University of California Press, 2006.

Zelizer, Barbie. *Covering the Body: The Kennedy Assassination, the Media, and the Shaping of Collective Memory*. Chicago: University of Chicago Press, 1992.

Zerubavel, Yael. "Patriotic Sacrifice and the Burden of Memory in Israeli Secular National Hebrew Culture." In *Memory and Violence in the Middle East and North Africa*, edited by Paul A. Silverstein and Usama Makdisi, 73–100. Bloomington: Indiana University Press, 2006.

Index

Page numbers in *italics* indicate photographs and illustrations.